D0566657

The
most
amazing
birds
to see
in Britain

PUBLISHED BY
THE READER'S DIGEST ASSOCIATION LIMITED
LONDON • NEW YORK • SYDNEY • MONTREAL

The most amazing birds to see in Britain

Contents

INTRODUCTION 6-7

GARDENS AND PARKS 8-41
FEATURE: LONDON'S WILDER REACHES 30-31

FARMLAND 42-75
FEATURE: PRECIOUS HAVEN 66-67

WOODLAND 76-125
FEATURE: A FOREST FOR ALL SEASONS 96-97

MOUNTAIN, MOOR AND HEATH 126-173
FEATURE: BIRDS OF THE BARREN HEIGHTS 146-147

WETLANDS 174-211
FEATURE: SECRET LIFE OF THE FENS 184-185

COAST 212-253
FEATURE: SEABIRD SPECTACLE 234-235

INDEX 254-255
ACKNOWLEDGEMENTS 255

Introduction

Millions of wild birds inhabit or visit the British Isles, enchanting observers from Land's End to the Shetland Islands, whether in a flock wheeling high in the sky or a single pair choosing their nesting site. Discover when and where to see the most spectacular species.

Positioned at a migratory crossroads on the edge of Europe, the British Isles are rich in birdlife with almost 600 species recorded here. This guide features 111 of the most remarkable species, each one selected for its striking appearance, unusual behaviour or distinctive calls.

A plain brownish wader for most of the year, the black-tailed godwit develops a spectacular plumage in the breeding season, while the ptarmigan changes colour with the seasons to blend in with its surroundings. Some birds adopt defensive strategies to protect their young – the fulmar's projectile vomiting keeps predators at bay while plovers feign a broken wing. Birdsong also adds to the appeal of these birds, whether it's the glorious song of the blackbird or the loud, persistent rasping of the corncrake.

How to use this book

For ease of reference, the birds are arranged alphabetically by habitat – gardens and parks, farmland, woodland, mountains and moorland, wetland and coast. However, birds are no observers of boundaries, often moving from one area to another, so birds featured in one habitat in this book may often be seen in other habitats.

Each entry includes a colourful description of the species, highlighting its distinctive characteristics. Useful field notes provide details on appearance, size, nesting and feeding habits and a map and calendar show where and when each bird is likely to be seen (see below).

Six features focus on key areas where birdlife can be seen and describe the effects of habitats on the birds that frequent them.

How to read the maps

The distribution maps show when and where each species is most likely to be encountered. Timing and location may help with identification.

Darkened blocks on the calendar (above) indicate the months when the bird may be seen in the British Isles.

- red dots show the sites of breeding colonies
- purple shows the usual breeding range of summer visitors
- green shows the areas where a resident species breeds and remains all year round
- blue shows the areas where a species is found in winter
- grey indicates where passage migrants occur

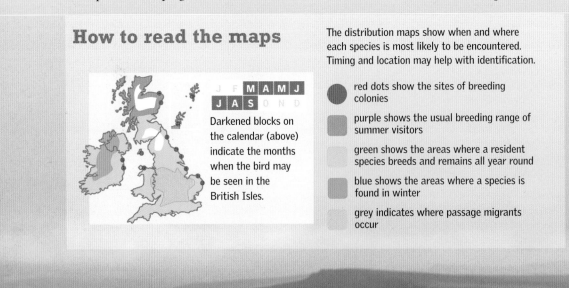

Where to see rarer birds

The following locations offer a good chance of seeing certain rarer species, although patience and a pair of good binoculars are often required. Search the internet to find the exact location of the reserves, parks and other sites listed below.

Bewick's swan
Arundel WWT Wetland Centre, Sussex; Martin Mere WWT Wetland Centre, Lancs; Ouse Washes RSPB reserve, Cambs; Slimbridge WWT, Glos; Welney WWT, Cambs

Bittern
Cley Marshes Norfolk Wildlife Trust reserve, Norfolk; Leighton Moss RSPB reserve, Lancs; Minsmere RSPB reserve, Suffolk; The WWT Wetland Centre, London (winter)

Black grouse
Corrimony RSPB reserve, Highland; Tulloch Moor RSPB reserve, Speyside

Capercaillie
Abernethy National Nature Reserve, Highland; Corrimony RSPB reserve, Highland

Chough
South Stack Cliffs RSPB reserve, Anglesey

Crested tit
Abernethy National Nature Reserve, Highland

Dartford Warbler
Arne RSPB reserve, Dorset; Dunwich Heath National Trust reserve, Suffolk; New Forest National Park, Hants; Studland and Godlingston Heath National Nature Reserve, Dorset

Golden eagle
Beinn Eighe National Nature Reserve, Highland

Goshawk
Forest of Dean, Glos; Kielder Forest, Northum; Thetford Forest Park (Forestry Commission), Suffolk; New Forest National Park, Hants

Hawfinch
Lynford Arboretum (Forestry Commission), Norfolk; Nagshead RSPB reserve, Glos; New Forest National Park, Hants

Honey buzzard
Haldon Forest Park raptor viewpoint (Forestry Commission), Devon; New Forest National Park, Hants; Wykeham Forest raptor viewpoint (Forestry Commission), Yorks

Hoopoe
Dungeness RSPB reserve, Kent; Sandwich Bay Bird Observatory, Kent

Lesser-spotted woodpecker
Church Wood RSPB reserve, Bucks; Holkham Hall Estate, Norfolk; Nagshead RSPB reserve, Glos

Marsh harrier
Leighton Moss RSPB reserve, Lancs; Minsmere RSPB reserve, Suffolk

Nightingale
Minsmere RSPB reserve, Suffolk; New Forest National Park, Hants

Nightjar
Haldon Forest Park (Forestry Commission), Devon; New Forest National Park, Hants; Thetford Forest Park (Forestry Commission), Suffolk

Osprey
Loch Fleet Scottish Wildlife Trust reserve, Highland; Loch Garten RSPB reserve, Highland; Loch of the Lowes Scottish Wildlife Trust reserve, Highland; Rutland Water Nature Reserve, Leics

USEFUL WEBSITES

The Royal Society for the Protection of Birds (RSPB) – www.rspb.org.uk

The Wildfowl & Wetlands Trust (WWT) – www.wwt.org.uk

The Forestry Commission – www.forestry.gov.uk

Wildlife Trusts – www.wildlifetrusts.org.uk

Gardens and Parks

Oases of calm, gardens and parks have a magnetic attraction for birds, ranging from resident goldfinches to exotic ring-necked parakeets. The lure of a regular food supply has enticed many birds away from their natural habitats to busy towns.

BLACKBIRD *Turdus merula*

Fluent, musical notes are the hallmark of this common thrush, its rich, languid song varying between individuals. In addition, the blackbird produces many different alarm calls, each relating to a specific threat.

The main singing role in the dawn chorus all over the country has been taken by the blackbird, and its mellow fluting is one of the most beautiful bird-songs heard in Britain – rated by some people even higher than that of the nightingale. The blackbird also produces a sweet, muted sub-song, hummed through a closed bill and sounding like a distant echo.

At dawn and dusk groups give voice to a persistent chorus of 'pink-pink' calls. Other sounds made by the blackbird are harsher. Its nervous, scolding 'mik mik mik' chatter gives notice of a prowling cat or a fox. Its tail-flicking 'chook-chook' shows mild anxiety, and in winter is a sure sign that a guarded communal roost is in the vicinity. When the need arises, the calls can develop into a somewhat hysterical, screaming rattle of full alarm. In summer, a thin 'seep', which is difficult to locate, alerts the blackbird's mate or chicks to the presence of danger, and a similar call is made to warn that a sparrowhawk or other avian predator is too close for comfort.

Spreading territories

A dynamic expansion into man-made habitats during the past 100 years has made the blackbird the most common resident breeding bird in Britain. Its rivals for that title include the wren and the dunnock, and in much of the north and west, the chaffinch. The blackbird used to be confined to woodland, but it has moved out into gardens, fields, parks, squares, commons, heaths and, in hill districts, to cloughs and combes. One reason it has been able to do this is its willingness to vary its diet. Also, it is aggressively territorial, so as the population increased

Young blackbirds may join migrant thrushes, such as redwings, to feed.

with successful breeding, a tendency to spread further afield followed. Numbers are enhanced in autumn and winter by migrants from Europe. Many of the blackbirds seen in Britain at this time are in fact non-residents.

The blackbird is the only one of Britain's three common breeding thrushes (the others are the song thrush and the mistle thrush) in which the male's plumage differs from the female's. A few males become well known in their areas for being partly white, some looking as if they have snowflakes on their backs. Female and, particularly, young blackbirds, with their more noticeable mottled underparts, are often mistaken for song thrushes.

IDENTIFICATION
Male jet black with golden yellow bill and eye-ring; female dark brown, lighter below, slightly mottled, with brown bill.

NESTING
Female builds neat cup of dry grass, dead leaves and mud in hedge, low tree or on ledge of a building; lays late March–July; usually 3–5 eggs, light blue-green with brown spots; incubation about 13 days, by female only; nestlings, fed by both parents, fly after 13 or 14 days; usually two or three broods, occasionally one, four or five.

FEEDING
Insects and their larvae, earthworms; fruit and seeds.

SIZE
25.5cm (10in)

| J | F | M | A | M | J |
| J | A | S | O | N | D |

Widespread in most habitats in Britain and Ireland; continental visitors in winter.

GARDENS & PARKS

BLUE TIT
Cyanistes caeruleus

Quick and adaptable when it comes to finding food, the blue tit has learnt to make exceptionally good use of birdfeeders in the garden, taking only a few minutes to discover a new supply of peanuts.

When it comes to problem-solving, the blue tit has few rivals. Faced with 'intelligence test' apparatus, blue tits have learnt to pull out a series of pegs or open matchbox drawers to get at food. Some years ago, blue tits solved a less artificial problem – they learnt how to get at the milk left on suburban doorsteps, by pecking at the foil of the bottle tops, and went further than that by choosing only the full-cream variety. The birds benefited from the cream's high fat content, especially in cold weather – and full-cream milk contains very little lactose, a crystalline sugar found in milk, which blue tits are unable to digest.

Sometimes these residents take part in an even odder activity. Blue tits, if they get inside a house, may have a mania for tearing paper. Strips are torn from wallpaper and from books, newspapers and labels. Putty and other objects may be attacked. No one really knows why they do this, but it may be what is known as a 'dissociated' hunting activity, as tits commonly pull bark off trees when they are seeking insects.

Unusual nests

When it comes to choosing a nest site, blue tits are equally adaptable. Any crevice, nook or cranny that gives protection from the elements and from predators will do. They have been known to build in drainpipes, tin cans and car radiators, and on lamp posts and

bus stops, among other places. Nest-boxes put up especially for them are particularly favoured. Blue tits readily take seeds and nuts from birdfeeders, and continue to do so in the summer so that all the insects they find can be fed to the young.

Originally, blue tits were woodland birds, and in winter they often join other species of tits, and the occasional goldcrest, nuthatch or treecreeper, in large, loose flocks that move through the woods.

The trilling song of the blue tit may be heard on a sunny day in January, and nest-boxes should be put up by the end of February, because blue tits start prospecting for nest-holes early in the year. The record for the largest clutch laid by any songbird – 19 eggs – is held by a blue tit, although a clutch of 8-10 eggs is more usual. Large clutches are an insurance against the blue tit's high mortality rate.

Blue tits readily use a nest-box with an entrance hole about 25mm (1in) across.

IDENTIFICATION
Wings, tail and crown of head blue; cheeks white; back green and underparts yellow; adult sexes alike; young birds duller green colour with yellow ring around head.

NESTING
Nests in tree hole, nest-box or crevice in wall; both sexes collect moss, grass, hair and wool as nesting material; lays late April–May; 8-15 or more eggs, white with red-brown spots; incubation about 14 days, by female only; young, fed by both sexes, fly after about 19 days.

FEEDING
Mainly aphids, caterpillars and other insects; some fruit, grain and seeds.

SIZE
11.5cm (4½in)

J	F	M	A	M	J
J	A	S	O	N	D

Woods (largest populations in deciduous woods, especially those with oak trees), parks and gardens in all areas, including cities.

GOLDFINCH *Carduelis carduelis*

Great agility and a narrow, pointed bill enable the goldfinch to probe the spiky heads of tall weeds in autumn, in order to extract the soft, feathery seeds, a feat beyond many other small birds.

The scientific name, *Carduelis*, is derived from *carduus*, the Latin for thistle, reflecting the goldfinch's predilection for this particular source of food. It is the only British finch that can reach inside teasles without difficulty, grasp the seeds in a tweezer-like grip and successfully extract them, a feat noted by naturalist Charles Darwin. The male has a slightly longer bill than the female, and so can do this even more easily.

Although in spring they may be quarrelsome with other species, especially when in competition for sunflower hearts and niger seeds at bird tables, goldfinches are generally sociable birds. In fact, the only time goldfinches may become aggressive, even towards other goldfinches, is when they are nesting and food is in short supply.

Caged songsters

Towards the end of the 19th century, the number of goldfinches in Britain had been brought dangerously low by intensive trapping for the cage-bird trade. In 1860 it was reported that 132,000 a year were being caught near Worthing in Sussex. A few years later, a House of Commons committee was told of a boy who took 480 in a single morning. The Society for the Protection of Birds (later Royal) made the saving of the goldfinch from the trapper one of its first tasks, and today small groups and family parties, aptly known as 'charms' of goldfinches, are a familiar sight, feeding on the heads of thistles and other tall weeds in late summer and early autumn. They can often be seen throughout the winter, feeding in flocks with other finches, but when the weather gets really cold, many goldfinches migrate to France, Spain and Belgium – some go as far as North Africa – and it seems that more females than males make the trip. The song for which the bird was caged in Victorian times is a tinkling variation of the most frequently heard flight-note, a liquid 'tswitt-witt-witt'.

It is given when the male is establishing his territory in large gardens and orchards, and sometimes in thick hedgerows or open woodland. Changes in agriculture have reduced the thistle beds among which the species feeds but, at the same time, the reservation of areas for quarries and other development has provided it with new foraging grounds.

In courtship, which always takes place near the nest, the male droops and partly opens its wings, sways from side to side and exhibits its bright yellow wing-flashes.

Young birds typically lack the adult's red and black head markings.

IDENTIFICATION
Pale brown back; black and white tail; wings black, with yellow band and white spots; red face, rest of head black and white; sexes alike.

NESTING
Female builds neat nest of roots, grass, moss and lichen, lined with wool and vegetable down, usually in spreading tree; lays early May–August; usually 5 or 6 eggs, pale blue, lightly spotted with brown; incubation 12 or 13 days, by female only; nestlings, fed by both parents, fly after 13 or 14 days; normally two broods, sometimes three.

FEEDING
Seeds of thistle, burdock, dandelion, knapweed and other weeds; fruit of birch, alder and other trees; some insects, especially for young.

SIZE
12cm (4¾in)

J	F	M	A	M	J
J	A	S	O	N	D

Farmland, gardens and other places with scattered bushes or trees, including towns; absent only from mountains and moorland.

GREEN WOODPECKER
Picus viridis

This most brightly coloured of British woodpeckers uses its sharp bill not only to hack into trees but also, unlike its smaller cousins, to probe soft earth in search of ants, a favourite food.

While most woodpeckers are found among an abundance of trees, short grass is essential for the survival of the green woodpecker, because that is where it is likely to find its main food, ants. Once it has found an ant colony, it brings its very long sticky tongue into play. This is like a precision instrument capable of delicate movement, and with it the woodpecker explores the passages of the nest, scooping out all it contains – ants, eggs, larvae and pupae. A green woodpecker may spend up to an hour emptying an ant hill. Although ridding a garden lawn of ant hills may be viewed as a useful service, the birds can be troublesome. Very occasionally they take fruit, and they have been known to damage beehives while trying to get at the grubs.

In country districts, this largest British woodpecker is sometimes called 'the yaffle', because its loud ringing call can sound almost like laughter. Its other country name, 'rain bird', probably arose through its call being heard more clearly in the atmospheric conditions before rain, and may also be bound up with some ancient mythology that endowed the bird with powers of augury. Yelping and squealing cries are most often heard from its young.

Varied habitat
The green woodpecker is found in all kinds of well-timbered country, from open woodland, heaths, commons and farmland to parks and large gardens. Its numbers have risen in northern England and southern Scotland in recent years, but the reason for this has not been established. One suggestion is that the widespread planting of conifers has led to an increase in wood ants, so more food for the woodpecker, yet the birds usually prefer broad-leaved woods to conifers.

Despite its ground-feeding habits, the green woodpecker has retained the woodpecker tool-kit of sharp beak and toes adapted for maximum stability, with two toes pointing forward and two to the rear, to enable it to drill nest holes in soft wood and hang tenaciously to tree trunks.

The bird's vivid greenish yellow rump is conspicuous in flight.

Male birds challenging other green woodpeckers for territory will sway their heads from side to side, and usually spread their wings, fan their tails and raise their crown feathers. In courtship, they tend to droop their wings and raise the spread tail. Sometimes male and female chase each other round a tree. Drumming on tree branches occurs only occasionally, and fairly weakly, and is concentrated on the nest site.

IDENTIFICATION
Crimson crown; bright green upperparts; grey-green underparts; yellow rump; stripe under eye is red in male, black in female.

NESTING
Both sexes bore hole in tree; woodchips left scattered on ground; lays April–May; 5–7 eggs, white; incubation about 19 days, by both sexes; nestlings, tended by both sexes, fly after 18–21 days.

FEEDING
Almost entirely ants; also some wood-boring larvae of beetles, moths and other insects; occasionally grain, acorns and fruit.

SIZE
31.75cm (12½in)

Widespread in woods in England and Wales, spreading in Scotland; not in Ireland.

HOOPOE *Upupa epops*

The soft, far-carrying call of the male, from which the hoopoe derives its name, advertises this bird's presence. Rarely seen, the hoopoe creates a startling impression, especially when raising its spectacular crest.

With its pink-brown plumage, a crest like a Native American's war bonnet and boldly barred black-and-white wings, the hoopoe is one of the most exotic birds to be seen in Britain. Sadly, however, for most people a sighting of the bird is likely to remain little more than a dream because the hoopoe is rare and unpredictable. Small numbers arrive each April or May as vagrants from the Continent, probably having overshot their European destination, although others may turn up at any time of the year,

especially in the southwest of England, and areas along the south coast. These striking birds are seen singly more often than in pairs, although hoopoes breed regularly across the Channel. In the 19th century, hoopoes were mercilessly tracked down by collectors whenever they appeared on these shores.

When they do come to Britain, they usually seek places with scattered trees, nesting in a hole in an old willow or a cranny in a farm building. The site may soon become insanitary,

18

Courtship leads to much display with the crest as the male, the tip of his bill pressed against a branch, bows to the female. During incubation, he provides all the food for both birds. The hoopoe feeds mainly on the ground, where it is surprisingly inconspicuous, waddling around on short legs, probing the soil for insect larvae with its long bill.

The hoopoe displays its black-edged crest in alarm or when alighting.

IDENTIFICATION
Pink-brown plumage; very broad black and white wings and tail in flight; black-and-white tipped pink crest, long curved bill; sexes alike.

NESTING
Breeds in southern Europe, rarely in Britain, in hole in tree or wall, or uses nest-boxes; usually no nesting material but droppings accumulate; lays May–June; 5–8 eggs, light grey to cream; incubation 18 days, by hen only; nestlings, fed by both parents, leave after 3–4 weeks.

FEEDING
Beetle grubs, locusts, grasshoppers, moths, ants, earwigs, flies, some spiders, centipedes, woodlice, worms.

SIZE
29.25cm (11½in)

for hoopoes do not keep their nests sweet. Both nests and young acquire a strong, unpleasant smell, partly due to a build-up of droppings but also to a change in the composition of the preen oil. One theory is that the stench may have evolved as a strategy to keep predators away. The nestlings' other defence is to hiss loudly. Hoopoes are sometimes perceived as filthy birds because of their smelly breeding habits.

Distinctive sounds
The male hoopoe's song is a rapid, far-carrying, clipped 'hoo-hoo-hoo', of the same pitch as the cuckoo's. Both sexes give harsh calls. Fluttering before its nest, the hoopoe looks like a gigantic black-and-white barred moth, but its flight is by no means as feeble as it seems. Lazy wing flaps give it a generally erratic and undulating action but, when the need arises, a hoopoe can out-manoeuvre a falcon.

J F M **A M J**
J A S O N D

Woodland edges, orchards and other open land in south of England; feeds on bare soil or short grass (including lawns).

HOUSE MARTIN *Delichon urbicum*

On arrival in Britain, house martins congregate near suitably wet ground. Each pair must collect up to a thousand pellets of mud in their stubby bills to build a cosy, cup-shaped nest.

A small colony of house martins' nests is still a familiar sight, clustered under the eaves of houses and barns. The solid structures are built of mud that must be found no more than 200m (650ft) away – any farther than that and the mud pellet will have dried out by the time the bird gets back to the nest site. The cosy nests have an entrance hole at the top, keeping the nestlings safe from would-be predators. Originally a cliff-nesting species – and a few still nest on cliffs in north and west Britain – house martins have adapted to a human environment, where walls and eaves simulate the overhanging rocks of their natural habitat.

Surveys suggest that house martins may be slowly decreasing in Britain, but the evidence is conflicting. Certainly there are local fluctuations in their numbers, and from early April to mid May and again from late August to October passage migrants add to the population. In

1966 they returned to inner London as a nesting species for the first time since 1889. A colony under the arches of Clifton Hampden bridge, near Oxford, reached 513 nests in 1952, but today it is largely deserted. Few colonies now exceed a few tens of pairs at best and most house martins nest in small groups of up to five or so.

House martins usually nest in small colonies.

Crowded nests

Nest building begins three or four weeks after their arrival in April, although if there is no rain and access to wet mud is restricted, nesting may be delayed. A pair will produce at least two broods and all the young birds often continue to roost in the nest until they migrate. Late in the season, as many as 13 birds have been counted, crammed into a single nest.

From August onwards, flocks of house martins begin to gather, often in company with swallows, before heading for their wintering grounds south of the Sahara, although exactly where these are remains uncertain. In flight, a conspicuous white rump makes the house martin the easiest of the swallow family to distinguish. They fly high in the sky, particularly in Africa where flocks usually remain at such high altitudes they are only just in range of binoculars.

House martins are thought to sleep on the wing, the little white feathers that cover their legs and toes ensuring heat is retained as they fly on through the cold night sky.

IDENTIFICATION
Blue-black above, white beneath, with white rump; tail less forked than swallow's; sexes alike.

NESTING
Both sexes build rounded nest of pellets of mud, mixed with fine grass and roots, under eaves of house, sometimes under bridge, in caves or on cliff; nest thickly lined with feathers; lays May–August; usually 4 or 5 eggs, white; incubation 14 or 15 days, by both parents; nestlings, fed by both parents, fly after 19–22 days; two broods, sometimes three.

FEEDING
Almost entirely insects caught on the wing, especially flies and small beetles.

SIZE
12.75cm (5in)

Widespread in and around villages and towns, and farmland; scarce in north and west Scotland and western Ireland.

GARDENS & PARKS

HOUSE SPARROW *Passer domesticus*

A master of adaptability, the house sparrow is quick to exploit every opportunity provided by living in close proximity to humans, readily taking to nest-boxes and learning to take nuts from birdfeeders.

Equally at home in bustling cities or rural villages, inland or by the sea, the house sparrow is adept at taking advantage of whatever situation it finds itself in. Largely confined to the neighbourhood of human settlements, it draws attention to itself with its chirping, bold behaviour and frequent squabbles, and has become so familiar that people often suppose it to be the most numerous bird in Britain. Until the early 1970s, the house sparrow was Britain's commonest breeding bird, but now it is surpassed in numbers by the chaffinch and the blackbird. Of all birds suffering severe declines in numbers, this one is perhaps the most unexpected, but the lack of insects to feed its young in summer, seeds in winter and holes for nest sites is responsible for a dramatic reduction.

Intrepid builders

The sparrow is fighting back, though, and continues to show its ingenuity in its choice of nest sites. In the past, these have included a hole in a street light, the coke oven of steel works in south Wales and a coal mine in Yorkshire. More usually it utilises nest-boxes, holes in masonry and gaps under roof tiles, and is able to evict house martins and take over their nests.

There were probably no house sparrows in Britain before the arrival of man. They are believed to have come with Neolithic men, spreading across Europe from Africa. Like starlings, they were introduced into North America and have spread widely there. The sparrow was once regarded as a pest, and clubs were formed to catch them and turn them into pies or puddings, which provided a useful source of protein for farmworkers and poor city folk.

In autumn the house sparrow moves to farmland to feed on ripening corn. Its habit of tearing garden primulas and crocuses – especially the yellow ones – may be linked to its diet, as at least part of the petal is eaten.

The house sparrow utters a variety of 'chirps' and 'cheeps' and has a double note, 'chissik', all of which are strung together to form a rudimentary song. The most important element of its courtship display is the 'sparrow party', which usually begins with a single cock displaying to a hen and bowing to her. Then others join in, all chirping loudly until the hen flies off, pursued by the whole flock.

IDENTIFICATION

Brown upper parts, streaked with black; grey crown and rump, red-brown shoulders and black bib; white wing-bar; more heavily built than tree sparrow; female brown, with streaked back and plain underside.

NESTING

Both sexes build untidy nest of dry grass in hole in building or tree, sometimes in open in thick hedgerow, when nest is domed; usually lays April–August; normally 3–5 eggs, white with grey and brown blotches; incubation 12–14 days, chiefly by hen; young, fed by both parents, fly after about 15 days; up to three broods.

FEEDING

Grain and weed-seeds; insects and their larvae; almost entirely bread and scraps in built-up areas.

SIZE

14.5cm (5¾in)

Sparrows often dust-bathe in suitable spots on open ground in high summer, making small hollows in the dry earth in the process.

J F M A M J
J A S O N D

Towns, villages and isolated houses or other buildings and farmland throughout Britain and Ireland, but recently in much reduced numbers.

RING-NECKED PARAKEET
Psittacula krameri

Parrots may be thought of as tropical birds, but one species is now thriving in southern Britain – an exotic feral invader, the ring-necked parakeet is both conspicuous and noisy.

Popular as a cage and aviary bird, the ring-necked parakeet was first noticed in the wild in London in the 1960s, however there are reports of free-flying birds breeding in Norfolk as early as 1855, disproving one fanciful theory that the birds escaped from the West Ealing film set of *The African Queen* in 1951. It is possible that several captive birds may have escaped into the wild, although some may have been released deliberately, possibly by sailors who didn't want to go to the expense of putting them in quarantine.

However they found their freedom, what is certain is that the birds readily adapted to the living conditions in which they found themselves and numbers are growing in the core area of the parakeet's range in southeast England, especially in London and the home counties. In relatively mild conditions, the parakeets have been able to establish the most northerly wild parrot population in the world. Having few natural predators to contend with has helped, as has the birds' ability to breed early, from January onwards.

Pushy feeders
The ring-necked parakeet's vast natural range includes the Himalayan foothills, so it can cope perfectly well with winters in the south of England, especially with handouts of food available at garden feeders and bird tables, a major reason for the success of the species. The parakeets drive off all-comers, even starlings, eagerly seeking the peanuts, sunflower and other seeds on offer.

Another reason for the parakeets' success is their aggressive ability to oust other hole-nesting birds from their nesting sites, a potentially serious problem for woodpeckers, stock doves and nuthatches, among other native species.

Ring-necked parakeets, also known as rose-ringed parakeets, are unlikely to escape notice on their flights to and from their roosts, which are often hundreds strong. A famous one at Esher Rugby Club contains thousands of birds. Obviously parrots in appearance, they are also very noisy, and their loud, screeching calls are often what make people aware of them, especially on the evening flights, when flocks hurtle past against sunset skies.

IDENTIFICATION
Rounded head; deep, hooked crimson bill; long, pointed tail; pale green plumage, darker flight feathers, bluish tinge on tail; male has black and pink ring round base of head and bluish nape.

NESTING
In hole in tree or building; lays January–June; 3–4 eggs, white; incubation 22–24 days, by female only; young, fed by both parents, fly after 40–50 days, stay with parents for few more weeks.

FEEDING
Buds, fruit (including apples, pears, cherries and hawthorn berries), seeds, peanuts and other food at birdfeeders.

SIZE
38-42cm (15-16.5in), of which up to 25cm (10in) is tail.

Parakeets nest in tree holes or other natural cavities.

| J | F | M | A | M | J |
| J | A | S | O | N | D |

Woods, parks and gardens, mainly in southeast England; numbers increasing.

GARDENS & PARKS

ROBIN
Erithacus rubecula

Fiercely territorial, the robin patrols its borders all year round. It declares ownership by singing loudly, sometimes even at night, puffing out its brilliant orange-red breast feathers, and fighting if necessary.

The robin's image as a symbol of peace and goodwill at Christmas time is rather misplaced, because it is one of the world's most aggressive birds. Usually, conflict among birds is restricted to territorial singing, ritual display and chasing with the occasional escalation into a real fight. A robin will fly up to a perch above its rival, puff out its breast feathers and raise its head and tail. If this isn't enough to intimidate the intruder, battle may commence. The territory holder will go for its opponent's head, pecking at the eyes and trying to penetrate the skull. Fights to the death are not uncommon.

The defence of territory is a robin's life and the main reason for its plaintive warbling song, which is heard all year, except for a brief moulting period in July. Pauses of a few seconds between snatches of song allow rival cock robins to get in their own songs, and so help to establish a pattern of robin territories. In winter the females sing, too, and hold territories of their own. Only when the cold is so severe that finding food takes precedence over every other activity do robins allow others of their species to intrude on their winter territories.

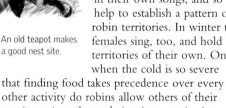

An old teapot makes a good nest site.

Night-time serenades

It has never been unusual to hear a robin singing during the night, but the habit increased with the coming of street lights. In the summer, the song is often mistaken and the bird delivering it assumed to be a nightingale.

In late summer, when the young birds have grown adult plumage, there is a great deal of disputing as territories and borders are established. In midwinter the female goes mate-hunting. She does the choosing. While the

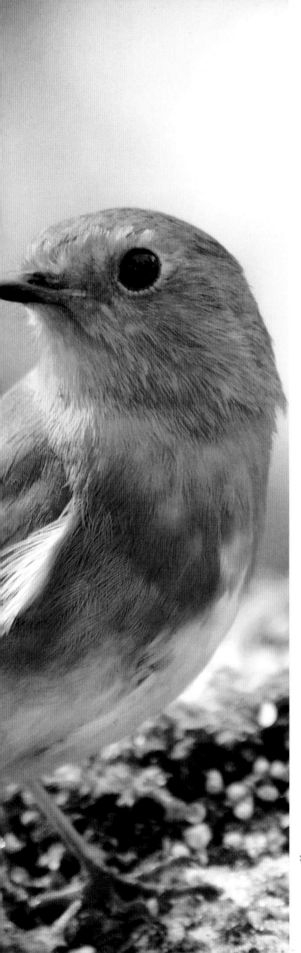

cock sings from his tree, she unobtrusively enters the undergrowth, and if she is tolerated for a few weeks, she begins to accompany him.

When in 1961, the British Section of the International Council for Bird Preservation was set the task of choosing Britain's national bird, they chose the robin, after a long correspondence in **The Times**. As well as belligerence, another characteristic of the robin is its tameness, which, according to the late David Lack, the world authority on robins, is a tribute to the British character. On the Continent robins are shy birds, keeping to deep woodland, but in Britain they are bold enough to dog the footsteps of a gardener who might turn over a worm or two for them.

Male robins will fight if threat displays are ignored.

IDENTIFICATION
Olive-brown above; orange-red breast, throat and forehead; whitish belly; sexes alike.

NESTING
Female builds domed nest of grass, dead leaves and moss in hollow in bank, tree hole, wall or ledge in shed; lays March–June; 3–6 eggs, white, usually with red-brown spots and blotches; incubation 13 or 14 days, by female only; young, fed by both parents, leave after 12–14 days; two broods, occasionally three.

FEEDING
Insects and larvae; fruit and seeds; earthworms.

SIZE
14cm (5½in)

J	F	M	A	M	J
J	A	S	O	N	D

Widespread throughout Britain and Ireland in woods, hedgerows, gardens, parks and other places with trees, shrubs and undergrowth.

GARDENS & PARKS

SONG THRUSH *Turdus philomelos*

The song thrush sings for most of the year. During the breeding season, one parent feeds the young while the other gives voice from a nearby treetop, the ringing tones of each aria lasting five minutes or more.

A rich and distinctive song gives this bird its name. Perched high in a tree at dusk, the song thrush may still be heard long after most other songbirds have finished their performances. The male starts singing in January, unless the weather is very severe, and continues steadily until July. Late in September he starts up again, and on fine days in October and November he sings almost as strongly as he does in spring.

Golden-buff under the wing marks out a song thrush from a redwing.

The clutch of sky-blue eggs in a song thrush's cup-nest seems symbolic of spring itself. The poet Robert Browning, nostalgic for April in England, gave a useful tip for identifying the bird's song: 'That's the wise thrush; he sings each song twice over.' The repetition of each loud, clear phrase – often more than twice – prevents confusion with either the mistle thrush or the blackbird. Common names for the song thrush include 'throstle' and 'mavis', and many people simply refer to it as 'the thrush'. Its scientific name comes from the Greek *philo*, meaning 'beloved' and *melos*, meaning 'song'.

Food search

When a song thrush hops across the lawn and cocks its head intently to one side, it is not listening for the stirring of worms in the ground, although it is certainly fond of earthworms. It is looking for food, tilting its head because its eyes are at the sides.

Snails are another favourite food, and a pile of broken shells often indicates that a song thrush has taken up residence in the vicinity. The bird has developed an ingenious method of getting to the animal inside – it smashes the snail against a stone, or 'anvil', to break the shell. The thrush returns time after time to its chosen stone.

Although the song thrush has a highly successful relationship with man, taking a wide variety of fruit, berries and insects in gardens, its numbers have decreased dramatically. Dry summers make life hard for the thrush because of the scarcity of snails; and earthworms, needing to keep their skins moist, remain buried deep in the soil. The song thrush is also badly hit by hard winters, not being particularly good at tolerating severe cold. Some move to France or even Spain for the winter, while others from Holland spend the colder months in Britain.

IDENTIFICATION
Brown above; breast buff, heavily streaked with chestnut and shading into white; smaller than mistle thrush, with no white on tail feathers; sexes alike.

NESTING
Both sexes build bulky cup-nest of dry grass and dead leaves, with lining of mud, in bush or hedge, low in tree or on ledge; lays March–July; 3–6 eggs, light blue with black spots; incubation 13 or 14 days, by female only; young, fed by both parents, fly after 13 or 14 days; usually two or three broods.

FEEDING
Snails, earthworms; insects and larvae; fruit and seeds.

SIZE
23cm (9in)

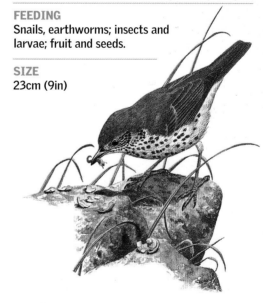

J	F	M	A	M	J
J	A	S	O	N	D

Woods, hedgerows, gardens and other areas with trees and shrubs for nesting; passage migrants and winter visitors from the Continent.

GARDENS & PARKS

London's wilder reaches

Just 20 minutes from central London lies the largest and wildest of its parks – a royal hunting ground that is now a haven for red deer and a wonderful variety of birds including exotic parrots.

Visit Richmond Park in autumn soon after dawn, and nothing seems to have changed since its creation in the 17th century. Autumn is the time of the red deer rut, when roaring stags test their strength with clashing antlers in the morning mists – a primal scene that would have been familiar to the English kings who once hunted here. Yet high in the ancient trees there is often a bustle and shrill screeching that is distinctly exotic. Hidden among the autumn leaves are hundreds of parrots. They are ring-necked parakeets – originally escapees from captivity, these parrots now thrive and breed in the wild, especially in outer London. At the end of the breeding season they gather in noisy flocks to roost in the park's trees for the night. Their presence demonstrates one of the charms of this magnificent parkland – a visit is often full of delightful surprises.

Richmond Park was once an area of scrubby woodland, small farms and pasture with scattered trees. Then in 1637 Charles I decided to enclose some 3¾ sq miles as a deer park. The local farmers were forced to move out beyond the high brick walls – an eviction that did nothing for the king's already shaky popularity – and some 2,000 red deer and fallow deer were moved in. Charles had little time to enjoy his new playground, for within five years England was in the grip of civil war. The park and walls remained, though, and by degrees the nibbling deer eliminated any new tree growth and transformed the scrubby landscape into grassland with tall trees.

Later, new woods were planted within protective fences and a number of ponds were excavated, resulting in the current patchwork of semi-natural acidic grassland, areas of bog and bracken, wetland, woodland and hundreds of ancient parkland oaks – many of which were mature in 1637. The whole park is now a National Nature Reserve.

Insect life

The varied habitats of Richmond Park provide refuges for a rich variety of plant and animal life, including more than 1,350 species of beetle and many other insects, such as moths and butterflies, various flies, grasshoppers, ants and dragonflies. These in turn attract birds, including green woodpeckers that use

In the many woodlands, a steady drumming sound may betray a great spotted woodpecker chiselling into timber to dig out wood-boring beetle grubs. These include the larvae of stag beetles, which feed deep in the decaying timber of the ancient oak trees. The woods also provide a home for the much rarer and smaller lesser spotted woodpecker, although it usually forages out of sight high in the trees. A ringing 'chwit chwit' signals that a nuthatch may be feeding acrobatically among the branches, but it is harder to spot the slim brown treecreeper as it spirals up tree trunks in search of bark-dwelling insects and spiders.

Welcome visitors

The inviting green haven of the park attracts a lot of visiting birds, which may either stay for a season or drop in on passage. In all, more than 140 species have been recorded here. Summer visitors include reed warblers and sedge warblers, which come to nest in the reed-bed at Pen Ponds, the divided lake created in the centre of the park in 1746. Dragonflies hatching from the ponds are pursued by summer-visiting hobbies that catch and eat them on the wing, and these agile raptors may even hunt the swallows and sand martins that hawk for midges over the water.

Winter brings migrant wildfowl to the ponds, including wigeon and gadwall. They join the resident mallard, pochard and tufted duck. There may even be the occasional fish-eating goosander. Most spectacular are the resident male mandarin ducks. Their ornate plumage looks like the product of artificial breeding, but is completely natural. Other winter visitors may include redwings and fieldfares – colourful thrushes that arrive from the far north to feast on berry crops in the park alongside the native thrushes and blackbirds. Up in the trees at this time, flocks of siskins and redpolls may be active, especially among birches and alders.

The real rarities, however, tend to turn up during the migration periods of spring and autumn. The great grey shrike, barred warbler and ortolan bunting have even been recorded on occasion.

Although the big gates close at dusk, walkers can remain in the park as long as they wish. Staying on after sundown in early summer can be a magical experience as the shrieking swifts fade into the upper air and the last calls of wildfowl echo across the lake. As darkness falls bats emerge, tawny owls in the woodlands begin to hoot, and time stands still.

High in the trees there is often a bustle and shrill screeching that is distinctly exotic. Hundreds of parrots now thrive and breed in the wild.

RING-NECKED PARAKEETS

their long tongues to probe anthills for prey, while stonechats perch on bushes watching for insects to snatch out of the grass. Meadow pipits feed in the rough turf, bursting up from underfoot with characteristically squeaky calls, and in spring perform parachuting song-flights. Their efforts are, however, eclipsed by the seemingly endless songs of the skylarks that soar overhead. Meanwhile, scurrying voles and other small mammals are sought by hovering kestrels, and by the little owls that often hunt by day from favoured perches among the trees.

STARLING *Sturnus vulgaris*

The starling's skills are not confined to reproducing the complex songs of a wide variety of other birds. This renowned mimic can also imitate car alarms, ringing telephones, wolf-whistles and even whinnying horses.

The male starling in particular is highly vocal, often adopting a favourite song perch to deliver his own rich and varied song, to which he adds convincing versions of other sounds he has happened to overhear. The calls and songs of tawny owls, chickens, blackbirds and swallows may appear in the starling's repertoire. One theory for why the male behaves in this way is that it helps to attract a female – the more complex the song, the maturer the bird, which may be attractive to a prospective mate.

Starlings, swarming in tens of thousands to their roost sites just before dusk, used to be a spectacular, noisy and inescapable part of life in many cities. Their high-pitched calls rose above the din of traffic and their droppings fouled streets and buildings. Many methods were used to drive them away, but it was the effects of intensive agriculture that eventually reduced them to much smaller numbers. Most town roosts have gone, although some exciting spectacles remain, as on Brighton pier, but it is in reedbeds and dense woods that huge roosts sometimes still appear in winter. The collective name for them is a murmuration, which may be something of a misnomer since they make more of a commotion than that term suggests.

Northern cousins

These winter flocks, which still perform magnificent swirling dances in the sky, are largely made up of visitors from Europe, some from as far away as Russia. Numbers of breeding birds in summer have declined by two-thirds since about 1970. A reduction in holes for nest sites may have had some effect in places, but it is largely lack of food that is to blame, as old pastures and meadows, full of insects, have been replaced by dense, tall grass, cut early and squeezed into plastic bags for silage. There is little there for any insect-eating bird to find, still less for a starling to feed to hungry chicks.

Leatherjackets – the larvae of craneflies – are one of the starling's favourites, and it has a surprising and effective

Starlings often nest in old woodpecker holes but any hole in a tree or cliff will do.

way of finding them. Once the starling has probed into the soil, it can open its bill to excavate a small hole in the earth. Since its eyes are located so far forward on its head, it can then peer down into the cavity to spot any likely meal. This is called 'open-bill probing' and is an unusual tactic for a songbird.

IDENTIFICATION
Iridescent purple, green and blue plumage, handsomely spangled with white or buff in winter; spangling more marked in female than male; jerky walk; swift, direct flight, sometimes varied by gliding.

NESTING
Usually nests in loose colonies; male builds untidy nest of dried grass and straw in tree hole, on cliff or building; female lines it with feathers or moss; lays April–May; 5–7 eggs, pale blue; incubation about 13 days, by both parents; nestlings, fed by both parents, fly after about 21 days; usually two broods.

FEEDING
Insects (especially leatherjackets), earthworms, spiders, snails, slugs; fruit, seeds, roots and berries.

SIZE
21.5cm (8½in)

J	F	M	A	M	J
J	A	S	O	N	D

All over Britain and Ireland except on high mountains; feeds mainly on grassland, from farmland and parks to garden lawns, also on shores, rubbish dumps and in town centres; winter visitors from Europe.

SWIFT *Apus apus*

Perfectly adapted to flying huge distances, the swift spends most of its life in the air, wheeling and gliding in graceful flight. Conversely, when obliged to descend to the ground, it is remarkably ungainly.

No birds are more aerial in their habits than swifts. Their legs, so seldom used, have evolved to become short and weak and, once on the ground, the birds are helpless and easily caught; but swifts never alight on the ground except by accident, and never perch on wires. Their family name, Apodidae, means 'without feet'. They feed on the wing, sometimes mate on the wing, and even sleep on the wing. At dusk, swifts circle higher and higher until they disappear from sight. It used to be thought that they returned after dark to roost at their nests, but it is now known that those not incubating eggs or brooding young remain aloft in the sky until sunrise, probably cat-napping on currents of rising air between short spells of flapping to regain height.

Despite appearances, swifts are not related to swallows and martins. Their closest relatives are the New World hummingbirds. To countrymen, the swift was once known as the 'devil bird', because of its habit of flying screaming round houses during late spring and early summer evenings. These forays often involve all members of a nesting colony. Swifts nest in any buildings

that offer dark, sheltered crevices and their nests are not easily seen. Females produce a slightly higher-pitched tone than males, and the sound of a pair calling together from the environs of the nest warns any other birds searching for a site that this one is already taken. If a strange swift does intrude on an occupied nest, fierce fighting may occur. One such battle, watched in a tower in Oxford, lasted 5¾ hours. There are also two records of swifts being found alive and interlocked on the ground beneath their nests.

Lifelong partnership

Swifts appear to pair for life. They have two courtship displays. On the nest, mating occurs after mutual crooning and preening, while in the air there is a spectacular chase before the birds mate on the wing. In long periods of cool and wet weather when prey is scarce, they can

Screaming flocks of swifts dash around rooftops.

survive for many days, even weeks, with very little food, living off their fat reserves. Swifts have been known to lose half their weight during such periods.

The swift is one of the latest migrants to arrive and one of the earliest to go. Not many are seen before the last few days of April or after the middle of August, which may be one reason why the swift is regarded as an emblem of summer.

Widespread visitor, except in northwest Scotland. Ranges widely over many habitats in its aerial search for food.

IDENTIFICATION
Black-brown plumage, except for whitish chin-patch; long, scythe-shaped wings; forked tail; sexes alike.

NESTING
Both sexes build nest of straw, grass and feathers, cemented with saliva, under eaves of building or in thatch, occasionally in rock crevice; lays May–June; usually 2 or 3 eggs, white; incubation usually 18–20 days, by both parents; young, fed by both parents, fly after 35 or 36 days.

FEEDING
Insects taken on the wing, especially flies, small beetles and moths.

SIZE
16.5cm (6½in)

GARDENS & PARKS

TAWNY OWL *Strix aluco*

The position of every tree and branch in its territory is etched into the tawny owl's memory, enabling it to hunt efficiently and silently in dense woodland at night. Once established, it rarely moves from its patch.

As soon as a young tawny owl becomes independent, it must establish a territory of its own and maintain it against intruders. It probably has a remarkable spatial memory that allows it to learn the layout of the area and get around with maximum efficiency, taking as much prey as possible with the minimum of effort.

The birds' diet can be studied fairly accurately by scrutinising their droppings. Tawny owls regurgitate pellets of undigested fur, bones and beetle wing cases.

A bird of copses and well-wooded parks and gardens as well as larger tracts of forest, the tawny owl is the most common owl over much of Britain, though absent from Ireland. Like most owls, it hunts by night and roosts by day, but if hard-pressed for food at nesting time, it will hunt in broad daylight. At other times, a roosting owl is superbly camouflaged by its mottled plumage, but can sometimes be located by following noisy parties of smaller birds, especially jays, blackbirds and chaffinches, which seek out the predator and mob it. The owl may not be dislodged by their clamour, merely sitting out the onslaught – it is not disturbed easily even at the sight of a human. The owl's astonishingly flexible neck allows it to turn its head almost full-circle, so that its large, unblinking, black eyes can be kept focused on an observer moving round it.

The owl pounces without warning, after spotting prey from a tree perch.

Nesting choices
The eggs are usually laid in a tree hole, but a pair may choose a convenient spot in a ruined building or on a cliff ledge, or take over a magpie's nest, a squirrel's drey or, in the absence of anywhere else suitable, a burrow in the ground. The female can be extremely fierce in defence of eggs or young. The owl will attack anything, or anyone, considered to be a threat, and its sharp talons can inflict serious wounds.

When Shakespeare wrote down the call of the tawny owl as 'tu-whit, tu-whoo – a merry note' he was, for once, being a poor naturalist. What he did was to combine two notes, the beautiful, breathy hoot, 'hooo: hoo, hu, hoooo-oo-oo', which is the male's song, and a loud, nasal, sharp 'kee-wick', a call used by both sexes at dusk to keep in contact in the dark. Young birds in late summer have a more vibrant, or whining, version of the 'kee-wick' call.

J	F	M	A	M	J
J	A	S	O	N	D

Woodlands throughout Britain; absent from Ireland; also occurs on farmland with trees, and in big gardens and city parks.

WAXWING *Bombycilla garrulus*

Occasionally, large hungry flocks of this strikingly crested bird from Scandinavia and Russia will descend on berry-bearing shrubs in suburban parks and gardens, seemingly regardless of humans or potential danger.

Every few years, and sometimes for several years in succession, there are mass irruptions of waxwings from their breeding grounds in northern Europe. A failure in the crop of rowan berries, their favourite food, may have forced them to move further afield; or there may have been a population explosion among waxwings after a particularly good rowan year. Britain gets a share of the larger dispersals, and although the invasions are erratic, they have been going on for centuries. A 'waxwing winter' was recorded as long ago as 1679–80.

There were four successive invasions in 1956–60, a series that beat all records. A massive irruption came in 1965–66, with the arrival of more than 11,000 birds recorded in two weeks, and numbers in the 1990s and since the turn of the century have sometimes been much higher.

Berry feast

By the time waxwings arrive in Britain, other birds have usually stripped the rowan bushes, so they gorge on the berries of ornamental trees and shrubs. In Norfolk, in February 1957, in two days a party of seven stripped the berries on 9.25sq m (100sq ft) of a cotoneaster growing in a cottage garden. One bird ate 390 berries, roughly its own weight, in 2½ hours. Other target vegetation includes hawthorn, pyracanthus, whitebeam and roses. They prefer red berries, a fact reflected in their unusually colourful droppings. This ability to home in on red-berry bearing plants has led to them being thought of as urban birds, and they turn up in city streets just as much as parks and gardens, wherever decorative shrubs have been planted, paying no attention to people or traffic noise.

Waxwings are highly sociable and call frequently, usually with a soft trilling 'sirrr'. They were once known as 'Bohemian chatterers'. In courtship, the handsome male displays his colourful wings, especially the secondary wing feathers. Their bright red wax-like tips, from which the bird derives its name, are shaped like elongated teardrops, each one an integral part of the feather. These may be a guide to sex and age since the waxy blobs are more numerous and longer in males and older birds, and may play a part in attracting a mate.

A flock of waxwings on the move are sometimes mistaken for starlings, but the birds can be distinguished by their longer, plumper bodies and less dart-like flight.

Waxy red tips on wing feathers are visible at close range.

IDENTIFICATION
Yellow and white markings and red waxy tips on wing; bright yellow tip to tail; prominent crest; black throat and eye-patch; chestnut and grey above, pink-brown below; looks like large plump finch at first glance; sexes alike.

NESTING
Does not nest in Britain; many that arrive probably breed in Finland; cup-shaped nest of twigs and moss built in conifer; lays May–July; 4–6 eggs, grey with dark spots; incubation about 2 weeks, chiefly by hen; nestlings, fed by both parents, leave after about 2 weeks.

FEEDING
Berries, including rowan, cotoneaster, pyracantha, viburnum, juniper, hips and haws.

SIZE
19cm (7½in)

Parks, gardens, woods, towns – anywhere with berry-bearing shrubs and trees, mainly in east; numerous in some years.

WREN
Troglodytes troglodytes

Often the loudest, shrillest song to be heard in the garden is produced by the wren. One of the tiniest birds, its diminutive frame trembles with the effort of maintaining such a vigorous and complicated tune.

This second smallest of Britain's regular breeding birds (it is only marginally larger than the goldcrest) has long been a national favourite; and considering its piercing, trilling song and perky stance with cocked-up tail, it is easy to understand why. Song is the male wren's main way of signalling territory ownership and attracting a mate, or mates.

The Jenny Wren – a nickname applied to the male as well as the female – has an absorbing life history. The male often builds several nests and entices his mate to select one. Two broods are normal and the male may take the first brood to roost in one of the 'rejected' nests while the female is incubating the second clutch. In surroundings where the food supply is poor, wrens are monogamous, but in richer habitats, males will set up more than one mate in the nests that they build.

Wren hunt

Despite the affection in which they are held, wrens were the victims of a cruel ritual that is still carried on in some parts of Ireland, although the birds are no longer caught. In the past, on St Stephen's Day (December 26), groups of youths in motley dress would beat the hedgerows, singing and trying to kill any wren they saw. The origin of the wren hunt is obscure, but the earliest record of it occurring was in Pembrokeshire in the late 17th century.

A wren may be glimpsed flitting between patches of undergrowth.

In winter, the wren's first line of defence against the cold is an efficient layer of feathers, roughly the same number as many larger birds, which it fluffs out to trap air against its body. In severe weather, though, when food is in short supply, keeping warm is a problem for these tiny birds, especially at night. Usually wrens are solitary birds, but

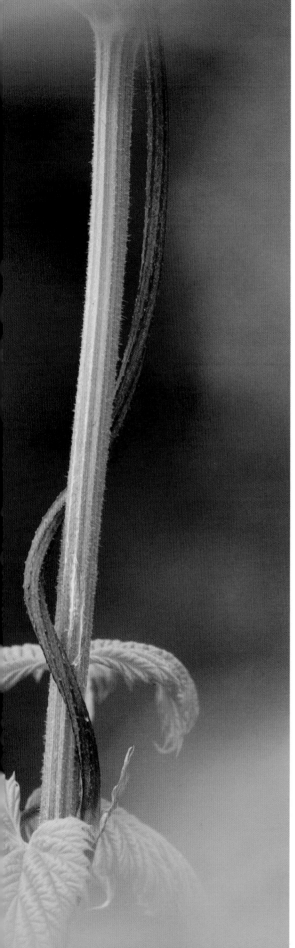

they have been found huddling together for warmth inside nest-boxes, in the eaves of houses – in one instance 96 wrens were counted – and ten birds have been found in a coconut shell. In severe winters, many of the birds perish but despite their heavy losses, wrens are capable of making remarkable recoveries, owing to their ability to produce large clutches and nurture two broods.

Wrens adapt to most environments, from large cities to remote treeless islands. Distinct races now inhabit the Outer Hebrides, Fair Isle, Shetland and even St Kilda, way out in the Atlantic. Wherever they are, wrens choose caves, or dark, cave-like places, for their nests, a reflection of their scientific name, which means 'cave-dweller'.

IDENTIFICATION

Red-brown, with barring on wings, tail and flanks; small tail, often cocked up; loud shrill song; loud 'churring' alarm call; sexes alike.

NESTING

Male builds several domed nests of moss, leaves and grass, in bush, creeper, woodstack or hollow in wall; female lines one with feathers; lays late April onwards; 5–7 eggs, white with fine red-brown spots; incubation about 14 days, by female only; nestlings, fed by both parents, fly after about 15 days; usually two broods.

FEEDING

Small insects and their larvae; a few spiders and small seeds.

SIZE

9.5cm (3¾in)

J	F	M	A	M	J
J	A	S	O	N	D

Found throughout Britain and Ireland in most habitats, from city centres to remote islands. It thrives in gardens, parks, farmland, heaths and woodland.

GARDENS & PARKS

Farmland

Often a patchwork of cultivated fields, pastures and hedgerows, traditional farmland provides the ideal habitat for many birds, including grey partridges seeking shelter among the crops, flocks of feeding rooks and skylarks soaring high above.

BARN OWL *Tyto alba*

Distinctive golden and white plumage gives the barn owl an unearthly look. The sight of one quietly scanning the ground from a perch, or gliding noiselessly through the dusk, is mesmerising in its impact.

The ghostly form of a barn owl looks white when it is caught in the flash of a car's headlights at night, quartering fields and meadows on softly feathered wings. In summer, though, when the bird needs extra food for its young, and towards the end of winter when food is so scarce that the bird is forced to hunt by day, its true colour can be seen – golden buff and ash grey above, with white underparts. The owl's buoyant, floating and briefly hovering hunting flight ends dramatically in a sudden noiseless swoop. To lose height as quickly as possible, the owl often folds its wings upwards and drops rapidly. At the last moment it swings its powerful talons forward, ready to strike. The rodent quarry has no warning and is usually killed outright, and the owl, gripping it firmly with its talons, takes it away to eat.

When hunting, the barn owl does not rely on sight alone. Experiments have shown that it can locate its prey on a pitch-dark night by its sense of hearing. Its ears are placed asymmetrically on its head, so that there is a fractional interval between the sounds picked up by each ear, and this gives it unusually precise powers of pinpointing the slightest sound.

Shrieking cries

Although the barn owl is renowned for its ability to fly in almost total silence, there is nothing muffled about the male's cry when he wants to attract a female or warn off a rival – a prolonged, strangled shriek. The female's response is uttered much less frequently and tends to break off in a less tremulous scream. During aerial chases, the pair may duet in a noisy, caterwauling performance. Loud, wheezy or snoring noises mainly come from hungry young, but may sometimes emanate from courting adults.

Barn owls were once fairly common and their decline is something of a mystery. It began long before some other birds of prey were affected by the build-up of pesticides in their bodies. The loss of grassland for feeding has had an effect; and with fewer empty buildings and hollow trees around, nesting sites are less easy to find. The owls do not build nests but lay their eggs on a heap of pellets made up of the indigestible fur, feathers and bones of their prey.

IDENTIFICATION
Golden buff and ash grey above with white face and underparts; female slightly greyer.

NESTING
No nest material; eggs laid on disgorged pellets; sites include old barns, ruined buildings, church towers, hollow trees, quarry faces, corn-ricks and nest-boxes; laying recorded in every month except January, but main period is April–early May; 4–6 eggs, white; incubation about 33 days, by female only; nestlings, fed by both parents, fly after 9–12 weeks; often two broods.

FEEDING
Shrews, mice, field voles, bank voles, water voles, brown rats, moles; small birds; beetles, moths; frogs, sometimes bats and fish.

SIZE
34.25cm (13½in)

Wings spread out in a threat display, a barn owl defends owlets from an intruder.

J	F	M	A	M	J
J	A	S	O	N	D

Widespread but local in agricultural country; scarce in northeast England, upland Scotland and northwest Ireland.

CORNCRAKE *Crex crex*

The call of the male corncrake is one of the most dramatic of natural sounds. Its volume and relentless insistence that once kept country folk awake on summer nights is now heard only in a few places.

The rasping voice of the corncrake, like a piece of wood repeatedly drawn against the teeth of a comb, was once a familiar sound in the countryside, but during the last 100 years the bird has become virtually extinct as a breeding species over much of Britain. Now they breed in western Ireland, where they are decreasing, western Scotland and the islands, and at one site in East Anglia, where the species has been reintroduced. In the Hebrides, for instance, farmers are allowing field margins and corners to become overgrown with the lush vegetation that the birds need for safe nesting, and are using more traditional mowing methods, including mowing from the centre outwards, to give the chicks time to escape the flailing blades.

The reason for the decline elsewhere lies in early cutting of grass for silage, rather than leaving it for hay, and the mechanised cutting methods that prove lethal to corncrakes. In the 19th century, many hay meadows were either scythed or at least mown later in the year than they are today, giving corncrakes time to rear their young in the long grass. The bird used to winter in small numbers in Britain, but is now reduced to the status of a summer visitor, when it feeds in fields of long grass and sometimes in damp, sedgy meadows or along hedges.

Corncrake nests and young can survive where unmechanised methods of reaping are used.

Secretive character

The corncrake is a relative of the coot and the moorhen and is sometimes called the landrail. Like many of the rails, it is shy and skulking, preferring to remain in deep cover for most of the time, and more often heard than seen. It flies only when hard-pressed, fluttering off for short distances on rounded wings with dangling legs. Despite this, it somehow manages to migrate to and from southeast Africa each year, crossing both the Mediterranean and the Sahara. On migration, it tucks its legs up into its feathers, as most birds do, and flies more strongly with its wings elongated.

The corncrake's monotonous 'crex-crex' call, heard mostly at dusk and at night, serves as a song with which to announce its territorial claims. Observations of captive corncrakes show that the male often builds a number of nests for the female to chose from, and the better the quality of the nest, the more easily the male will find a mate.

IDENTIFICATION
Brown, streaked darker above, with grey on face and breast and chestnut on wings; paler below, with dark bars on flanks; sexes alike.

NESTING
Ground nest of dried grasses well hidden in thick vegetation, and may be domed; lays May–June; usually 8–12 eggs, pale cream, heavily spotted with red-brown and grey; incubation about 16 days, mainly by female; chicks, tended by both parents, leave nest a few hours after hatching, fly after about 5 weeks.

FEEDING
Grasshoppers, earwigs, beetles, craneflies and other insects; slugs, small snails, earthworms and millipedes; some vegetable food, such as rush seeds.

SIZE
26.75cm (10½in)

Summer visitor to grasslands in western Scotland and islands, and Ireland; after 100 years of decline, very slowly increasing; reintroduction programme in eastern England.

CUCKOO
Cuculus canorus

This strikingly marked summer visitor has an ingenious method of ensuring its young are reared successfully – it leaves the task to other birds. Every other day, the female deposits a single egg in another bird's unattended nest.

The timing has to be right for the cuckoo, which is the only British bird to rely on other species to rear its young, a process known as brood parasitism. Incubation by the host bird should not have started when the female deposits her egg, and the female host may even still be in the process of completing her clutch. Each cuckoo lays up to 25 times in a season, and removes one of the host's eggs so that the overall total remains the same. Each egg is laid in a different nest, although individual females choose the same host species. Dunnock, meadow pipit and reed warbler are the most commonly selected hosts, although more than a hundred other species have been recorded.

Summer's herald

The first cuckoos of the year usually arrive in the second or third week of April from their winter quarters in Africa. March cuckoos are not unknown, but more often such early birds prove to be singing collared doves. No sound in nature is awaited more keenly in Britain than the loud, repeated song of the cuckoo. The male's double-noted courtship song, with its promise that summer is not far off, is a national institution, important enough in Britain's country calendar to be dignified by letters to *The Times*. The song can, in fact, be trisyllabic, 'cuck-cuck-oo', and the male also utters a strange, almost laughing 'gwuk-gwuk-gwuk' call when excited. The female has a loud, bubbling trill.

After their arrival, cuckoos spread out over almost the whole of the British Isles into any kind of country where they can find foster parents for their young, but the song that once rang out over farmland, woods and thickets, heaths, sand dunes, moorland and hills is heard less frequently now due to a recent dramatic decline in numbers.

The adult birds fly south in July and early August, while the newly fledged young tend to linger until September after leaving their foster parents. Then they migrate, finding their way unaided to their winter quarters – a remarkable example of the bird's inborn ability to navigate.

An adult cuckoo looks rather like a male sparrowhawk (but with pointed wings), while a young red-brown cuckoo resembles a kestrel.

IDENTIFICATION
Grey head and back, barred underparts; distinguished from sparrowhawk by slender bill, pointed wings and graduated, spotted tail; sexes alike, though in a rare variety female is chestnut-coloured and barred above and below; juveniles are brown and barred, with white spots on the head.

NESTING
Female fosters young on other birds, replacing an egg from host's nest with one of her own; lays 12 or 13 eggs in different nests, similar in colour to host's eggs; incubation 12–13 days; nestlings fed by host birds, fly after 14–21 days.

FEEDING
Insects, chiefly large caterpillars; also spiders, centipedes and earthworms; nestlings share host bird's diet, usually insects.

SIZE
33cm (13in)

| J | F | M | A | M | J |
| J | A | S | O | N | D |

Summer visitor widespread throughout Britain and Ireland but has declined recently.

CURLEW *Numenius arquata*

When the curlew delicately inserts its long, down-curved bill deep into soft ground, it uses the sensitive tip to locate unseen prey, which it then grasps firmly enough to extract from the clinging soil.

The curlew's bill is about three times as long as its head and is flexible enough to be opened at the tip only, which means there is very little danger of the bird losing prey once it has been seized. The curve makes it easier for the curlew to extract prey intact from mudflats and to probe around in small spaces inside burrows. Any prey that is found must be pulled out before it can be swallowed, a process that usually involves a good deal of vigorous head jerking. On average, the female's bill is longer than the male's.

Britain's biggest wader, the curlew was once confined as a breeder to moorland, but it extended its range to low-lying farmland and lower heaths and bogs early in the 20th century. This trend has since been reversed and numbers in Wales, for example, have declined by four-fifths in just 30 years, leading to fears of the curlews' inevitable disappearance there before long. In winter, curlews often feed in flocks, wading over coastal marshes and mudflats.

Haunting song

A loud, melancholy 'coor-li', the cry that gives the curlew its name, is the clearest sign of the bird's presence for most of the year. The full song, with its beautiful rising and falling crescendos and bubbling trills, is associated with establishing territorial rights and, in spring, this stirring sound announces that the breeding season is beginning. The males perform the song while they fly in wide circles and then glide down on extended wings to claim territories in the breeding area.

When female curlews arrive at the breeding place, sometimes as early as February, the males follow them in a crouching walk, circling them when they stop. Having spent the winter separately, the same pairs join up again and may even reclaim the same nesting site as the previous year, defending it against rivals. Newly paired adults indulge in more prolonged displays.

The customary caution of the birds is especially pronounced in the early stages of incubation, when male and female will change places on the nest in wary silence. But later, when the eggs have hatched, the parents become aggressive, running towards intruders and sometimes taking off to sweep down on them, uttering harsh, barking calls in an attempt to drive away the perceived danger. Despite this a fair number of chicks are lost to foxes and crows.

IDENTIFICATION
Grey-brown with long legs and downward-curved bill; white rump; larger than similar-looking, scarcer whimbrel and without stripes on crown; distinctive 'coor-li' cry; sexes alike.

NESTING
Nests in hollow, lined with grass or heather, among low vegetation; lays April–May; 4 eggs, buff, brown or olive, spotted with darker brown; incubation about 30 days, by both parents; chicks, tended by both parents, leave a few hours after hatching, fly after 28 days.

FEEDING
On coast, small molluscs, crustaceans, worms, small fish and sometimes seaweed; inland, insects and their larvae, worms, molluscs and at times berries and weed-seeds; occasionally grain.

SIZE
56cm (22in)

The curlew's distinctive white rump and long bill are conspicuous during its rather slow, gull-like flight.

| J | F | M | A | M | J |
| J | A | S | O | N | D |

Breeds mainly in uplands of western and northern Britain and Ireland; winters on estuaries and coasts throughout British Isles.

FARMLAND

GREY PARTRIDGE *Perdix perdix*

Athletic leaping in the air is part of the grey partridge's courtship ritual. At other times, this ground-loving bird lies low, exploding from cover at the last minute, wings whirring loudly, if danger threatens.

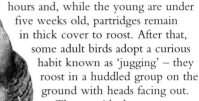

The grey partridge rarely flies very far. When disturbed, it speeds away in a twisting flight, but soon returns to the ground, gliding down on down-curved wings. It prefers to spend its life hidden among cereal crops and fallow fields, with nearby hedges, bushes, grassy banks and ditches to provide cover. Subtly complex colouring helps it to avoid detection.

Although the partridge also nests on rough grassland, moorland edges and heaths, its favourite nest site is among the thick vegetation at the base of a hedge, with access to fields and pastures where food for the chicks can be gathered. The grubbing out of hedgerows has badly affected the partridge but the widespread decline in numbers throughout the past 40–50 years has been caused mainly by a pesticide-induced reduction in suitable insect food for the chicks. Not only have chemicals been used to control the insects themselves, but herbicides have killed the food plants, which has also reduced the seed food available to adult partridges. Autumn-sown cereal crops that eliminate winter stubble have cut down the partridge's food supply still further and all this is exacerbated by increased danger from ground predators, such as foxes.

Active courtship

In autumn, partridges gather into family parties, known as coveys. They break up into breeding pairs in late January and early February, and at this time the cock birds become aggressive in defence of their territories. In courtship, pairs of birds often spring into the air and chase one another. In one recorded case, a number of birds formed a circle before pairing off.

The grey partridge holds the record for the greatest number of eggs laid by a British bird. There are generally 12–18 eggs in a clutch, but the maximum number recorded is 29. This may be the result of two females laying in the same nest, but more often a clutch is the product of just one bird. The entire clutch hatches in the space of a few

Camouflaged plumage protects female and chicks.

hours and, while the young are under five weeks old, partridges remain in thick cover to roost. After that, some adult birds adopt a curious habit known as 'jugging' – they roost in a huddled group on the ground with heads facing out.

The partridge's most frequently heard call-note, a loud, high-pitched, creaky 'keev-it', resembles a key turning in a rusty lock and often degenerates into a rapid cackle, 'it-it-it', when the bird is flushed. Years ago, this sound was practically synonymous with the cultivated fields of Britain's farmland but in many areas it has disappeared altogether.

IDENTIFICATION

Brown plumage, barred with chestnut on flanks and chestnut tail; neck and under parts grey with dark horseshoe on breast; hen less boldly marked than cock.

NESTING

Hen makes scrape in ground lined with dried grass and leaves, often approached by runway, and usually in thick vegetation; lays late April–May; usually 12–18 eggs, pale olive; incubation about 24 days, by hen only; chicks, tended by both parents, leave after a few hours, fly after about 2 weeks.

FEEDING

Mainly grain and buds, flowers, leaves and seeds of low-growing plants; animal matter includes insects, spiders, small snails and slugs.

SIZE

30.5cm (12in)

J	F	M	A	M	J
J	A	S	O	N	D

Mainly on farmland in lowland Britain and Ireland; declining very rapidly. Conservation on some large shooting estates still produces healthy populations.

KESTREL *Falco tinnunculus*

Tail feathers splayed into a fan shape, wings outspread, the kestrel hangs in the wind, seemingly immobile, as it scans the ground below. This remarkable ability to hover helps the bird target its prey.

The hunting technique for which the kestrel is famed is often, in fact, a slow glide into the wind. The bird holds its wings still, with just a few occasional small flapping movements to prevent it being blown backwards. All the bird is in motion apart from its head, which is fixed in relation to the ground. When a mouse or a vole is spotted, the kestrel drops in stages, never taking its eyes from its quarry, until finally it pounces, grabbing the rodent in its talons and swiftly dispatching it with a bite.

The kestrel's distinctive hovering flight gave rise to its country name, 'the windhover', and inspired the poet Gerard Manley Hopkins to compose a poem under that title. A kestrel was also the 'star' of director Ken Loach's classic 1969 film *Kes*. Like all birds of prey, the kestrel is protected by law throughout the year, although it is not in desperate need of this protection. Farmers recognise the bird as a useful ally against mice, rats, voles and harmful insects, and enlightened gamekeepers are prepared to

The kestrel's splayed tail gives it extra control in the air.

are part of the ritual. The male also catches and presents food to the female as part of the pair-bonding process. In another courtship ceremony that has been recorded, the male was seen to beat upwind, then fly down fast at the female. She was sitting in a bush, and just when he seemed about to strike her, he shot up in the air. This performance was repeated several times. Kestrels pair for the season and sometimes remain paired for life.

IDENTIFICATION
Pointed wings and long tail; male has blue-grey head rump and tail, with black band at end of tail; female has barred tail, also with black band; hovering flight is distinctive.

NESTING
No nest built; eggs laid on cliff ledge, or high building, in tree hole or abandoned nest of other bird; lays mid-April–May; usually 3–5 eggs, white, with heavy red-brown markings; incubation about 28 days mainly by female; nestlings, fed by both parents, fly after 27–30 days.

FEEDING
Mainly mice, voles and young rats; also frogs, earthworms and insects; sparrows and other birds in towns.

SIZE
34.25cm (13½in)

overlook the occasional game-chick it takes, because of its value as a destroyer of pests. Partly because it does not have to face persecution, and partly because it can adapt to different terrain, the kestrel remains one of the commonest of Britain's day-flying birds of prey, although it is less common than it used to be. It is equally at home in farmland, moorland and along sea cliffs.

In recent years, the kestrel has become more of an urban bird, and is renowned as a hunter along motorway verges, where its hovering skills can be easily observed, although to save energy while hunting, it may use a convenient perch, such as a tree, bridge, fencepost or pole, from which to watch for prey.

Aerial games
The kestrel's main call-note is a shrill 'kee-kee-kee-kee', heard mainly during courtship. Aerial chases, high in the sky, and sometimes in circles,

| J | F | M | A | M | J |
| J | A | S | O | N | D |

All types of open country including urban areas; most numerous in rough grassland.

LAPWING *Vanellus vanellus*

In spring, the male lapwing's already long crest grows longer still and his face markings become more distinct. He attracts a mate by performing striking aerobatic manoeuvres over the breeding territory.

As the breeding season approaches, the male lapwing establishes his territory. His flamboyant, tumbling aerial courtship display is a delight to watch. Diving, swerving, rolling and twisting, apparently out of control, the bird plunges down, the air rushing through its wings making a vibrant throbbing or 'lapping' sound while he utters his wild 'p'weet-p'weet, peewit-peewit' song.

His call-notes are elaborations of the long drawn-out wheezy 'pee-wit' calls of both sexes. The lapwing, or peewit, derives both its common names, as well as most of its many old country names, such as 'piewipe' and 'peasieweep', from the sounds it makes.

As well as the aerial display, the courting male makes scrapes in the ground – to serve as potential nests – by rocking forward on to his breast and showing off his orange-brown rump patch to entice a prospective mate.

Sociable groups

Like other plovers, lapwings are highly gregarious outside the breeding season. As they fly together in big, loosely bunched flocks, an eye-catching twinkling effect is created by hundreds of flashing black-and-white wings. They often form mixed flocks with golden plovers in winter, when numbers are significantly boosted by migrants from Europe.

All year, lapwings feed over farmland, both arable and grass, but when breeding they are also fairly common in damp, rushy fields, coastal marshes and moorland. In winter many join other waders on freshwater margins and sometimes on sands and mudflats along the coasts, although if the weather gets very cold, flocks of lapwing may be seen heading south and west in search of warmer climes.

Originally a bird of undisturbed grassland, the lapwing adapted readily to thrive on farmland, but like so many farmland species, it has undergone a dramatic decline as a breeding

The male displays his cinnamon rump while making a nest-scrape.

bird, especially in the southern England and Wales. Drainage and the increased use of autumn-sown cereal crops, which are too long and thick by spring for nesting lapwings, are the main culprits.

Lapwings were once so common that their eggs were regularly collected in large numbers, and sold as a delicacy. Plover's eggs were often served in their shells in moss-lined baskets, but since the 1960s the eggs may be collected only at certain times and under licence.

IDENTIFICATION
Medium-sized, looks black and white at a distance; rounded wings and short tail, clear in flight; at rest, long crest conspicuous; in bright sunshine can look brilliant green above; male has longer crest, whiter face and blacker breast.

NESTING
Female selects one of several ground scrapes made by male, often on slight rise, and lines it with dried grasses; usually lays late March–May; usually 4 eggs, olive-buff or olive-green, heavily marked with black; incubation about 27 days, mostly by female; chicks, usually tended by female only, leave in a few hours, fly after about 5 weeks.

FEEDING
Mainly insects, especially wireworms and leatherjackets; also earthworms, sometimes brought up by stamping feet.

SIZE
30.5cm (12in)

J	F	M	A	M	J
J	A	S	O	N	D

Open country throughout most of Britain and Ireland; breeds chiefly on farmland, especially among fields with bare soil and short grass; some on wet grassland, marshes and other damp habitats; visits estuaries and shores in winter.

PHEASANT *Phasianus colchicus*

Originating in Asia, this is the most exotic-looking bird to be found roaming the countryside, and due to its popularity as a gamebird, one that has had a greater influence on the landscape than any other.

No firm evidence can be found to support the theory that the Romans brought the pheasant to Britain. It was first definitely recorded in 1059, a few years before the Norman Conquest. The bird's true home is in Asia, from the Caucasus across to China, and it was birds from the western part of this range, the Caucasus, that were originally introduced to Britain. This form became known as the Old English pheasant, but from the 18th century onwards there were repeated introductions, from eastern Asia, of forms with a white neck-ring. As a result, present-day birds are an amalgam of types – those with and those without the white neck-ring in roughly equal proportions.

The pheasant's success in Britain is due partly to human nurturing and partly to its adaptability. Reedbeds and other wetland vegetation are where it prefers to live in its native lands, but in Britain it also thrives in shrubby woodland edges and on farmland with woods nearby. One reason is that although it lives mainly on the ground, it likes to roost in a tree. Every year, gamekeepers incubate eggs, care for chicks, control predators and then release millions of reared birds into woods in preparation for the shooting season, which runs from 1 October to 1 February. Management of the environment to suit pheasants was once ruthless, and detrimental to other species, but these days it is usually excellent for wildlife in general, and especially for other birds such as warblers, tits and woodpeckers.

Wild success
Well established as a wild breeding species, on heaths and commons as well as in copses and among beds of reeds and

Pheasants fly up steeply in alarm, with loud wing-beats and hoarse 'ku-tuk-ku-tuk' calls.

sedges, the pheasant has increased in almost all areas of Britain during the past 25 years. It has the typical whirring flight of a gamebird, alternating with gliding on down-turned wings, and it can rocket explosively upwards when disturbed. The cock crows with a loud, hard 'korr-kok', and often responds to a shot or distant explosion by crowing. In spring, the male

gathers a harem of females, from two to 15 or more, noisily displaying his beautiful plumage along with the gaudy red facial wattles and ear-like tufts that become swollen with blood. He regularly patrols his territory, deterring rivals by stopping at intervals – every 10 to

15 minutes at the height of the season – to crow and flap his wings vigorously, making a distinct drumming sound.

IDENTIFICATION
Cock has mainly copper plumage; hen is mottled brown and shorter-tailed; green, grey and black-barred forms of the cock are common.

NESTING
Hen scrapes hollow in ground, often under thick vegetation, lines it scantily with leaves and grass; occasionally nests in old bird's nest in tree; lays late April–June; usually 8–15 eggs, pale olive; incubation 22–27 days, by hen only; chicks, tended by hen, leave nest when a few hours old, fly after 12–14 days.

FEEDING
Wide variety of animal and vegetable food, from fruits and seeds to wireworms, caterpillars, grasshoppers and other insects; occasionally lizards, field voles and small birds.

SIZE
Male: 83.75cm (33in) including 45.75cm (18in) tail
Female: 58.5cm (23in) including 23cm (9in) tail

J	F	M	A	M	J
J	A	S	O	N	D

Woods and farms throughout Britain and Ireland, except far northwest Scotland.

QUAIL
Coturnix coturnix

A powerful, three-note song that seems to emanate from a field of cereal crops may be the only sign of a quail's presence – but a misleading one since this little bird has the ability to throw its voice.

So shy and secretive are quails that they would hardly ever be detected were it not for the male's repeated, simple, liquid song in summer. The sound, although astonishingly loud and far-carrying, is maddeningly hard to pin down to a particular spot, with an effect similar to that produced by a ventriloquist.

In the breeding season, the cock bird advertises its presence with a persistent 'quic-ic-ic' call, which is sometimes written as 'wet-my-lips'. The hen calls a soft 'bru-bru' until contact is made. Then the cock bird runs up and circles her, puffing up neck and breast feathers, stretching his neck and dragging his wings along the ground. Once the birds are paired, the singing usually stops. However, a male may have more than one mate, sharing a single nest.

The quail's normal habitat is farmland, especially light chalk and limestone soils, where the male's song can be heard coming from fields of clover, lucerne and young corn, and also from hayfields, fields of root crops and tussocky grassland. A great deal remains to be discovered about the species' feeding habits, but the seeds of weeds and grasses apparently form the main part of its diet. If disturbed, the quail will fly off at the last minute, its flight fast and twisting, but it soon drops down into cover again.

Fluctuating numbers
The unpredictability of Europe's only migratory gamebird means that although usually a few hundred arrive in Britain in the spring, every so often, in 'quail years', these numbers increase dramatically, sometimes to more than 2,000. The downland-rich counties of Dorset and Wiltshire are the migrants' main destination, with good

Longer-winged than other gamebirds, the quail flies fast with few glides, often dropping quickly into cover.

numbers choosing the crop fields of East Anglia, English-Welsh border country and southern Scotland. In quail years, though, the visitors can turn up almost anywhere in Britain, wherever suitable cover and nesting sites can be found.

This little bird – its body is marginally longer than a skylark's, although much plumper – is declining across much of its European breeding range as a result of intensive farming practices, increasing drought conditions in its wintering grounds in central Africa, and the ravages of hunters' guns on both sides of the Mediterranean. Hunters have always taken their toll of quail, but in the early part of the 20th century the birds were netted live, too. London was one of the main exporting centres for this trade, halted by law in 1937.

IDENTIFICATION
Sandy-brown above, paler below; light streaks on flanks; liable to be confused with young partridge, but is distinguished by buff streaks on head and absence of chestnut on tail; cock has long pale stripe over eye; hen drabber than cock, with black spots on breast.

NESTING
Hen makes scrape in ground among crops or grass, thinly lined with grass or leaves; lays late May–June; usually 7–12 eggs, pale cream, marbled with shades of brown; incubation 18–21 days, by hen only; chicks, tended by hen, leave after a few hours, begin to fly after about 11 days.

FEEDING
Mainly seeds of grasses and weeds; also snails, caterpillars.

SIZE
17.75cm (7in)

J F M A **M J**
J A S O N D

Lowland farmland throughout the British Isles; numbers fluctuate.

ROOK *Corvus frugilegus*

Rooks are sociable birds, with winter roosts among the most impressive of any landbird and their communal life so well developed that it has even given rise to fanciful stories of 'rook parliaments'.

Rooks form their biggest feeding flocks in autumn and winter, when migrants from northern and eastern Europe join the throng on suitable farmland. The birds roost in nearby woods and copses, and their morning and evening flights to and from their favoured feeding haunts are as regular as clockwork. This particular mix of agricultural land for feeding and nearby tall trees for roosting is crucial for the rook – one is no good without the other.

Autumn is also the time when rooks start to form pair bonds in readiness for the next breeding season. The male courts the female with food offerings and displays of physical prowess, bowing and cawing to her both on the ground and in the treetops. Spectacular aerial acrobatics, involving tumbling, twisting and diving, may also be part of the ritual but could also serve to confuse birds of prey or to advertise the location of the roost to other rooks.

Early breeders

The reason courtship takes place in autumn is so that nesting can begin early – some females lay their eggs in February, although March is more usual – and the young can fledge before the soil invertebrates on which they feed become scarce in summer.

Although rooks nest in colonies and feed in flocks, they have a strong sense of territory. Mayhem often breaks out in the spring as pairs defend a small area around their nests, threatening and driving off intruders. Sometimes rooks steal sticks from the nests of neighbouring pairs while the rightful owners are away collecting more nesting material, and once incubation has begun, males may try to mate with sitting females. Misinterpretations of aggressive behaviour in the defence of territory have led some observers to claim that they have seen a circle of rooks sitting in judgment on 'criminal' birds.

Treetop rookeries, loud with hoarse cawing, are often located near buildings and may be found in cities. Occasionally, the nests may even be built on man-made structures, such

A distended throat pouch indicates when a rook is carrying food.

as pylons, rather than in the usual ash or oak trees. In Scotland, some birds nest in Scots pines. Wherever they are sited, the rookeries are usually permanent communities. Pairs of rooks use the same nest each year, repairing it for each new breeding season. Rookeries vary considerably in size. Many contain just a few dozen nests, but one colony in northeast Scotland once held as many as 9,000 pairs.

IDENTIFICATION
Black with purple gloss; bare, grey-white patches on face and base of bill; wedge-shaped tail; thick thigh feathers give 'baggy breeches' effect; young do not have face patch; sexes alike.

NESTING
Nests in colonies, normally in trees; both sexes build untidy nest of sticks, lined with dry grass, leaves and roots, and often added to each year; lays late March–April; usually 3–6 eggs, pale green to grey or pale blue, heavily flecked with grey and brown; incubation about 18 days, by female only; nestlings, fed by both parents, fly after about 30 days.

FEEDING
Wireworms, leatherjackets and other insects and larvae; earthworms, snails, grain and weed-seeds, fruit; sometimes carrion, shellfish.

SIZE
45.75cm (18in)

J	F	M	A	M	J
J	A	S	O	N	D

Widespread, especially in lowland farmland with tall trees for nesting; absent only from treeless uplands and large towns.

FARMLAND

SKYLARK *Alauda arvensis*

In strict contrast to its unspectacular appearance, the skylark's heavenly song is its true glory, although the sound may seem to come from an empty sky, because the bird often flies too high to be seen.

For Wordsworth, the skylark was an ethereal minstrel, a pilgrim of the sky. For Shelley, it was a blithe spirit, showering the earth with a rain of melody, and lesser poets before and since have added their praises until it has become one of Britain's best-loved birds. Its sustained warbling song, which can last for five minutes or more without a pause, is usually delivered when the bird is flying high in the air, often out of sight or nearly so. The skylark is the only British bird that habitually sings while ascending almost vertically, keeps singing while hovering and goes on singing while spiralling back down to the ground.

In the breeding season, skylarks nest in any kind of open country, from sand dunes at sea level to peat bogs and moors on the mountains as well as open grassland and farmland. The males' singing has the twin objectives of defending territory and attracting females, and is heard from late January to early July. At other times of the year, particularly in August and September when the annual moult is in progress, they are fairly silent. Male and female remain together during the breeding season and, if both birds survive the winter, may pair up again the following year.

Ground cover

Aside from the renowned song flights, the skylark spends most of its time on the ground, looking for food, nesting and roosting. Changed farming techniques – especially the predominance of autumn-sown crops that deny the skylark the chance to feed on stubble in winter and become too tall and dense for nesting in spring – have brought about widespread declines in numbers. A spring morning when the air is full of skylark song is an unforgettable but sadly much rarer experience these days.

As late as 1931, skylarks were trapped for food, and also to keep as cagebirds. Special reflectors known as lark mirrors were sometimes used to dazzle the birds so that they could be netted more easily. Skylarks now have full legal protection.

After the breeding season, skylarks are often gregarious, gathering in flocks to feed and to move to their winter territories. Flocks may number a hundred birds or more, but they mostly remain practically invisible, well camouflaged by their streaky brown plumage. Upland breeders move to lower ground for the winter, and home-bred birds are joined by winter visitors and passage migrants from Europe.

The skylark sustains its song for several minutes while in its vertical song-flight.

IDENTIFICATION
Streaky brown; white outer tail feathers show in flight; characteristic soaring song-flight; small crest and white line along trailing edge of the wing; sexes alike.

NESTING
Hen builds cup nest of grass, sometimes lined with hair, on ground; lays April–August; usually 3 or 4 eggs, white, thickly speckled with brown; incubation about 11 days, by hen only; nestlings, fed by both parents, leave nest after 8 days, fly after 16 days; two or three broods.

FEEDING
Seeds of charlock, chickweed, sow thistle, sorrel and other weeds; leaves of clover and other plants; earthworms, caterpillars, beetles and their larvae, spiders and other small ground animals; some grain.

SIZE
17.75cm (7in)

J	F	M	A	M	J
J	A	S	O	N	D

Widespread in open habitats; joined by migrants from northern and eastern Europe in winter.

Precious haven

Centuries of traditional farming in the Yorkshire Dales have created ideal habitats for birds that, elsewhere in Britain, are being driven off the land by modern agricultural practices.

Beating slowly across a hay meadow in the Yorkshire Dales, a barn owl catches the late afternoon light in its wing feathers and, for a few magical seconds, the creamy buff of each vane is lit up as if with an inner glow. It pauses and hovers, wings flashing, then twists and plunges into the long grass with outspread talons. A moment later it rises again, a limp shape clutched in one foot, and flies off. At least one of its chicks will eat tonight.

For a barn owl, the Yorkshire Dales are perfect hunting grounds, rich in prey. Covering 680 sq miles of the central Pennines, the National Park is mostly grassland and moorland, with some 277 sq miles of farmland in the dales themselves – long valleys leading down from the high fells, overlooked by rugged limestone scars, etched with stone walls and dotted with isolated field barns. Most of this land is used for grazing sheep and, in the valley bottoms, making hay to feed farm animals in winter. Over much of Britain pastures and meadows have been transformed by the practice of adding fertiliser to encourage lush grass that smothers other plants. Traditional haymaking is rarely practised and instead the grass is cut early and preserved as green silage. But here in the Yorkshire Dales the lime-rich soil is not fertilised, and local farmers still employ the old practice of allowing the meadow grass to grow until late July or August, then cutting it and letting it dry in the field. This allows all the other plants that grow among the native grasses to flower and set seed, and the result is a wonderfully rich flora with as many as 30 different plant species in every square metre.

Rich pickings
Such floral diversity creates a stunning spectacle in early summer, but it also forms the basis of a flourishing ecosystem. It encourages a host of insects, such as the butterflies that must have access to particular food plants for their caterpillars, as well as grasshoppers, beetles, bees and hoverflies. Small mammals, such as voles and wood mice, also thrive here.

Much of this teeming life is invisible to the human eye, but not to the grassland and farmland birds that flock to the region in spring to nest and raise their young. They include the ground-nesting skylark – its liquid, silvery song, delivered from a high, hovering flight, is an almost constant soundtrack to any walk through the Dales in spring. The yellow wagtail, an elegant summer migrant from Africa, particularly favours the traditionally managed haymeadows. Loss of such habitats elsewhere has caused widespread population declines in both these species nationally, yet here in the Yorkshire Dales they still flourish. The voles and mice that scurry through the grass are targeted by hovering kestrels and patrolling barn owls. Often active during the day, an owl may land momentarily, its gorgeous golden and grey plumage subtly merging with the dry grass. The region also has a reintroduced population of red kites – beautiful raptors that feed largely on carrion.

Higher up the valleys the rough grass supports nationally important breeding populations of waders, such as curlews with their evocative bubbling song, and lapwings that display over their nesting sites with gloriously reckless swoops and dives. The lapwing, in particular, has been hard hit by intensive farming regimes that lead to its nests being overwhelmed by tall crops or crushed beneath farm machinery, but here on the upland pastures of the Yorkshire Dales it has only sheep to contend with.

Rugged fells
The high fells above the dales are mostly heather moorland, owing to heavy rain washing nutrients and soluble lime out of the soil and turning it acid. Such land cannot be profitably farmed, so the moors are largely left to hardy sheep and upland birds. The fells are the nesting grounds of dunlin, snipe and golden plovers, as well as noisy redshanks, which alert every bird in the area to human presence with their loud, ringing 'tew-tew-tew' alarm calls. Meadow pipits are everywhere, bursting up from the grass with their thin, squeaky calls and, in spring, parachuting down with an accelerating trill of simple song. They are often targeted by merlins – small, fast falcons that seize other birds in flight in the manner of miniature peregrines. These too are to be seen – especially at Malham Cove, where a regular peregrine nesting site can be viewed through telescopes provided during the breeding season as part of a scheme run by the RSPB and the Yorkshire Dales National Park Authority. Other crags are occupied by nesting

Often active during the day, an owl may land momentarily, its gorgeous golden and grey plumage subtly merging with the dry grass.

BARN OWL

ravens, and their deep, croaking cries echo through the fells and dales, especially in spring when they are reclaiming their territories.

Such birds offer high drama, and the rocky streams that flow down the dales provide equally memorable encounters. For these are the haunts of the grey wagtail and dipper – a plump, short-tailed bird resembling an oversized white-breasted wren that has the extraordinary habit for a songbird of hunting aquatic insects underwater. Undaunted by the rushing flow, it plunges in and walks upstream beneath the surface, clinging to the rocks with its strong toes. It often stays in the Dales throughout the year, even hunting beneath the ice on occasion. For many of the breeding birds, though, the chill of autumn is their cue to be gone, and they will not return until the following spring.

STONE-CURLEW *Burhinus oedicnemus*

Sitting motionless in a nest-scrape on the ground, the stone-curlew is practically invisible. Its brown-patterned plumage blends perfectly with the stony soil – big yellow eyes providing the only clue to its presence.

Despite its name, this ungainly bird is only distantly related to the curlew, although it is a wader and its plaintive cry of 'coo-lee' is similar to the sound made by its namesake. In fact, the stone-curlew is a member of a small family of unusual birds known as thick-knees – from their stout knees, which, as in other birds, are actually ankle joints – and its closest relatives may be oystercatchers. Mainly active between dusk and dawn, the bird's big, staring yellow eyes give it a fierce look but allow it to see in the gloom when foraging for insects.

Grassland nester

A rare summer visitor, arriving in March from its wintering grounds in southern Europe and Africa, the stone-curlew is at the northwestern tip of its range in Britain. The bird is adapted to life in an open, treeless landscape and its favoured habitats in England are the dry sandy heaths of Breckland and east Suffolk, and the chalk downland of the southern counties. Much of this habitat has been converted from grass to crops in the past 70 years and the survival of the species in Britain now largely depends on the birds' ability to make sure their breeding season coincides with farmers' cultivation of spring-sown crops, such as carrots and kale. However, the short cropped grassland of Salisbury Plain still offers nesting opportunities and intensive efforts at conservation, notably in Breckland, have met with some success. The rapid decline in numbers has slowed, and the population may even be starting to build up again.

Courting birds face opposite ways.

Stone-curlews are believed to mate for life and they may return to the same nesting territory each year. Their courtship displays include bowing and touching bills, and the birds have been seen running about excitedly, picking up straws, flints and other small objects and tossing them over their shoulders.

Stone-curlews are gregarious, even in the breeding season, calling to one another in the evenings and at night. The sound builds to a haunting crescendo until it seems they are all wailing together, either in excitement or distress. They form flocks when migration time comes in October, but despite their sociable nature they are wary, bobbing their heads when suspicious and 'freezing' when taken by surprise. Both adults and chicks in the nest crouch low, stretching out their heads and remaining immobile in this pose.

IDENTIFICATION

Large, staring yellow eyes; broad whitish band across head; pale yellow legs, round head and short bill; sexes alike.

NESTING

Both sexes make scrape, near vegetation but not normally among plants; lined with white stones or rabbit droppings; lays late April–July; 2 eggs, buff, usually with heavy brown blotches; incubation about 26 days, by both parents; chicks, tended by both parents, leave soon after hatching, begin to fly after about 40 days; sometimes two broods.

FEEDING

Snails, slugs, ground insects and their larvae, earthworms; sometimes mice, voles, frogs, and chicks of partridge and pheasant.

SIZE

40.5cm (16in)

Downs, heaths and arable farmland in southern and eastern England.

FARMLAND

SWALLOW *Hirundo rustica*

After a hazardous journey from Africa, swallows arriving in spring somehow manage to find their way back to exactly the same spot they left the previous autumn, and set to work repairing their nests.

The saying 'One swallow does not make a summer' is based on accurate observation of the birds. When swallows begin to return from their winter quarters, mainly in South Africa, at the end of March or early April, they arrive at first in ones and twos, and ringing has proved that they often return year after year to the same nest. It is not until mid or late April that they are here in force, and summer is on the way.

They must have been familiar birds for centuries to be drawn on for a folk proverb, but today there is evidence that swallows are decreasing. From many areas there are reports of declines, with more intensive and hygienic farming causing a reduction in the large flying insects on which they feed. Most swallows in Britain nest in farm buildings, and improvements in milking parlours and barns have hit their food supplies by reducing the numbers of insects.

Swooping flight
Swallows are superb and graceful aerial hunters, specialising in hawking for flying insects. The bird has a tiny bill with a large gape, so is able to envelop the insect before snapping its beak shut. Swallows often fly low, sometimes almost

touching the ground, and then they will suddenly swerve and climb. They not only hunt but also drink on the wing, dipping down to take water from lakes, ponds and streams. Where food is plentiful, swallows will return again and again to the area, sometimes circling overhead. Relatively forward-looking eyes help them to judge distances when chasing agile insect prey.

Swallows nest in loose colonies and females tend to choose the male with the longest tail streamers as a mate. Display seems to be the tail streamers' main purpose, although they also aid aerial manoeuvres. The bird's most common call-note is a twittering 'tswit,

tswit, tswit' and the alarm note 'tsink, tsink'. The twittering song is given from a perch or on the wing.

Swallows, martins and swifts look somewhat alike because what scientists call 'convergent evolution' has made swifts develop a build similar to that of the other two species, with all three adapted to a life spent catching flying insects. Swallows and martins are closely related, and they often congregate on migration or when feeding, but swifts belong to the Apodiformes, a quite distinct Order of birds.

IDENTIFICATION
Steel-blue upper parts; chestnut forehead and throat; long streamers on forked tail; female's tail is slightly shorter than male's.

NESTING
Both sexes build saucer-shaped nest of mud and dried grasses lined with feathers, usually on ledge or rafter in building; lays May–August; usually 3–6 eggs, white, heavily speckled with red-brown; incubation about 15 days, by hen; nestlings, fed by both parents, leave after 18–21 days.

FEEDING
Flying insects, sometimes including dragonflies and butterflies.

SIZE
19cm (7½in)

The swallow's chestnut throat and forehead are apparent in low flight.

J F **M A M J**
J A S O N D

Widespread in open country, near buildings for nesting and usually near water.

TURTLE DOVE *Streptopelia turtur*

Small and boldly patterned, the turtle dove claims territory with a steep, energetic flight, fanning its tail and uttering a wheezy cry. Its soporific coo-ing is saved for the warm, lazy days of summer.

The 'voice of the turtle', referred to in the Song of Solomon, is a sleepy, romantic sound, evocative of a summer's day, and it is this call that gives the bird its name. 'Turtle' is derived from the French *tourterelle*, which approximates the gentle sound the bird makes. However, the deep, purring croon becomes more of a wheeze during the turtle dove's vigorous territorial display. The male climbs steeply, tail spread, then glides down, often circling to perch again on the tree from which it launched itself. In courtship display, the male bobs in front of the female half-a-dozen times in quick succession, with breast slightly puffed out and bill pointing downwards.

The male bows in its courtship ritual.

Later, a very different kind of display involves parent birds, seemingly helpless, fluttering to distract predators from their young. The turtle dove has a curious habit of jinking to one side or the other as it flies off at speed.

Summer visitor

The turtle dove is the smallest and slimmest of Britain's five breeding pigeons, and is the only summer migrant. It avoids hills and prefers open arable farmland and parkland with plenty of hedgerows and scrub to dense woodland, although it is not averse to large gardens or even open woods. It breeds quite commonly in the south and Midlands, but its numbers thin northwards and westwards, having declined dramatically in the past 20–30 years. In many areas where it was once frequent, it has disappeared. Turtle doves are traditionally a main quarry species for the hunters of countries around the Mediterranean and slaughter took place on a massive scale as the birds flew across the Continent. An EU ban on spring hunting of migrants should have put a stop to this practice, but the law is being flagrantly flouted in some areas and illegal hunting remains a serious problem. Modern agricultural methods and damage to wintering grounds in sub-Saharan Africa, caused by drought and increasing desert conditions, are also to blame for the decline of this beautiful little dove.

The bird's favourite food is the seed of the common fumitory, a weed of arable fields, but weed-seeds have been eliminated from huge areas of agricultural land. The turtle dove's late arrival in Britain – at the end of April or the beginning of May – is probably related to the short supply of the seeds early in the year.

IDENTIFICATION
Slim with red-tinged upper parts and pink breast; black and white striped patch on neck; long tail with white tip; sexes alike.

NESTING
Female builds flimsy platform of fine twigs, sometimes lined with roots, in tree or shrub, about 1–3m (4–8ft) up; lays May–July; usually 2 eggs, glossy white; incubation about 14 days, by both parents; nestlings, tended by both parents, leave after 18 days, fly a few days later; usually two broods.

FEEDING
Seeds, mainly from common fumitory, chickweed, charlock and grass; sometimes small molluscs.

SIZE
28cm (11in)

J F M **A M J** **J A S** O N D

Parkland, farmland, open woodland and tall, dense hedges, mainly in southern and eastern England.

YELLOWHAMMER *Emberiza citrinella*

For most of the year, the yellowhammer is fairly inconspicuous but each spring the male develops brilliant lemon-yellow plumage, especially on its head, and perches in full view to give voice to its distinctive song.

The breeding tactics of the yellowhammer rely on its unmistakably colourful appearance and its equally recognisable song. The traditional 'little-bit-of-bread-and-no-cheese' (a Scottish version is 'deil-deil-deil-tak ye') may be heard from almost any roadside hedge from late February until the middle of August, and in some years through to early November, as the bird persistently advertises its presence.

The yellowhammer's song is also a familiar sound on bushy heaths and commons, especially chalk downlands, and sometimes on farmland where there are few hedges, or only dykes or field banks. It is often delivered from a favourite song-post.

Once a female shows interest, courtship includes a chase in which cock pursues hen in twisting flight, at the end of which the pair may fall to the ground and mate. The cock may also parade around the hen, wings and tail spread and crest erect.

The pair usually nest low down in bushes, or in vegetation at the base of a hedge, and the male continues to trill his song from the upper branches. One old country name for the yellowhammer is 'scribble lark', which is thought to have its origin in the pattern of thin squiggles that covers the eggs, although the yellowhammer is not related to the lark.

Country bird

Like most other buntings – all of them are seed-eating birds, with short, conical sharp-pointed beaks – the yellowhammer avoids areas of human settlement. It rarely enters a garden, even in the countryside, yet it is not particularly shy of people. In winter, after the moult when the birds resume their duller colouring, yellowhammers become gregarious, and often flock with other seed-eaters to feed nomadically over stubble fields, where they can find them, and near grain stores. If disturbed, the whole flock will disperse as one to nearby bushes and trees, and return slowly, in ones and twos, to continue feeding. Their call-notes are a sibilant, liquid 'twit-up' and a somewhat grunting 'twink' or 'twit'.

The loss of stubble fields in autumn and of wide field margins that harbour insect food, as well as a reduction in weed-seeds due to the use of herbicides, are all partly to blame for the recent decline in yellowhammer numbers. Some yellowhammers from Europe come to Britain in winter, but there is no evidence that native birds leave for warmer countries, or even that within these islands there is much drift southwards.

IDENTIFICATION
Cock has bright yellow and chestnut breeding plumage; hen duller, more streaked with brown; bright chestnut rump and white sides to tail.

NESTING
Hen builds nest of dried grasses, lined with finer grass and hair, well hidden, on ground, bank, hedge, ivy or on wall; rarely more than about 1m (4ft) up; lays April–August; usually 2–5 eggs, white or pale pink with brown or purple-brown squiggles; incubation about 13 days, by hen only; young, fed by both sexes, fly after 11–13 days; two broods, sometimes three.

FEEDING
Largely seeds of weeds, with some grain and wild fruit; also insects and small ground animals.

SIZE
16.5cm (6½in)

The plain chestnut rump contrasts with streaked brown and black upperparts.

| J | F | M | A | M | J |
| J | A | S | O | N | D |

Widespread though declining in open areas with scrub or hedges; feeds on stubble and other fields in winter.

Woodland

Whether oak coppices or primeval pine forests,
woodlands are inhabited by a fantastic
diversity of birds. From the exquisite song of
nightingales to the raucous cries of jays, the
sounds can be wonderfully evocative.

BLACKCAP *Sylvia atricapilla*

A powerful warbling song emanating from a small clump of trees may well be that of a blackcap. These little warblers can even be found near railway lines as they tolerate a high degree of disturbance.

The blackcap's rich and melodious song has won it a reputation as the 'northern nightingale'. The 'mock nightingale' is another old name for it. The 18th-century naturalist Gilbert White described the bird's song as a 'full, sweet, deep, loud and wild pipe'. The male, usually perched in cover as deep as he can find near the nest site, pours out his powerful warbling, varied with phrases mimicked from other birds' songs, and ending abruptly. The song is higher pitched and less sustained than that of the garden warbler, with which it is often confused. The blackcap's call-notes are a harsh 'churr' and an excited 'tau-tau', rapidly repeated when the bird is alarmed.

Most blackcaps are summer visitors, arriving from late March – but mostly in April – and spreading out over much of England and Wales, although fewer birds reach Scotland or Ireland. Some of these blackcaps have taken to staying on for the winter months but most of the birds seen in Britain at this time are migrants from northeast Europe and Germany. Changes in the migratory habits of European blackcaps over the last 30 years mean a number of them arrive in the autumn just as most of Britain's summer breeders are leaving for southern Europe and North Africa. The relatively mild climate and the availability of food in winter are among the reasons the northern birds come to Britain. Winter blackcaps can be quite aggressive, driving away tits and other small songbirds from feeders and bird tables. They will take most offerings, including peanuts, and are not averse to eating bread, cheese and other scraps.

Hidden nests

Blackcaps nest mainly in broad-leaved woodland where there is tangled undergrowth including brambles and rose briers or evergreen shrubs, particularly rhododendrons. In this coarse vegetation they build their neat nests of dry grass and roots, lined with finer strands of grass and hairs. These nests are attached to the surrounding plants with 'basket handles'. Blackcaps have become surprisingly adaptable, though, and populations in Britain have doubled since 1945. The birds usually remain hidden among vegetation as they feed, and their flights from one patch of cover to the next are short and jerky.

The male blackcap adopts a wide variety of courtship postures. Sometimes he raises his cap feathers and fluffs out his body feathers; sometimes he droops his wings and at other times he flaps them; and he may also spread and raise his tail.

Identification

Male has grey-brown upper parts and a glossy black cap; female is browner above and has red-brown cap.

Nesting

Slight nest, built chiefly by hen, of dried grass lined with hair and rootlets, in bushes or other coarse vegetation; lays May–July; usually 4 or 5 eggs, white tinged with green and marbled with brown; incubation about 12 days, by both parents; nestlings, fed by both parents, leave after about 10 days.

Young birds all have dark brown caps.

Feeding

Flies, caterpillars and other insects; fruit and berries in autumn.

Size

14cm (5½in)

Broad-leaved or mixed woods, scrub with trees; parks and gardens. Widespread, except in northern Scotland and northern half of western Ireland.

WOODLAND

79

BRAMBLING
Fringilla montifringilla

These gregarious winter migrants are unpredictable. In some years they descend on Britain's woodlands in flocks many thousands strong to feast on beech mast, but when this is scarce they turn up in gardens.

From late September, bramblings flock into Britain, travelling across the North Sea from their breeding grounds north of the Baltic and spreading out all over these islands, except the far north and west of Scotland and the west of Ireland. They vary their routes south, wandering extensively, and sometimes appearing in huge numbers in a particular region in one year and hardly at all the next. In some years, most of the European population of around 20 million birds may be concentrated in just one valley in central Europe. Nothing like that many come to Britain, however,

although total numbers have been known to reach nearly 2 million.

Beech mast is the staple item in the birds' winter diet. They use their strong, sharp-edged bills to cut open the tough husks to get at the seed inside. When supplies run low, or are covered by snow, bramblings often join other finches and move on to farmland, visiting any stubble fields they can find in search of grain and weed-seeds. The birds also take advantage of bird food on the ground in gardens.

Changing plumage

The cock bird's handsome breeding plumage is seen only briefly in Britain before the bramblings return to Scandinavia and Siberia in March and April. In common with its close relative, the chaffinch, but in contrast to most songbirds, the brambling acquires its bright colours not by moulting and growing new feathers but by wearing away the pale tips of existing ones. The bird's mottled winter plumage provides excellent camouflage as it scours the woodland floor for beech mast and other seeds.

The male's spring song – rather like the 'dzwee' of the greenfinch – is rarely heard in Britain, and the melodic, fluting song given in the breeding season is even rarer. Until 30 years ago there was only one known case of bramblings nesting in Britain – in Sutherland in 1920 – but since 1979 they have bred in Scotland and eastern England on several occasions. They often turn up in pinewoods before migrating back to their breeding grounds, where they become territorial, moving into conifers and birch woods to build their nests.

In winter the best way of identifying a brambling is by its call-note, a rather grating, nasal 'tsweek', or by the 'chucc-chucc-chucc' cry it gives in flight.

In winter, mixed flocks of bramblings and other finches search for seeds, especially beech.

Identification
White rump; orange-buff breast and shoulder patch in male; male's head and upper parts glossy black in summer, mottled brown in winter; female has dull brown upper parts.

Nesting
Builds deep cup nest in tree; lays mid May–July; usually 6 or 7 eggs, green-blue to olive-brown with dark spots and streaks, incubation probably about 12 days, by female only; nestlings, fed by both parents, leave after about 14 days.

Feeding
Weed-seeds, beech mast, grain; sometimes berries; insects in spring.

Size
14.5cm (5¾in)

J F M A M J
J A S O N D

Widespread in winter, concentrated in woods and other areas with beech trees; sometimes in gardens, on farmland and at sewage works.

WOODLAND

BULLFINCH *Pyrrhula pyrrhula*

A bird of many contradictions, the bullfinch produces an uninspiring, creaky warble in the wild but it is a songster of remarkable talent and clarity when taught to sing while in captivity.

The bullfinch's phenomenal song-learning ability made it popular as a cagebird in the Victorian era. Many bullfinches were imported from Germany and taught to sing by their human owners repeatedly whistling the same tunes to them. 'Whistling bullfinches', when hand-reared, formed a strong attachment to their keepers, which is another contradiction since the birds are highly strung and have been known to drop dead when handled. In the wild, they are shy birds, retiring quickly from human presence. Only a soft, but far-carrying, indrawn, melancholy whistle, usually written down as 'deu', indicates where they have gone. Their quiet, squeaky song is rarely heard for unlike that of other songbirds, it is not used to proclaim territory.

Life-long mates

Many ornithologists believe that bullfinches mate for life. Certainly, once two have formed a bond, they do not seem to split up for the winter, as do most small birds. Whenever a glimpse is caught of the black-capped, pink-breasted male, his mate will be flitting a little way behind, looking like a toned-down copy with the colours filtered out. Although the bullfinch's name is sometimes thought to come from its bull neck, it may instead be derived from the German Blodfink or Blutfink, which means literally 'bloodfinch', inspired by the colouring of the male.

Handsome though it is, the bullfinch has made enemies in many parts of the country because in late winter and early spring it literally nips fruit trees in the bud. A single bird has been seen to eat the buds on a plum tree at the rate of 30 a minute, and fruit growers have often complained about their depredations.

However, although the birds' numbers were on the increase after the 1950s,

since the 1970s they have declined dramatically with the loss of orchards and an enormous reduction in the availability of winter seeds. The dwindling number of hedgerow trees and the tidying up of big, overgrown hedges have also added to the bullfinch's travails, depriving the birds of food as well as the deeply hidden nest sites they seek.

Attacks on fruit trees and ornamental shrubs occur mainly when the bird's natural food source is scarce, from January to April. Its short, rounded bill, with especially sharp cutting edges, is an excellent adaptation for this purpose, but even in fruit-growing districts the bullfinch also takes many weeds and tree-seeds.

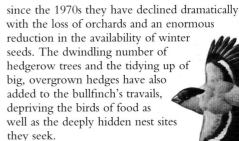

The bullfinch's white rump is conspicuous in flight.

Identification
Black cap; rose-pink breast; grey back; white rump; female much drabber than male.

Nesting
Female builds nest of twigs, moss and lichen in thick hedge, bramble, brake or other deep cover; lays late April–July; usually 4 or 5 eggs, green-blue, sparsely streaked and spotted with purple-brown; incubation 12–14 days, mainly by female; nestlings, fed by both parents, fly after about 14 days; two broods, sometimes three.

Feeding
Tree-seeds, weeds and berries; buds of fruit trees in late winter and early spring; caterpillars fed to young.

Size
14.5cm (5¾in)

J	F	M	A	M	J
J	A	S	O	N	D

Widespread except in extreme north and northwest; most numerous in southern England and southern Ireland.

WOODLAND

CAPERCAILLIE *Tetrao urogallus*

The largest of all grouse, the capercaillie indulges in some extraordinarily wild behaviour to attract a mate. It aggressively defends its patch against all comers, including dogs and people as well as rival males.

In the spring, male capercaillies perform a flamboyant courtship ritual on traditional group display grounds, called 'leks'. They gather before sunrise, fan their tails, throw back their heads and strut up and down on their chosen area, uttering a strange song, one of the weirdest in the world of birds. It begins with a resonant rattle, continues with a noise like the drawing of a cork and pouring of liquid out of a narrow-necked bottle, and ends with a knife-grinding rasp. If neighbouring males meet on the boundary of their territory, a fierce battle may ensue. Instant fatalities are rare, but injuries are not and a wounded male may well die later. As dawn approaches, the females gather, perching in the branches of surrounding trees, and the excitement level rises. The males start to leap up in the air, flapping their wings noisily. The female birds enter the lek in small groups, and gradually each one chooses a mate and waits to be courted. Some males have a queue, while others display in vain. They all continue to defend the boundaries of their territories exceptionally boldly.

Reintroductions
Towards the end of the 18th century, the capercaillie, the largest British gamebird, and the biggest of the world's grouse, became extinct in these islands – a victim of the disappearance of many natural pine forests, and of the guns and snares of huntsmen. Then in the late 1830s a collection of 55 birds was brought from Sweden to the Marquis of Breadalbane's estate in Perthshire, and the capercaillie quickly re-established itself in the pine forests there and in the surrounding areas.

Today it occurs in the greater part of its former range in the Scottish Highlands, although for largely unknown reasons, its numbers have declined significantly over the past 20 years. Fox predation, woodlands being over-grazed by deer and sheep, and chicks not surviving late spring rains could all be contributory factors. Previous attempts to establish capercaillie in other parts of the British Isles, including Cannock Chase

in Staffordshire and Grizedale Forest in Cumbria, have failed.

The cock capercaillie is much the largest bird likely to be seen in a pinewood, and could be mistaken for an escaped and unexpectedly airborne turkey. A large male can weigh up to 7.75kg (17lb) and for such a heavy bird is surprisingly nimble, spending time in the treetops during winter, feeding on conifer needles.

The female adopts a submissive posture in courtship.

Identification
Fan tail; plumage grey-black with dark green breast and brown tinge on wings; female smaller, chestnut breast, ruddy brown and mottled.

Nesting
Hen makes scrape in the ground, lined with vegetation, usually grass and pine needles, often at foot of pine tree; lays late April–May; 5–8 eggs, pale yellow speckled with brown; incubation about 4 weeks, by hen; young, tended by hen only, can flutter after 2–3 weeks, but are not fully grown until much later.

Feeding
Conifer shoots; fruit and berries in summer; occasionally insects.

Size
Male: 83.75cm (33in)
Female: 63.5cm (25in)

J	F	M	A	M	J
J	A	S	O	N	D

Old conifer woods in north-central Scotland.

CRESTED TIT *Lophophanes cristatus*

A pointed, black and white chequered crest makes this bird stand out from the crowd. It is the only small British songbird to have such a prominent arrangement of feathers on its crown.

The second smallest of the tits found in Britain, being just marginally longer than the coal tit, the crested tit's distinctive appearance ensures it is not easily confused with any other species. The spiky crest and black and white speckled head stand out even more because of its white cheeks with their curve of black.

The crested tit is a common bird in European conifer forests and mixed woodlands, but in Britain it is to be found only in Scotland. Extensive felling of Scottish woodland during the 17th and 18th centuries drove the crested tit into a small area of the Highlands, where it lived in the Old Caledonian forest. Now, because of re-afforestation, the species is moving back into areas from which it was once lost but the advance is a slow one since crested tits prefer mature pine forests. Nesting areas are still mainly limited to pinewoods in Highland, with a spread in recent years to Moray and Aberdeenshire. Crested tits may be seen in England on rare occasions but these are almost certainly vagrants from Europe. Those found in Scotland are of a separate subspecies, *scoticus*, and are highly sedentary. They have never been recorded as breeding outside Scotland.

Tree feeder

Among the conifers and the pines, the crested tit behaves like the coal tit and treecreeper, clinging to the tree trunks to pick off insects and their larvae, and it sometimes hangs from branches, like most tits, to take the seeds of conifers and juniper berries. The crested tit collects food in early winter to store for use in times of scarcity, but

Tree bark is a source of insect food.

in extreme weather it has been known to visit garden bird tables, in company with other tits. Its vocabulary is mostly restricted to a soft 'tsi–tsi–tsi' contact note and a soft churring sound.

Courtship consists of a special fluttering flight by the male, and he may also adopt a display posture by raising his crest and fluttering his wings. He goes on to chase the female through the high conifer branches, and feeds her while she incubates the eggs. Although natural holes in trees and fence-posts may be used, the female usually excavates a nest-hole in a rotten pine stump. The only other species of British tit to do this is the willow tit.

Identification
Black crest feathers edged with white; black semicircle behind the eye; grey-brown back; sexes alike.

Nesting
Tree hole, natural or excavated; male may help to gather deer hair, feathers and wool for nest-building; lays late April–May; usually 5 or 6 eggs, white with red-brown spots; incubation about 14 days, by female only; nestlings, fed by both parents, fly after about 18 days.

Feeding
Aphids, caterpillars and other insects; sometimes conifer seeds and juniper berries.

Size
11.5cm (4½in)

J	F	M	A	M	J
J	A	S	O	N	D

Ancient native Scots pine forest and some native Scots pine plantations, between the Spey Valley and Moray Firth.

WOODLAND

CROSSBILL

Loxia curvirostra

The crossed mandibles of this small, parrot-like finch enable it to get at nutritious seeds that other birds cannot reach and therefore avoid competition for its dinner. When food is scarce, it simply moves on.

Variation in bill shapes to suit a special kind of diet is marked in the finch family, and the crossbill is a specialist among finches. The several species of crossbills are the only birds that have the tips of their bills naturally crossed – an adaptation that enables them to pick seeds out of cones. The birds move sideways along branches, parrot-fashion, to reach the cones.

Very young birds have uncrossed bills.

Two separate species of crossbill are regularly to be found in Britain – the common crossbill (*Loxia curvirostra*) and the Scottish crossbill (*Loxia scotica*). The parrot crossbill (*Loxia pytyopsittacus*) is an occasional migrant to Britain, and the two-barred crossbill (*Loxia leucoptera*), a bird of northern Europe, is a vagrant, rarely seen. The common crossbill is widespread in Scotland, Wales and much of England and Ireland. The Scottish crossbill remains in the Highlands only, and at 17cm (6¾in), is slightly bigger than the other species. Scottish crossbills are the only birds unique to Britain, but their status is complicated by the presence of a few breeding parrot crossbills.

Bill adaptations

All four species show slight variations in their bills, the crossing of mandibles having evolved to take account of the birds' favoured conifers and the different-shaped cones that they have to prise apart to get at the seeds within. Seeds of Scots pine, spruce, larch and other conifers make up the majority of their diets, although occasionally they will take wild fruit and insects such as flies and beetles. If they have to venture along small twigs to reach a cone, they will sometimes snip off the cone and take it away to deal with on a more substantial branch.

This reliance on conifers makes crossbills nomadic. Should the trees fail to produce sufficient cones, the birds must travel in search of another supply, which causes irregular 'invasions' of common crossbills across the North Sea into Britain. Mass irruptions of the birds every few years are believed to be triggered by the lack of spruce cones in Scandinavia. In this case,

common crossbills start to arrive on the east coast of Britain in late June or early July, and they later spread to any part of the country where conifers have been planted.

The song of the crossbill is soft, twittering and rather similar to that of the greenfinch, but its flight-note, an explosive, metallic 'jip-jip', is unmistakable. The crossbill's courtship displays include a sexual chase and courtship feeding.

J	F	M	A	M	J
J	A	S	O	N	D

Widespread though sporadic and shifting breeder in coniferous woodlands; scarcer in Ireland.

Identification
Crossed bill; adult male crimson with orange tint, young male duller; female yellow-green; both have dark brown wings and tail.

Nesting
Female builds substantial nest of twigs lined with grasses in conifer; usually lays February–March; 3 or 4 eggs, green tinged with purple-red marks at blunt end; incubation about 13 days, by female; nestlings, fed by both parents, leave after 18 days.

Feeding
Seeds of pine, larch, spruce and other conifers; very occasionally fruit, weed-seeds and insects.

Size
16.5cm (6½in)

WOODLAND

GOLDCREST *Regulus regulus*

The voice of the goldcrest is so soft and high-pitched that some are unable to hear it. It also has a remarkable ability to live close to its physical limits, whether crossing the North Sea or raising two broods.

Resilience is the watchword for the goldcrest. Resident breeders are joined in winter by large numbers flocking in from northern and eastern Europe in a bid to escape the harsh weather conditions prevalent in that part of the world. Their arrival a day or two before woodcocks gave rise to the goldcrest's old name of 'woodcock pilot'. Some remain near the south and east coasts, but others spread out, dispersing in mixed woodland, suburban parks and gardens, anywhere where there are conifer trees. They often form flocks with tits and other woodland species. However, despite the bird's ability mostly to withstand British winters, numbers are always severely reduced by extreme cold, partly due to their size and partly to the lack of insects on which they feed. In some exceptionally hard winters they have been almost wiped out, but after a few years, they always manage to re-establish their numbers.

Lively and fearless, the goldcrest is Britain's smallest bird, and it makes up in pugnacity for what it lacks in size. Cock birds have been known to fight to the death over a hen in the breeding season, and the hen will defend its nest by flying out to peck at any animal intruder, or keep watchful guard from a short distance away against a human.

First-choice nest site

The nest is usually built in a conifer, often a spruce or fir tree. The goldcrest will choose one of these in areas of mixed woodland, even if there are only one or two growing there, and it will sometimes choose to nest in churchyard yew trees. Goldcrests will colonise conifer plantations from the stage where the trees are roughly 2m (6ft) tall. However, they usually look for twigs from which they can sling their snug, pocket-like nests at heights of up to about 15m (50ft) or even higher. The female may lay as many as a dozen tiny eggs, adding up to one and half times her own bodyweight, and may lay a second clutch in another nest while the first brood is only half-grown. For a while after

Nest is sited at the end of a twig.

the breeding season, goldcrests are likely to be seen on heaths and commons and in other open places, as well as among conifers and in deciduous woods.

In courtship, the cock spreads and raises the black-bordered orange crest that gives the bird its name. Its call-note is a thin 'zi-zi', higher pitched than the cries of a coal tit or treecreeper, and its high-pitched song – a distinctive 'cedar-cedar-cedar-cedar-sissa-pee' – is one of the first that birdwatchers lose should hearing deteriorate with age.

Identification
Yellow-green plumage with double wing-bar; male's crest is orange, female's more yellow; both have black border at base.

Nesting
Usually in conifer, but sometimes in deciduous tree, bush or creepers, 1–15m (3–50ft) high, or more; both sexes build elaborate nest of spiders' webs, moss and feathers, suspended by 'basket handles'; lays April–June; usually 7–10 eggs, white or pale yellow, freckled with brown; incubation about 15 days, by hen only; young, fed by both parents, fly after about 20 days; usually two broods.

Feeding
Flies and other insects; spiders.

Size
9cm (3½in)

J F M A M J
J A S O N D

Mostly coniferous woodland, but also churchyards with yew trees, parks and large gardens.

GOSHAWK
Accipiter gentilis

The goshawk rarely draws attention to itself, preferring to sit quietly among the trees waiting for unwary prey – but in spring, it throws caution to the wind, wheeling high in the sky in an exuberant courtship display.

Goshawks are most likely to be seen when they are courting, or re-establishing pair bonds. Dramatic aerial displays may involve both birds, performing together above the breeding wood, with fluffed-out bulging white undertail coverts. Other than this, they are secretive birds, and although numbers are increasing slowly, they are still by no means numerous.

Goshawks stopped breeding in the wild in Britain in the 1880s, having been persecuted by gamekeepers for their hunting activities, but by the mid 1960s they had returned to several of their old haunts, and goshawks are now protected under the Wildlife and Countryside Act. The goshawk prefers coniferous forests, although it will settle in mixed woodland, and needs open countryside over which it can hunt. The Kielder Forest in Northumberland and Hampshire's New Forest are among its strongholds. Birds that escaped or were deliberately released by falconers helped the re-colonisation, along with truly wild birds apparently arriving unaided from Europe. These days, enlightened landowners welcome the presence of goshawks, even though they may take a few game chicks, because they control woodpigeons, which feed on crops and are regarded as pests.

Efficient hunters

Big and powerful, goshawks are adept at taking quite large prey, including pheasants and crows, as well as starlings, thrushes and smaller birds. They also target mammals, such as rats, voles and rabbits, and even squirrels and hares, relying on surprise as their main strategy. The goshawk sits concealed on a perch, waiting for a suitable quarry. It often has several perches in an area, moving

The long tail has a rounded tip while the wings are broad and relatively rounded.

between them after a few minutes spent on each one. It may pursue its prey through the trees, but with its bulky frame, a sudden swoop is often more effective than a prolonged chase.

The goshawk removes feathers and often intestines from its catch on a plucking post, which can be a tree stump or a thick horizontal branch. In the breeding season, a male will have several plucking posts near the nest and will take the meal back so that the female can tear off morsels to feed to the chicks. The nest, a large shallow, untidy structure, is usually built high in a conifer tree, as far away from the chance of human disturbance as possible. Since it has such a messy diet, the goshawk needs to bathe regularly in fresh water to clean its feathers, bill and talons.

Female goshawks are the size of buzzards, but the smaller males may easily be mistaken for female sparrowhawks. The goshawk has a more deep-chested body, shorter tail and longer wings, which are often held in an 'S' curve in flight.

Identification
Upper parts dark grey-brown (female browner), underparts and head strongly patterned; wings short, broad and rounded; stout, hooked bill.

Nesting
Large nest, loosely built of branches and twigs, lined with pine needles and bark; lays April–early May; usually 3–4 eggs, dull bluish white; incubation 35–38 days by female; nestlings, fed by female for about 2 weeks, fledge at about 5 weeks, independent at 10 or 11 weeks.

Feeding
Other birds and mammals.

Size
Male: 50cm (20in)
Female: 60cm (24in)

Well-wooded areas in various parts in Britain; also hunts in open habitats.

WOODLAND

HAWFINCH _Coccothraustes coccothraustes_

The huge bill that gives the hawfinch a top-heavy appearance is entirely practical. Its massive power can be used to crack cherry stones or, more delicately, it can be engaged in a courtship gesture known as 'the kiss'.

Undoubtedly the hawfinch's most significant feature is its incredibly strong conical bill, which is operated by highly developed muscles on each side of the head. Two pairs of finely serrated, horny pads, one in the palate of the upper jaw and one in the lower jaw, hold a fruit stone steady while the hawfinch brings to bear an enormous crushing force of 27–43kg (60–95lb) to crack it open with ease. Cherry stones are one of its favourite foods in autumn and winter. Hawfinches ignore the flesh of cherries, choosing to wait until the ripe fruit has fallen from the tree and then feeding on the stones on the ground. They crack open the stones of sloes and damsons in the same way.

Haws, hips and holly berries also form part of their diet. Hawthorn berries are sometimes eaten, too, but these are not a major food for the hawfinch. Its scientific name _Coccothraustes_ comes from the Greek words meaning 'I break the kernel'.

Long-term resident

The hawfinch, Britain's largest finch, started nesting in these islands only about 170 years ago. It breeds in deciduous woodland and in orchards, large gardens and bushy places with scattered trees. Hawfinches are shy birds, preferring to remain amid dense foliage in summer, and perch in the topmost branches of tall trees. They adopt a parrot-like waddle when moving along branches, and on foraging visits to the ground hop rather heavily. In winter they often move into more open country, forming small feeding flocks. Hawfinches have declined or even disappeared in many areas where they were once found, although their secretive habits make it difficult to estimate numbers since they are often overlooked.

The song of the hawfinch is feeble, halting and seldom heard, but in flight the bird has a loud and distinctive clipped 'tick'. The male's courtship display includes puffing out the head and breast feathers, bowing and drooping the wing-tips, as well as showing off his curiously shaped notched black flight feathers, which have an iridescent green and purple sheen. The gesture when the pair gently touch bill tips in what looks like a kiss is, in fact, courtship feeding.

The hawfinch's plumage is a subtle and unusual combination of orange, grey and rich brown and it has a rapid, whirring, front-heavy flight. When disturbed on the ground, it flies up almost vertically to conceal itself among tree branches.

The young hawfinch lacks a black bib and has dark bars on its belly.

Identification

Upper parts red-brown, underparts peach; black bib and wings with white shoulders; white on wings and tail conspicuous in flight; massive bill is grey-blue in summer, yellow in winter; female duller.

Nesting

Female builds cup of roots and grass founded on twigs and moss, usually on a high branch; sometimes lined with hair or fibres; lays late April–May; usually 4–6 eggs, pale blue-green or grey-green with dark brown marks; incubation about 12 days, by female only; nestlings, fed by both parents, leave at about 11 days; sometimes two broods.

Feeding

Mainly fruit stones and large seeds; also buds and shoots; sometimes peas, haws and beech mast; occasionally insects.

Size

17.75cm (7in)

J	F	M	A	M	J
J	A	S	O	N	D

Mature deciduous and mixed woods, especially with hornbeam. Scattered distribution; most common in southeast England. Rare in Scotland and Wales; absent from Ireland.

WOODLAND

A forest for all seasons

Preserved by archaic laws that date back to the 11th century, the varied landscapes of the New Forest offer the chance to catch sight or sound of any one of a medley of remarkable birds.

Deep in the green shade of the New Forest, the calm is shattered by a frantic screeching and snapping of twigs as two jays burst out of an oak tree, along with a big brown bird that, at first sight, looks like a buzzard. As the jays tumble apart their pursuer suffers a moment of indecision – and loses them both. It settles for a moment to rearrange its feathers, turning to reveal the glaring orange eye of a goshawk.

A broad-winged hunter that specialises in chasing other birds through dense woodland, this magnificent raptor is one of the most elusive birds of prey. Persecution during the 1800s drove it to extinction in Britain by the early 20th century, but it has clawed its way back and now several pairs nest in the New Forest. They are fitting residents of a landscape that remains one of the largest tracts of near-wilderness in southern England, for despite its name the New Forest has hardly changed for more than 900 years. A patchwork of ancient woodland, heathland and rough pasture covering some 220 sq miles, its character was defined way back in 1079 when the area was declared a royal hunting ground by William I. The local people retained the right to graze their animals, but not to fence off farmland. These forest laws are still upheld, and as a result the whole area – apart from a few timber plantations – remains unenclosed country where cattle, pigs and ponies roam freely along with the wild deer.

Woodland species

More than half of the New Forest is grassland, heath or bog, and always has been. The medieval meaning of the word 'forest' did not imply woodland, only that the land was set aside for hunting. Yet the area also includes one of the finest remnants of ancient broad-leaved woodland in Europe – a luxuriant tangle of oak, beech, hazel and holly, of all ages and states of decay, with a rich ground flora of herbaceous plants. In spring and summer their lush foliage and nectar provide food for swarms of insects, which nesting songbirds gather by the million to fill the gaping bills of their young.

Many of these breeding birds are spring visitors. They include the redstart, the spotted flycatcher and the wood warbler. The trembling trill of the wood warbler is one of the more distinctive sounds of the broad-leaved woodland. These migrants join resident breeders, such as the marsh tit with its sneezing 'pit-chew' call, the chunky nuthatch and mouse-like treecreeper, and scarce species, such as the secretive lesser spotted woodpecker and the big-billed hawfinch. Conifers in mixed woodlands are visited by tiny, shrill-voiced goldcrests and much rarer firecrests, as well as siskins and redpolls, feeding high in the trees. The conifers also attract flocks of crossbills, which use their twisted bill tips to prise open ripe cones so they can insert their tongues to extract the scaly seeds. All these birds are targeted by the resident sparrowhawks and goshawks, while a wider range of prey is taken by the numerous buzzards that breed in the forest. There are also a few honey buzzards – remarkable raptors that prey mainly on the larvae of wild bees and wasps.

Open heaths

The woodlands are punctuated by open, grassy 'lawns' that attract breeding woodlarks and tree pipits. In spring both make themselves conspicuous by their song-flights – especially the woodlark, which has one of the most melodious of all courtship displays. Both also occur on the open heaths – extensive tracts of vivid yellow gorse and glowing purple heather that, in places, extend to the horizon. These heaths support fewer bird species than the woodlands, but those that do live here are often far more conspicuous.

They include the stonechats that perch on tall bushes giving their distinctive 'chac-chac' call, like two stones being knocked together. In summer there are whinchats and wheatears, and the occasional hobby – a dashing, long-winged falcon that specialises in seizing large dragonflies in its talons and eating them in flight. The skulking, red-eyed Dartford warbler is much harder to see, however. Notoriously reclusive, it tends to hide in dense gorse or heather, only betraying its presence with buzzing calls, although a male may perch more prominently to give its scratchy warbling song. Even more elusive is the nightjar, an exquisitely camouflaged nocturnal hunter that is almost impossible to see on its daytime roost. It becomes active after sunset, announcing itself with its strangely mechanical churring song and appearing as a fleeting, sharp-winged silhouette as it pursues moths through the night sky.

The nightjar flies south to Africa for the winter, as do the hobby and many other heathland and forest birds, but others arrive. Short-eared owls and hen harriers patrol open heaths, and a few great grey shrikes spend the cold months here. In the woods bare branches make scarce residents, such as hawfinches and woodpeckers, easier to see, especially if a dusting of snow reflects light up into the trees. For while the ringing birdsong of spring is one of its chief attractions, this forest is a delight in all seasons.

One of the finest remnants of ancient woodland in Europe... lush foliage provides food for insects, which nesting birds gather by the million.

LESSER-SPOTTED WOODPECKER

HONEY BUZZARD *Pernis apivorus*

Unusually for a bird of prey, the diet of this raptor consists mainly of insects, particularly bees and wasps. The honey buzzard hunts down its quarry, digging out nests with its strong feet and stubby claws.

The sight of a honey buzzard covered in a mass of angry wasps or bees is a rare but spectacular one. The bird discovers the whereabouts of a bee or wasp nest by waiting and watching, and following the insects' flight path. Once a nest has been located, the buzzard wastes no time in excavating it, using its long toes and rather blunt claws to rake the woodland floor and dig down to the honeycomb, which is full of nutritious larvae. Tough, scaly legs and short thick feathers on face and head protect the bird from stings.

In fact, the honey buzzard's name is misleading, since the bird is neither a buzzard nor does it eat honey. Its head is smaller and narrower than a buzzard's, and its bill is also smaller with an almost dainty hook, adapted to investigating honeycombs rather than tearing flesh,

The head is held forward on a slim neck.

Sadly, many are killed illegally each year by hunters in the Mediterranean, especially in Italy and Malta.

Despite honey buzzards being fairly secretive birds, the male performs a dramatic courtship display over its woodland territory – a series of steep earthward dives, followed by an upward sweep, climbing higher each time. Sometimes the bird seems to hover for a moment, raising its wings over its back and clapping them together rapidly several times.

The nest is built high in the branches of a spruce, oak or beech tree in mature woodland. The birds often take over an old crow's or buzzard's nest and use that as a platform for their own construction. The call is infrequent, a plaintive 'peee-ha'.

Identification
Pigeon-like head, blue-grey in adults; yellow eyes and blue-grey bill with black tip; juveniles have dark eyes and yellow bill with more black on tip; wings broad at centre, narrower at base; tail long and narrow with 3 bands.

Nesting
Large structure of sticks, lined with leafy twigs; lays late May–early June; 2 eggs, occasionally 3, white heavily blotched with reddish or purplish brown; incubation 30-35 days mainly by female; nestlings fly when 33-45 days old.

Feeding
Bees, wasps, hornets, ants and their larvae; occasionally small mammals, nestlings, lizards, worms and frogs.

Size
52–60cm (20½–23½in)

although it will take small mammals, young birds, frogs, lizards and worms when its insect food becomes scarce.

Growing population
Very few honey buzzards actually breed in Britain, but numbers are slowly increasing and are swelled by the presence of passage migrants. Once restricted to southern England, nesting birds have now reached Scotland and Wales. They arrive in May from their wintering grounds in Africa, south of the Sahara. Flocks on their way to Europe tend to congregate in Gibraltar, Istanbul, Messina in southern Italy and Falsterbo on the southern tip of Sweden, so as to keep sea crossings as short as possible. They prefer to fly over land in order to take advantage of rising warm air currents.

The birds leave again in August and September, and their short stay coincides with the time when bees and wasps are most plentiful.

Summer visitor to woodlands, especially with conifers, mainly in the warmer south and east of England.

JAY *Garrulus glandarius*

The jay's main survival strategy is to collect huge quantities of acorns and hoard them as emergency winter food supplies. Untouched stores of these acorns play a key role in the spread of oak trees.

In autumn, jays search through oak trees for acorns to pluck from the branches, and also forage for them on the ground. A jay is able to open its bill wide enough to swallow an acorn, and can carry three or four at a time, holding them in its throat pouch while it flies off to find a suitable site to bury them. Under roots, moss or leaves, inside a fallen log or even in a shallow hole in the earth are favourite places. Later, in hard weather, the jay returns to its hidden stores to feed. Any forgotten acorns take root, so jays are important in the distribution of oaks. In winter, jays seem to depend largely on their larders among the oak trees to see them through the weeks when food is scarce. In the breeding season, they sometimes prey on the eggs and nestlings of other birds but at other times they are mostly vegetarian.

In summer, jays prefer open woodland with tall undergrowth, and keep to the woods far more than any of the other British members of the crow family. They also visit hedgerows, town parks and gardens, but are seldom far from trees. The jay's exotically coloured plumage and screeching 'skaak-skaak' cry make it a conspicuous bird at most times of the year but in the nesting season it's quiet, and hard to see as it slips from branch to branch under a thick cover of leaves.

White patches show up clearly in flight.

As well as its characteristic screech, the jay has a wide vocabulary, including a loud, ringing 'kiew' note, a cat-like mewing, and a sound like a chuckle, which may be copied from the magpie. It also mimics other birds, especially predators, including the tawny owl, carrion crow and sparrowhawk, and produces various alarm calls. In common with some other crows, the jay occasionally utters a subdued warbling song.

The jay is the most brightly coloured of the crow family, and its electric blue primary covert feathers were frequently used in millinery and the making of fishing flies. It raises its salt-and-pepper crest when alarmed or excited.

Identification
Brown-pink plumage; blue wing-coverts barred with black; black and white crown feathers; white rump seen in flight; sexes alike.

Nesting
Both sexes build nest of twigs, lined with rootlets and hair, in bush or tree, usually 1–6m (4–20ft) from ground; lays April–June; usually 3–6 eggs, green-tinged with olive-brown freckles; incubation about 16 days, by female only; nestlings, fed by both parents, leave after 20 days.

Feeding
Acorns; eggs and young birds; insects and larvae in spring and summer; occasionally worms, mice and lizards.

Size
34.25cm (13½in)

Group activities
In early spring, jays become social birds, gathering for ceremonies in which they chase one another on slowly flapping wings. Outside the breeding season, they move about in pairs or small parties. Courtship consists chiefly of posturing and spreading the wings and tail.

J	F	M	A	M	J
J	A	S	O	N	D

Woodlands in most of the British Isles, but not in northern Scotland or part of western Ireland.

LESSER SPOTTED WOODPECKER
Dendrocopos minor

Bursts of rapid, high-pitched drumming are a sign of the lesser spotted woodpecker as it advertises its presence to potential intruders on its territory, and attempts to attract a mate.

The rattling, mechanical sound that the lesser spotted woodpecker produces by striking its bill rapidly against tree bark is weaker and more prolonged than its relative the great spotted's confident drumming. This is mainly because it chooses small, dry branches, maybe with loose or cracked bark, on which to perform. In spring, males drum hundreds of times each day. The lesser spotted woodpecker keeps to well-timbered country but avoids conifers. Little bigger than a sparrow, it is far from easy to pick out among the small branches high in deciduous trees, where it spends much of its time.

Lesser spotted woodpeckers have never been common anywhere in Britain, and are now declining substantially – they are hardly known north of Lancashire and Yorkshire – so there is something of a challenge in tracking them down. The loss of old orchards and other mature trees, and the tidying up of commons, parks and hedgerows, have contributed to the decline because the birds need old, decaying wood. They excavate their nest-holes in it and bore into it to find their insect larvae food. Tree felling following Dutch Elm disease and the great storm of 1987 accelerated the trend.

Fleeting glimpse
The crimson-crowned male may sometimes be sighted as he flits from branch to branch, searching for insect larvae, or moves from tree to tree in a slow courtship display flight, spreading wings and tail. Sometimes a pair can be seen side by side after a courtship display, perched stock-still on a branch.

The lesser spotted woodpecker often nests in orchards or rural parkland.

The same pairs tend to join up each year, although they don't spend the winter together. Then, lesser spotted woodpeckers may forage along hedgerows and in woods in company with mixed flocks of tits, nuthatches and goldcrests.

The lesser spotted woodpecker's flight is slow and hesitant, with typical woodpecker 'bounds'. Its calls are a 'tchick' note, weaker and more sibilant than those of the great spotted woodpecker, and, more often, a 'pee-pee-pee' call like the wryneck's but lacking its ringing quality.

The shrill calls of the nestlings often draw attention to the nest-hole, which the parents bore in decaying tree trunks or branches at almost any height up to about 21m (70ft) from the ground. A shaft about 18–25cm (7–10in) long leads from the entrance to the nest chamber, which is bare except for a few wood chips. The great spotted woodpecker has a taste for its cousin's nestlings, and should one approach, the parent birds mob it noisily in an attempt to chase it away.

Identification
Black and white plumage; wings and lower back barred; male has crimson crown, female's is white.

Nesting
Both sexes bore nest-hole in decayed wood; lays late April–June; usually 4–6 eggs, glossy white; incubation about 14 days, by both parents; nestlings, tended by both parents, leave after about 21 days.

Feeding
Mainly grubs of wood-boring beetles and moths; also grubs of gall-wasps, flies and spiders; some fruit, mainly currants and raspberries.

Size
14.5cm (5¾in)

J	F	M	A	M	J
J	A	S	O	N	D

Woods and hedgerows in England and Wales; not found in Scotland or Ireland.

LONG-EARED OWL *Asio otus*

Indicators of excitement or alarm, purveyors of courtship messages, or camouflage aids – the purpose of the long-eared owl's feather tufts may be any of these, but they have nothing to do with its hearing.

The long-eared owl's real ears are concealed in the feathers on each side of its head, under the edge of the facial disc. Situated asymmetrically, they give it acute directional hearing. The ear-like tufts on top of its head are simply elongated head feathers, which it can flatten at will, as it does in flight.

As well as being useful for signalling, the tufts break up the owl's distinctive silhouette when it roosts during the day. Aided by the excellent camouflage of its streaky brown-grey plumage, the owl blends in with its surroundings perfectly as it sits quietly on a tree branch, flattening itself against the trunk. Even so, if smaller birds, which often make up part of its diet, happen to find one hiding in a tree, they will mob it mercilessly.

At other times, the owl's presence may be given away by pellets lying on the ground beneath a favourite roosting tree. A recent study of the diet of long-eared owls in Northern Ireland showed that the long-tailed field mouse, or wood mouse, is easily its favourite food, supplemented by house mice, brown rats, pigmy shrews and various small birds.

Chased away

The bird breeds in many parts of the British Isles, although it is not common in Wales, the Midlands or southern England. This may be due to the presence of the tawny owl, which is the more dominant of the two species. A tawny owl has been known to drive off and even kill

any long-eared owl that strays into its territory. In Ireland, where there are no tawny owls, the long-eared owl is well established.

Normally, the long-eared owl chooses pinewoods, and its low, moaning hoot is one of the most eerie sounds of the woodland night. It also nests on heathland, dunes and marshes, and sometimes it searches for prey over open country.

Barred wing-tips and tail and dark 'wrist' patches are noticeable in flight.

The male has a special courtship display flight. He claps his wings together, then jumps up in the air. When angry, he threatens with outspread wings, hissing and snapping. As well as hooting, he has a barking call at breeding times, and the young have a hunger cry that sounds like the squeaking of an unoiled hinge.

The long-eared owl is normally strictly nocturnal, entering and leaving roosts at twilight, but it may fly during the day on migration. British breeders are largely sedentary but are joined from October to mid May by winter visitors from northern Europe.

Identification
Long 'ear' tufts; plumage buff with pale mottling and dark streaks; yellow eyes; sexes alike.

Nesting
Often uses old nest of magpie, raven or other crow, or a squirrel's drey; sometimes builds on ground; lays March–April; 4 or 5 eggs, glossy white; incubation 25–28 days, by female only; young, fed by both parents, leave after about 25 days.

Feeding
Mice, rats, voles, shrews; finches, sparrows and, at times, birds as large as jays; some cockchafers and other beetles.

Size
35.5cm (14in)

J	F	M	A	M	J
J	A	S	O	N	D

Widespread in woodland and tall hedges near open country; continental visitors in winter.

WOODLAND

LONG-TAILED TIT *Aegithalos caudatus*

More than half this little bird's total length is taken up with its tail, which is especially conspicuous in flight. Tiny plump bodies trailing stiff, thin tails make a flock of long-tailed tits unmistakable.

From bill to tail-tip, the long-tailed tit is considerably longer than any other of the tits, except the great tit, but by weight it is one of the smallest of British birds.

Pairs of long-tailed tits start building their elaborate nests in late February or early March. In the fork of a tree or bush, at almost any height from around 1–20m (4–70ft) from the ground, they piece together lichen, cobwebs and animal hair to form a distinctive oval-shaped domed nest. The construction has an entrance hole near the top, and has earned them the country name of 'bottle tits', as well as 'barrel tits' and 'bum barrels'. The

long-tailed tits work from inside the nest, and when the basic structure is finished, they add a lining of up to 2,000 feathers, and camouflage the outside with cobwebs. The nest is finished in time for egg-laying, which takes place sometime between late March and early May, and the fit is so snug that the parent birds have to

Roosting birds huddle in tightly packed clumps for warmth.

fold their long tails over the back of their heads when they go inside.

Community living

The long-tailed tit is one of few British birds to practise what is known as co-operative breeding. Birds with no offspring of their own help to look after a neighbour's brood, and since the neighbour is usually related, the birds form extended family groups. These tend to stay together for the winter, roosting communally on as sheltered a tree branch as they can find, and nestling close to conserve as much heat as possible. Their small size makes long-tailed tits particularly susceptible to cold weather and in harsh winters the mortality rate is high. They bounce back with milder weather, though, and there is evidence of a recent modest increase in numbers.

In the breeding season, long-tailed tits are found on the outskirts of woods and in woodland clearings. Some spread out to hedgerows and thickets but, unlike great tits and blue tits, they rarely visit suburban gardens. However, this may be changing as they have started to adapt. Their main food is insects so they are not generally attracted to bird-table offerings, but in winter they may occasionally take seeds and even peanuts from feeders, although they still usually keep to the woods.

There are two types of special courtship flight – a fast sexual chase through the leaves and a slower solo flight by the male.

Long-tailed tits do not have a territorial song, but they do utter a variety of call-notes – a spluttering 'tsirrup', a soft 'tupp' and a thin 'si-si-si'.

Identification
Distinctive black and white tail, longer than body; pink, black and white plumage; sexes alike.

Nesting
Intricate domed nest, covered with lichen and cobwebs, built by both sexes in tree or bush; lays late March–early May; usually 8–12 eggs, white with red-brown freckles; incubation about 16 days, mainly by female; nestlings, fed by both parents, leave after about 14 days; parents often helped to feed young by neighbours with failed brood.

Feeding
Mainly insects and spiders; occasionally seeds. May visit hanging feeders.

Size
14cm (5½in) including 7.5cm (3in) tail

Widespread, but more abundant in the south.

107

MISTLE THRUSH *Turdus viscivorus*

A wild, ethereal song, delivered from the tallest treetops, advertises the presence of the mistle thrush. The males sing all year round and are in full voice by January, seemingly oblivious to wind, rain and cold.

This largest of Britain's native thrushes is known in the vernacular as 'storm cock', which pays tribute to the way it sings in all weathers, even in a raging winter gale. The male's loud, ringing song does not have the mellowness of a blackbird's fluting, or the elegantly repeated phrases of a song thrush, but it is often the finest bird music to be heard on a gusty January day. It has an odd but distinctive quality, sounding distant even when the bird is fairly close.

The mistle thrush's main common name, though, is derived from its fondness for the sticky berries of mistletoe. This is an important food for the species in Europe rather than in Britain, where it concentrates more on holly and hawthorn.

After the breeding season is over, mistle thrushes take to rugged open country, such as downs, moors and marshes, moving about in small family parties. They feed on whatever berries they can find, including yew, and thus help in the distribution of those plants. Sometimes, a single mistle thrush (or a pair) will take possession of a richly laden bush, defending it against all-comers – starlings, blackbirds, song thrushes, redwings, fieldfares and even other mistle thrushes. It will drive away any other bird intent on raiding its precious food supply with loud calls and swooping attacks.

Fearless defender
The mistle thrush is an early breeder, and its bulky nest built in an exposed position high in a tree may contain eggs in late February – long before there are any leaves to give it shelter. At this season mistle thrushes, always wary and suspicious, are at their most aggressive. They may attack a person or bird venturing too near the nest, or even swoop down to threaten a cat. On the ground, they have an upright, alert stance, and move in bounding hops.

Mistle thrushes frequently attract attention with the grating rattle of their flight-call and alarm note, a sound like a comb being scraped on a piece of wood. This is in strict contrast to their far-carrying, almost absent-minded song. At times they will even sing on the wing. In flight their wings close at regular intervals for a perceptible time, and the white under-wing appears to flash on and off. Unlike the song thrush, the mistle thrush often rises up quite high after taking off, quickly reaching the treetops, and it generally flies higher than its smaller, gentler relative.

White under-wings and tail tip help identify the mistle thrush.

Identification
Grey-brown above, very pale beneath, with round chestnut spots; white outer tail feathers; distinguished from song thrush by bolder spots, larger size and often by more upright stance; sexes alike.

Nesting
Both sexes build bulky cup-nest of grass, twigs, earth and moss, usually high in tree; lays late February–June; usually 4 eggs, pale blue to buff, with red-brown spots and blotches; incubation 13 or 14 days, by female only; young, fed by both parents, fly after 14–16 days; usually two broods.

Feeding
Fruit and berries; insects and their larvae, earthworms, snails.

Size
26.75cm (10½in)

J	F	M	A	M	J
J	A	S	O	N	D

Widespread in open woods and other areas with tall trees for nesting and song-posts, and open ground for feeding.

WOODLAND

NIGHTINGALE *Luscinia megarhynchos*

The haunting song of the nightingale, breaking the quiet of a summer's evening, has made it the most celebrated of all British songbirds. The impact it makes is out of all proportion to the bird's plain appearance.

In volume, in variety of notes, and in the vigour with which it is poured out, the song of the nightingale is unforgettable. It consists of a rapid succession of repeated notes – some harsh, some liquid – including a very loud 'chooc-chooc-chooc' and a fluting, pleading 'pioo', building up slowly into a crescendo. The nightingale is a master of timing – the melodramatic phrasing is emphasised by irregular pauses between notes, making its song so compelling. The breathtaking sound can sometimes be heard up to a mile away.

As well as the song, there are also call-notes – a soft, chiffchaff-like 'hweet' and a harsh 'tacc-tacc' – and the bird has two alarm notes, which are a scolding 'krrrr' and a grating 'tchaaaa'.

In spite of their name, and contrary to popular belief, nightingales are as likely to be heard singing by day as by night. But their virtuoso performances are best heard in the stillness of a warm evening in late spring, when the males compete to attract females arriving from wintering grounds in tropical Africa. The females arrive ten days or so after the males. When the birds sing by day, it is partly to warn other males to keep off their territory.

Rarely seen

For every ten people who have heard a nightingale sing there can hardly be one who has actually set eyes on this shy bird. When they do come into the open, which is rare, they are inconspicuous. Only their song draws attention to them. Victorians tried to keep them as cagebirds because of it, but none of the birds lived long.

A juvenile, heavily spotted and mottled, differs from a young robin in having a longer reddish-brown tail.

Sometimes the captives would beat themselves to death against the cage's bars within a week. The birds were much more numerous then than they are now. The current decline is probably due to loss of habitat. The nightingale breeds in dense cover, choosing coppiced woodland with plenty of undergrowth, thick untidy hedges and tangled brambles. It hides its nest as carefully as it conceals itself, building close to the ground among thick undergrowth.

In courtship display, the male spreads his tail and moves it up and down, fluttering his wings and bowing so that his bill reaches down below the level of the perch.

Identification
Brown plumage; rather like a large warbler, with red-brown tail and grey-brown underparts; whitish throat; sexes alike.

Nesting
Female builds nest of dead leaves lined with grass and hair, on or close to ground; lays May; usually 5 eggs, olive-green or dark olive; incubation about 14 days, by female only; nestlings, tended by both parents, leave at about 11 or 12 days.

Feeding
Mainly ground insects; also earthworms, spiders, some berries.

Size
16.5cm (6½in)

Wooded or scrubby areas with dense cover, often near water; mainly in south and east of England.

NUTHATCH *Sitta europaea*

The diminutive nuthatch, more adroit than any woodpecker, climbs vertically up tree trunks in jerky leaps. It also has the remarkable ability to reverse direction and travel headfirst back down again.

The nuthatch is one of only two birds in the world that can climb down trees as easily as it climbs up them, which is a great help when it is investigating crevices in search of insect food. Its strong legs and feet are set well back on its body, and it has very strong claws, which all help to keep it securely attached to the bark.

Nuts and seeds are other favourite foods, especially hazelnuts in autumn, and the bird gets its name from its habit of wedging nuts in the bark of a tree and splitting them open with vigorous blows from its 'hatchet' bill to get at the kernel inside. It often attacks the nut from above, and the loud sound of its tapping gives away its presence in the wood.

In the past few years, nuthatches have spread north and west. When they disappeared from central London parks in the late 19th century (they returned in 1958), it was suggested that atmospheric pollution, covering the trees with soot, had driven them out. This may be the reason why nuthatches are not usually seen near industrial centres.

The nuthatch makes its nest entrance just big enough to squeeze through.

Calls galore

The bird has a remarkable range of call-notes, mostly ringing or piping calls, such as 'chwit-chwit' or more frequently 'chwit-it-it'. Other notes in the range are a tit-like 'tsit'; a sibilant 'tsirrup' reminiscent of the long-tailed tit; and in the breeding season two or three loud repetitions of 'twee', as well as a note that sounds like a boy's whistling. Yet another call-note sounds like the shrill chatter of the kestrel.

In its courtship display the male often flies slowly, or postures with feathers fluffed out and wings and tail spread. The nest is always in a hole, and the birds generally choose a site more than 2m (6ft) up a tree, but nuthatches will use nest-boxes, too, and occasionally they build in a wall or a haystack. The nuthatch instinctively plasters mud around the entrance to its nest, reducing its size to keep out larger birds, such as starlings, which will readily oust a pair of nuthatches from a suitable tree hole, given the opportunity. If the nuthatches' chosen site is a nest-box, the female still plasters the entrance with mud, even though it is already the right size. The dried mud is so strong that often a hammer and chisel have to be used to remove it at the end of the season so that the box can be cleaned.

Identification
Black eye-stripe; white throat; slate-grey upper parts; buff underparts; sexes alike.

Nesting
Builds nest of bark flakes or dead leaves, usually in tree hole; lays late April–May; 6–10 eggs, white, spotted with red-brown; incubation about 14 days, by female only; nestlings, fed by both parents, fly after about 24 days.

Feeding
Mainly hazelnuts, beech mast, acorns; also beetles, earwigs and small caterpillars.

Size
14cm (5½in)

J	F	M	A	M	J
J	A	S	O	N	D

Deciduous woods and mature gardens with trees in England and Wales; has recently started breeding in southern Scotland.

113

REDSTART
Phoenicurus phoenicurus

A flash of bright, rusty red, low down in a tree or bush reveals the presence of a redstart, flicking its tail as it darts away. This elegant summer visitor constantly quivers its tail to send messages to its mate.

The fiery chestnut tail of the redstart gives the bird its name – 'steort' is an Old English word for tail, and its scientific name *Phoenicurus* is from the Greek for 'crimson-tailed'. It helps to make the male, with his white forehead, black throat, red breast and grey mantle, one of the handsomest of Britain's smaller birds, and its purpose seems to be communication. The tail is mainly used in courtship display. The male bows, stretches out his neck, droops his wings and splays his tail feathers to show a blaze of flame-red, then chases the female from perch to perch. Both sexes quiver their tails all the while.

Redstarts breed in almost any habitat where they can find holes for nesting – woodland, parks, gardens and riversides with old trees, and they will breed in treeless districts if stone walls or quarries provide nesting sites.

They are most common in old woodland, especially in hill country, but may turn up in open country on their migration flights between Africa and Britain. Male redstarts arrive a few days before the females, usually at night, and claim territories with song. They stop singing while nest building is going on, probably so as not to draw attention to the nest site, but begin again once egg laying starts.

The female redstart is brown above and paler below.

Drop in numbers
Over the past 130 years the redstart has declined as a breeding bird in eastern and southeastern England, and now breeds mainly in the north and west. Redstarts that appear elsewhere, especially down the east coast of Britain, from late March to mid

June and again from July to October, are mostly passage migrants, on their way to and from breeding grounds in northern Europe. These appearances may sometimes be dramatic, because certain weather conditions can produce what are known as 'falls' of redstarts – the birds literally drop out of the sky to escape dense cloud and heavy rain that make it impossible for them to navigate, and they land randomly in their hundreds, tails quivering.

Redstarts are shy and elusive birds. They repeatedly flutter from branch to branch or make hovering sallies into the air to catch flying insects, and they often collect food on the ground. The brief song begins strongly with a squeaky warble, then peters out in a twitter of feeble notes. Some male redstarts mimic notes from other species. The call is a long, plaintive 'hooeet' and the alarm note a loud 'twee-tucc-tucc'.

Identification
Bright chestnut tail and rump; male distinguished from black redstart by chestnut breast and white forehead; female duller, with no white on forehead.

Nesting
Female builds nest of grass, lined with hair, in natural hole or hollow in ground; may use nest-box; lays mid May–June; usually 5–8 eggs, pale blue, very occasionally speckled; incubation about 13 days, by female only; nestlings, fed by both sexes, leave after about 16 days.

Feeding
Mainly insects and their larvae; also spiders and small worms; some berries.

Size
14cm (5½in)

J	F	M	A	M	J
J	A	S	O	N	D

Widespread in British woods and parkland; mainly in northern and western uplands (most numerous in Wales); rare in Ireland.

WOODLAND

SISKIN
Carduelis spinus

A dramatic change in feeding habits has contributed to the success of the siskin. Once restricted to northern conifer forests in summer, the siskin discovered garden feeders and now stays on in winter to breed.

This small yellow-green finch, once much admired as a cagebird under the name of 'aberdevine', feeds on the seeds of spruce, pine, alder and birch. Up until the 1960s, the birds generally lived and bred in the conifer forests of northern Scotland and the pine plantation areas of Ireland, and moved south in the winter just to escape the cold. Seemingly, they never wandered into gardens in search of food. The first recorded time a siskin visited a bird table was in 1963 – an extremely cold winter – in Guildford, Surrey. Siskins are roving birds, often joining feeding flocks of redpolls, and they roost communally. Possibly by this means news of an alternative food source seems to have spread among the siskin population and, by the 1970s, siskins were regular visitors to the garden, hanging tit-like from birdfeeders to eat the seeds on offer. Now they even establish a pecking order on the feeder, with dominant birds taking precedence – and they also take peanuts, although the once popular idea that siskins preferred red containers now appears to be a myth.

In winter, siskins and redpolls often feed together in the treetops.

Nesting opportunities
The fact that siskins have moved south to breed is also due to the spread of conifer plantations, which has been of huge benefit to these birds. Now siskins breed regularly in newly afforested areas where they were formerly unknown – in East Anglia, Wales, Northumberland, Devon and Hampshire. Although they prefer extensive coniferous woods, these once garden-shy birds will nest in large gardens if there are pine trees present, choosing the end of a branch at least 5m (15ft) from the ground on which to build their neat, cup-shaped nests.

The males put on a display flight over the nesting territory, and their song, a sweet, twittering succession of notes ending with a creaking sound, is mainly heard from the middle of February to the end of May. In courtship, the

male chases the female and postures before her with feathers fluffed out and wings spread. This is different from the posture the male adopts when defending a food supply – wings spread and raised, head feathers fluffed up and gape exposed threateningly.

The cock siskin is much yellower than any other British finch except the male greenfinch, and is the only one, apart from the greenfinch, to have yellow patches at the base of its tail. The female is duller than the male.

J	F	M	A	M	J
J	A	S	O	N	D

Coniferous forests and mixed woodland; in winter, visits parks and gardens, usually near water, with birch and alder trees and birdfeeders.

Identification
Yellow-green plumage, with dark streaks on back and flanks; male has black bib and crown; female less yellow and streakier than male; bounding flight typical of finches.

Nesting
Both sexes build compact nest of twigs, lichen, moss and wool, lined with roots, hair, down and feathers, high in conifer; lays April–June; 3–5 eggs, pale blue, spotted and streaked with purple-red; incubation usually 11 or 12 days, by female only; nestlings, fed at first by female only, fly at about 15 days; usually two broods.

Feeding
Mainly seeds of trees and weeds; insects during breeding season.

Size
12cm (4¾in)

WOODLAND

117

SPARROWHAWK *Accipiter nisus*

Well adapted to woodland hunting, the sparrowhawk waits in dense cover. Then, displaying remarkable speed and agility for a bird its size, it weaves unnoticed through the trees to catch its quarry offguard.

The fast-flying sparrowhawk relies on surprise attack as a hunting technique. It will dash along one side of a hedgerow, concealed by the vegetation, and suddenly dart up and over it to burst on an unsuspecting cluster of finches, grab one of them and dash away again. If its prey escapes, the hawk rarely tries to repeat the attack, but flies on until it sees another chance to pounce. In search of prey, it will sometimes glide in a circular, prospecting flight, or soar into the sky, to plunge with folded wings. Sparrowhawks never hover in the way that kestrels do.

A long tail and comparatively short and broad, rounded wings give the sparrowhawk its agility. Its long legs and long mobile toes, which are armed with very sharp talons, enable it to reach deep into bushes and other foliage or cover to snatch its quarry hiding within.

Stealthy hunter

The sparrowhawk tends to concentrate on ground-feeding flocks of songbirds, such as sparrows, chaffinches, blackbirds and other thrushes, skylarks, yellowhammers, starlings and pipits, as well as robins, tits and warblers. While these small birds are the male sparrowhawk's main targets, the larger female will occasionally kill birds as big as a woodpigeon, and females have been known to take pheasants and grouse. As a result, sparrowhawks were persecuted by gamekeepers, until they were given legal protection. These hawks stalk their prey in urban parks as well as woodland, and are also seen in gardens, where they naturally take advantage of the large numbers of small birds attracted to bird tables and hanging feeders.

In the 1960s, the sparrowhawk suffered badly from farmers' use of poisonous agricultural chemicals, becoming extinct in eastern parts of England. Since the worst of the pesticides were banned, sparrowhawk numbers have made a comeback throughout the country.

The male hunts single-handedly while the hen is brooding, landing at one of his plucking posts with his prey and calling his mate to feed with a harsh, chattering 'kek-kek-kek-kek'.

Later, both parents work hard to feed their young, since the nestlings will each eat two or three sparrow-sized birds a day. A plucking post may be a tree stump or fence post, and the sparrowhawk will use two or three regularly, all within a short distance of the nest. It holds the prey firmly with its strong feet and talons while removing the feathers with its sharp hooked bill. Plucking posts can be easily identified by the piles of feathers around them.

Identification
Short, rounded wings; long tail; male has slate-grey upper parts and reddish-brown barred underparts; larger female has browner upper parts, dark brown bars on underparts and white stripe over the eye.

Nesting
Nest built of twigs in tree, frequently by female alone, lined with thin twigs; lays May; usually 4–6 eggs, white tinged with blue with red-brown blotches; incubation about 30 days, by female only; nestlings, tended by both parents, leave after 24–30 days.

Feeding
Sparrows, finches, starlings, other small birds; occasionally mice, voles and young rabbits; insects.

Size
Male: 28cm (11in)
Female: 38cm (15in)

The male has distinctive barred underparts.

Widespread in woodland; hunts along woodland edges and hedgerows.

TREECREEPER
Certhia familiaris

This little bird spends its life in trees, spiralling jerkily up one trunk before flying down to the base of another and starting again, all the while probing the bark in search of its insect food.

Many woodland birds are more likely to be heard than seen, and the treecreeper is one of the more elusive of this group. It spends most of its time, as its name suggests, creeping up trees, using a fast, mouse-like shuffling action as it progresses up and around a trunk in fits and starts, occasionally moving quickly sideways to investigate a sudden movement or to tug at some stubborn insect. When it flies to another trunk, it starts at the foot of the tree again because, unlike the nuthatch, it is unable to move downwards, but it is agile in searching upside-down on the underside of a bough.

The treecreeper is perfectly suited to all this restless activity. Its plumage, which is intricately patterned with brown, russet, gold and grey, resembles bark and lichen, providing excellent camouflage, especially in dappled sunshine. The stiff feathers of its long, frayed-looking tail are used as a prop when climbing. Its long, curved claws allow it to cling on to the bark, and hang from the undersides of branches, with ease and its slender downcurved bill is superbly adapted for investigating nicks and crevices. It does have a noticeable silvery white front but, if threatened, the bird will press itself against the trunk to hide its breast feathers. In flight, which is undulating and erratic, the wings look broad and long, and pale banding becomes clearly visible.

The treecreeper's longish, stiff tail has pointed tips.

Minute nests

The treecreeper builds its nest behind loose bark, tucked away behind a tiny entrance hole that is easily overlooked, although tell-tale pieces of nesting material may stick out through cracks. The space may be too narrow for the female to turn round but such a tight fit keeps out any would-be predators.

Hard winters punish this small bird, but after Wellingtonia trees – introduced from California –

became established, treecreepers learned to make hollows in the soft, insulating bark to use as snug roosting places. Treecreepers may roam beyond their territories in winter with parties of tits and other small birds, although they seldom venture very far, and they sometimes gather in temporary communal roosts when the weather is cold.

The song, always delivered from a tree, is a high-pitched 'tee-tee-tee-titit-dooee'. The most frequent call-notes are a high-pitched and rather prolonged 'tseeee' and a tit-like 'tsit'. Courtship includes chases, a bat-like display flight, wing-shivering and feeding. The male continues to provide the female with food until the eggs hatch.

Identification
Mottled brown above, silvery white beneath; white eye stripe; only small British land-bird with a curved beak; sexes alike.

Nesting
Probably both sexes build nest of dried grass and rootlets, lined with feathers, wool and bark chips, sited behind loose bark or ivy roots or in other tree cavities, occasionally in nest-boxes, exceptionally in wall crevice or old shed; lays April–June; usually 6 eggs, white, with red-brown spots at blunt end; incubation about 15 days, probably mainly by hen; nestlings, fed by both parents, leave after about 14 or 15 days; sometimes two broods.

Feeding
Invertebrates, such as spiders, woodlice, weevils and other small beetles, earwigs, small caterpillars; grain and weed-seeds.

Size
12.75cm (5in)

J F M A M J
J A S O N D

Woodlands in most parts of Britain and Ireland; visits large gardens and hedgerows, especially in winter.

WOODLAND

WOODCOCK *Scolopax rusticola*

During the day, the woodcock rests among the leaf litter and debris on the woodland floor, but at dusk the male indulges in an extraordinary courtship flight, accompanied by strange calls and ritual head turning.

At dawn and dusk in spring and summer, male woodcock meander slowly just above the trees in an erratic 'roding' flight. When the moon is full, they may fly considerably higher. This is a territorial display that each male performs with the objective of attracting the attention of a female on the ground below. As it flies, the woodcock gives two calls – a throaty, frog-like 'og-og-og' note, repeated several times, and a high-pitched, explosive, whistling 'twisick' like a sneeze. A female that is ready to mate will respond with a softer version of the sneezing call and, guided by this, the male will drop down steeply and begin the courtship display, which includes bill tapping.

The leisurely roding flight is quite different from the woodcock's way of flying when it is flushed from its hiding place in the undergrowth. Then it leaps into the air to dodge rapidly through the trees, quickly disappearing into cover again. This has made the secretive woodcock a popular gamebird. It is considered a challenging quarry and is still legally shot outside the usual close season. The woodcock has been eaten in Britain since Roman times, or earlier, and its small, pointed pin feathers – one found on each wing – were once in demand for use in fishing flies and as watercolour paint brushes.

Woodland haunts

The woodcock, a relative of the snipe, is a wading bird that has taken to the land, especially to the kind of woodland that is opened up by clearings and rides. With eyes set high in its head, and well to the back, it has the all-round vision that enables it to look out for enemies even when it is probing in the ground with its long bill for earthworms and insects. It lies up quietly during the day, its mottled plumage making it hard to see as it rests on the woodland floor. At twilight it flies to nearby damp, marshy

or boggy ground to feed, returning to its daytime haunts just before dawn.

Roding occurs mainly between March and early July, when the birds are raising their two broods. If danger threatens before the young have learnt to fly, the female may 'airlift' them to safety, either clutching the chicks in her claws or tucking them between her legs and body.

The woodcock has an owl-like appearance in flight, but its long bill gives it away.

Migrant birds arrive in winter, joining resident woodcock. They fly in across the North Sea, and often drop on to the first piece of rough cover they encounter near the coast, moving inland later.

Identification
Stout; long bill; russet plumage with barred head and underparts; sexes alike.

Nesting
Nests in a scrape lined with dead leaves; lays mid March–June; usually 4 eggs, grey-white to brown, thickly marked with chestnut and ash-grey blotches; incubation about 21 days, by female only; chicks, tended by both parents, leave after a few hours; two broods.

Feeding
Earthworms, beetles, other insects and their larvae; small molluscs; some seeds and grass.

Size
34.25cm (13½in)

J	F	M	A	M	J
J	A	S	O	N	D

Widespread in young conifer plantations and other damp woodland; some nest on bracken-covered moorland; in cold winter weather may feed in streams.

WOOD WARBLER *Phylloscopus sibilatrix*

This summer visitor is one of only a few British birds to have two distinct songs, one a soft melancholy whistle and the other an intense, cascading trill, delivered wholeheartedly while the bird trembles all over.

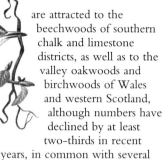

The 'warbler' part of the bird's name is a tribute to its song, or rather to both of them. The most frequently heard is a powerful trill, starting with a series of 'stip' notes repeated with accelerating speed until it reaches a loud, silvery 'sirrrr'. Each phrase lasts around four seconds and as it reaches its climax the male opens its bill wide, pointing it upwards, and shivers its wings and body. The sound has been said to resemble 'a spinning coin on a marble slab'. The second song is a much mellower, liquid 'dee-ur', which is also the bird's anxiety note; in the song it is plaintively repeated seven or more times.

The wood warbler is the largest of Britain's three leaf warblers – the scientific name *Phylloscopus* means leaf-searcher – and it is rarely seen or heard outside of its clearly defined habitat. The other two are the willow warbler and the chiffchaff. Mature woodlands with a closely knit canopy of leaves and sparse undergrowth with plenty of leaf litter meet the wood warbler's exacting requirements. In these surroundings, wood warblers find the insect life on which they feed throughout the summer. The birds hover to pick up insects from the underside of leaves, often high up near the treetops, or sally from their perches to snap up food on the wing. Their colouring resembles the sun-dappled foliage of the upper canopy allowing them to blend in easily. However, they nest on the ground among the leaf litter, using a convenient hollow. The nest's dome often shows above ground level.

Heading west
Wood warblers' preference for a particular type of woodland means they are less common in the south and east than in the north and west of Britain. Nevertheless, fair numbers are attracted to the beechwoods of southern chalk and limestone districts, as well as to the valley oakwoods and birchwoods of Wales and western Scotland, although numbers have declined by at least two-thirds in recent years, in common with several other woodland birds. Outside the breeding season, wood warblers keep to the trees, eking out their diet with wild berries before they migrate back to Africa. They usually leave in August but are seldom seen on the British coast. They are thought to break their journey in southern Europe.

In courtship, the male has two styles of flying. It quivers its wings rapidly or flaps them slowly.

Identification
Yellow breast; white belly; yellow-green above; yellow streak above eye; colouring duller in autumn; larger and more brightly coloured than chiffchaff or willow warbler; sexes alike.

Nesting
Female builds domed nest of grass and leaves, lined with grass and hair, in natural hollow; lays May–June, usually 5–7 eggs, white, thickly spotted with dark red-brown; incubation about 13 days, by female only; nestlings, fed by both parents, fly after about 12 days.

Feeding
Insects, mainly small caterpillars, beetles, flies and aphids; some wild berries in autumn.

Size
12.75cm (5in)

Widespread in Britain, mainly in the west; highest density in Wales, rare in Ireland.

The male bird often delivers its trilling song while flitting in a 'butterfly' display flight from tree to tree.

Mountain,
Moor and Heath

Wild, elemental and exhilarating, rugged peaks,
open moors and sandy lowland heaths offer a
stunning combination of glorious landscapes
and striking birds, from strutting grouse and
soaring eagles to mysterious nocturnal nightjars.

BLACK GROUSE *Tetrao tetrix*

Highly ritualised and elaborate courtship displays are the forte of black grouse. Every year the birds crowd together in the same places to strut, leap and flutter, threatening rivals and mating as often as possible.

The remarkable courtship ceremonies of the polygamous black grouse take place at communal display grounds known as 'leks'. There may be several leks in a district and the males, or blackcocks, arrive at their chosen site in March, about a month before the hens. In his advertising display, the male inflates his neck and chest, erects the red wattles above each eye, droops his partly open wings and fans his lyre-shaped tail over his back so that the undertail coverts form a shield of white at the rear. Then he carries out formal, jousting encounters with his neighbours, sometimes remaining stationary and at other times making little mincing runs or jumping up and down. This performance is mostly mock aggression although occasionally battles become more serious, and territories, or courts, within the lek can change ownership as males on the outskirts try to force their way to the centre.

Male has a distinctive lyre-shaped tail and white wing-bar.

Female has notched tail.

The mature and more vigorous males, occupying central positions in the lek, secure the most matings – as many as 80 per cent in some leks. Sometimes old blackcocks resume their lek displays in the autumn.

Two calls

While all this is going on, blackcocks frequently call, either crowing – a wheezy, tearing sound – or 'rookooing', a musical, dove-like bubbling song. This cooing carries a long way.

The females move through the lek, being courted by each male in turn. The blackcock parades round, often tilting his tail and body, although he may also sink down in front of the female. Mating follows if the female crouches.

The sexes meet merely for mating purposes and the male takes no part in nesting duties. The female, confusingly known as the greyhen, is brown, duller and smaller than the male, which provides some protection as she incubates the eggs.

The bird's diet is almost entirely vegetarian, although it will take insects occasionally, and the female feeds the chicks on insects. Birch buds are the black grouse's favourite food, and it also has a taste for young conifer shoots.

Black grouse favour moorland fringes where heather merges into birch scrub, or rough pasture that borders conifer woods. They were once widespread on the heaths and moors of southern England, but the last few pairs on Dartmoor and Exmoor have disappeared and the present most southerly populations – in Wales – are declining alarmingly. In northern Britain, despite local, temporary increases due to new forestry planting, there has also been a general decline over the past 100 years.

Identification
Male has lyre-shaped tail with white under-feathers; glossy blue-black plumage with white wing-bar; female smaller, with chestnut and buff plumage and forked tail.

Nesting
Female makes scrape in ground, often among rushes; lays May–June; 6–10 eggs, buff with sparse red-brown spots; incubation about 27 days, by female only; young, tended by female only, fly after 2–3 weeks, but are not fully grown until much later.

Feeding
Conifer shoots and birch buds; some beetles and other insects.

Size
Male: 53.25cm (21in)
Female: 35.5cm (14in)

J	F	M	A	M	J
J	A	S	O	N	D

Moorland fringes in Scotland, northern England and Wales, often near forests or young plantations; recent re-introduction to Peak District.

MOUNTAIN, MOOR & HEATH

DARTFORD WARBLER *Sylvia undata*

Resilience lies at the heart of this little bird's remarkable story. From a low point of a mere 20 survivors, the Dartford Warbler now numbers in the thousands and is regaining lost ground.

In Britain, the Dartford warbler is at the northern edge of its range, which makes it more surprising that it remains all year. Most other warblers migrate, but this small, reddish-breasted bird stays on, to face what can sometimes be harsh weather, and pays the penalty. It is extremely vulnerable to cold and after the severe winters of 1962 and 1963, the population crashed to ten pairs, but by 1966 this had doubled. Further mild winters enabled numbers to increase to about 500 pairs by 1970, to 950 pairs by 1991 and 1,700 pairs by 1994. Now there are about 2,000, including 70 in Wales and others in East Anglia and even the West Midlands.

The climate is not the only influential factor in the warbler's revival. Each spring, the winter's survivors set about repopulating their habitat, and although much of the gorse heathland that they prefer has been swallowed up by farmland and by the advance of suburbia, the protection and management of at least some of what remains has helped the birds. In fact, the gradual recovery of the Dartford warbler is a great advertisement for the conservation of lowland heath.

Birds flit furtively between bushes.

Southern success

The species was first recorded in Britain in 1773, when two of the birds were shot on Bexley Heath, near Dartford, and on investigation they were found to be widespread across southern England. At the beginning of the 19th century, they were still found south of the Thames and continued to be until just before the Second World War. Then came the succession of hard winters and the Dartford warbler became one of Britain's rarest breeding birds, until its later upturn in fortunes.

All that can usually be seen of this handsome but secretive bird is its long tail vanishing rapidly into a gorse bush, but in winter some Dartford warblers become nomadic and may break cover, venturing out to forage on rough ground.

Then, on still, sunny days in spring and early summer, the male often performs his thin, scratchy song from the topmost spray of a gorse bush, or while flying up and quickly back down again, his red-rimmed eyes alert to potential danger. On dull or overcast days, though, the bird usually remains in deep cover, even to sing.

Other courtship displays include raising the head feathers so they look bushy, ruffling the throat feathers and pumping the tail up and down and side to side. The birds may pair for life.

Identification
Both sexes have a long tail, often cocked; male in winter has dark brown upper parts and slate-grey head, with dark, wine-coloured underparts; head greyer in summer; female slightly browner than male.

Nesting
Male builds 'trial' nests; final nest built mainly by female, in gorse or long heather, of grass, roots and stalks, with spiders' webs; lays April–June; 3 or 4 eggs, dirty white speckled with grey, sometimes tinged with green; incubation about 12 days, chiefly by female; nestlings, fed by both parents, leave after about 13 days; normally two broods, occasionally three.

Feeding
Insects and their larvae; some spiders.

Size
12.75cm (5in)

J	F	M	A	M	J
J	A	S	O	N	D

Dry, lowland heaths and commons with gorse and heather in southern England. The British breeding population is Europe's most northerly.

DOTTEREL *Charadrius morinellus*

In a curious case of role reversal, the female dotterel is more brightly coloured than the male and takes the lead in courtship. Once the eggs are laid, she takes no further interest, and may even find another mate.

Unusually among birds, dotterels play a curious game of hide-and-seek as part of their courtship. The male hides among the stones of the barren mountain tops where the birds spend the summer, and the female, when she finds him, pecks at his neck feathers. In display flights, the female takes the initiative, chasing the male and then leading him to a scrape where the nest will be built. The duties of hatching the eggs and

tending the young are left to the male, while the female joins others of her sex, or occasionally finds another partner and lays another clutch, in which case she may share the incubation of this second family.

The male has an elaborate method of protecting the chicks should danger threaten. He runs along the ground in a crouch, looking like a small mammal, flies aggressively towards

sites before moving northwards. Historically, stopover places were known as 'dotterel fields', and a region of south Cambridgeshire has a 'dotterel day' in the second week of May.

Trusting outlook

The dotterel is well known for its confiding nature. Its name has been linked to 'dotard' and 'dotty', and its scientific name *morinellus* means 'little fool'.

About 950 pairs are believed to nest in Britain above 762m (2,500ft), mostly in the Cairngorms and on nearby summits. The dotterel is often referred to as a relict species – the last survivors from a much colder time. Their main breeding areas are on the Arctic tundra of Scandinavia and Russia, and in Scotland the birds are at their western limit. Their long-term future is threatened by disturbance but mostly by a changing climate.

Female dotterel.

Identification
White eye-stripes, meeting in a V at nape of neck; white breast band; chestnut underparts; faint bar on wing visible in flight; female brighter than male.

Nesting
Nests on ground in scrape lined with lichen and moss; lays May–June; usually 3 eggs, buff, stone or red-brown, thickly blotched and streaked with dark brown; incubation about 27 days, by male only; chicks, tended by male, leave within 24 hours, fly after about 28 days.

Feeding
Mainly insects; also spiders and crowberries; occasionally snails and earthworms.

Size
21.5cm (8½in)

J F M **A M J** **J A S O** N D

Scarce breeder on northern mountains, mostly in Scottish Highlands; migrants pause at traditional sites, especially in East Anglian fenlands.

the intruder and then flops back to the ground, acting as if he has a broken wing.

The tameness of the dotterel, and its need for a specialised upland habitat, make this member of the plover family a rarity in Britain. Around 100 years ago, dotterels were widespread on the higher hills from Highland south to the Pennines. Migrants, flying from their winter quarters in North Africa in small parties known as 'trips', used to visit a few places in eastern and southern England each spring – and often they were promptly shot and eaten. Trips of dotterels still spend a day or two at their traditional resting

Male feigns a broken wing to distract attention from the nest.

MOUNTAIN, MOOR & HEATH

GOLDEN EAGLE *Aquila chrysaetos*

In flight, the golden eagle's massive wings form a distinctive, graceful arc, tips separated into 'fingers' as though feeling for air currents, and giving an impression of unequalled power and control.

For sheer majesty there is no bird to compare with the golden eagle. This huge bird of prey soars above Highland peaks, primary feathers splayed at the tips of wings spanning 2m (7ft), as it scans the sky and ground below for quarry. Then it accelerates towards the target at a breath-taking speed of up to 90mph and thumps down to pin a red grouse, ptarmigan or blue hare to the ground. Eagles may take lambs occasionally, although these are usually weaklings. They also eat carrion – a habit that, at one time, cut back the bird's range. In regions where sheep-dips based on dieldrin pesticides were used, eagles were poisoned if they ate dead sheep. Dieldrin has now been banned throughout the EU. However, golden eagles still face a grave threat of being poisoned by baited carcasses – there have been 14 confirmed victims of this illegal practice since 1998.

Feathers on the back of the head and nape have a golden tinge.

The golden eagle inhabits remote mountain regions and wild open moorlands, in Britain favouring the Scottish Highlands and islands, where the population has remained steady at about 420 pairs for many years. Suitable habitat exists elsewhere but overgrazing by sheep and deer and afforestation resulting in lack of prey have discouraged the bird from spreading. A pair did nest at Haweswater in the Lake District for several years, but the female died in 2004.

Eagles pair for life, and usually have two or three eyries, pitched between heights of roughly 450m and 600m (1,500ft and 2,000ft), which they use in rotation. Territories and nesting places are used by generations of birds. In courtship, the pair soar in spirals over their territory and plunge earthwards with half-closed wings, sometimes rolling over in mid-air so close that their talons appear to link.

Re-used nests

The chosen nest, an immense basket of sticks built on a mountain crag, tall pine or sea cliff, is added to year by year – repaired before the breeding season and often decorated with fresh greenery. The eggs take about a month and a half to hatch and must remain covered for most of the time because they are very susceptible to a drop in temperature. The eagles may abandon the nest if disturbed. One egg usually hatches about a week before the second and as the downy eaglets grow, the nest becomes fouled with a litter of bones, the remains of food brought by their parents. The first hatched receives most of the food and attention, and the second chick rarely survives.

Golden eagles are usually silent but they have a shrill yelp at the nest and a thin whistling alarm call.

Identification
Almost uniformly dark, with golden tinge on head; heavy, powerful bill; exceptionally long wings; young birds have white in wings and tail.

Nesting
Both sexes build or repair nests in November or December; lays March or April; usually 2 eggs, white, with red-brown markings; incubation about 40 days, mainly by female; nestlings, fed by both parents, leave after about 12 weeks.

Feeding
Blue hares, grouse, ptarmigan, lambs and carrion.

Size
Male: 76.25cm (30in)
Female: 89cm (35in)

Mountains and islands in Scotland; reintroductions in northwest Ireland.

135

GOLDEN PLOVER *Pluvialis apricarius*

A rich mottled plumage makes the golden plover one of the most recognisable waders. When the bird adopts a play-acting strategy to protect its young, it makes an even more striking sight.

Running away with a wing drooping as though broken is a prelude to the golden plover's thrashing distraction display, the aim being to lure away the fox, dog, human intruder or other potential predator with the chance of an easy target. When these handsome birds arrive at their breeding areas on the high moors, they take part in communal courtship ceremonies. The males skirmish, running at each other with raised wings, and leapfrogging. Several males will chase one female. Later, when the eggs are being incubated, the off-duty parent will keep watch from a hummock near the nest, ready to launch itself at an animal or bird intruder, or perhaps to start the distraction display.

The mournful call-note and liquid song of the golden plover, nicknamed the 'goldie' by birdwatchers, are characteristic summer sounds on the open moorland. However, these birds are not as common as they once were. Their breeding range contracted steadily during the 20th century. They no longer breed on any of the Somerset moors, and there has been a sudden and dramatic decline in numbers in Wales, due to a combination of habitat loss, disturbance and climate change.

Winter flocks

In autumn and winter the birds move south to farmland, estuaries and saltmarshes, where they are joined by incomers from Iceland, Scandinavia and Russia. They tend to return to traditional winter-feeding grounds, and the same fields and valleys have been used for decades, perhaps hundreds of years. The plovers move from one field to another in fast-flying 'V'-shaped flocks, or in long lines or in dense, oval masses, and their home ranges may extend over several square miles. They often join feeding flocks of lapwings, and the combination attracts black-headed gulls. The gulls steal some of the worms pulled up by the waders but in return give early warnings of danger, so the waders can feed continuously without the need to be on the lookout for much of the time.

When disturbed the mixed flocks soon separate in flight, the goldies wheeling and turning, forming complex patterns against a background of slower flying lapwings. Golden plovers are among the fastest flying of all British birds in level flight, reaching speeds of 60mph. A heated debate about whether or not the golden plover was Europe's fastest gamebird led to one of the protagonists, who happened to be the managing director of the Guinness brewery, starting up what has become an international institution – the book of *Guinness World Records* – in order to settle just such esoteric arguments.

Foraging birds move in short runs, with pauses to pick up worms, slugs or seeds.

Identification
Large black areas on face and underparts, with spangled black and gold upper parts; duller in winter and loses black markings; sexes alike.

Nesting
Both sexes make scrapes, then female chooses one to line with twigs, lichen and grass; lays late April–June; usually 4 eggs, creamy, green-tinged or buff, spotted and blotched with dark brown; incubation about 30 days, by both parents; young, tended by both parents, leave after 1 or 2 days, fly after about 30 days.

Feeding
Insects (especially beetles), insect larvae, spiders and worms; snails and small shellfish; weed-seeds, algae and moss.

Size
28cm (11in)

J	F	M	A	M	J
J	A	S	O	N	D

Mainly on northern moors in summer; widespread in winter; recent decline in breeding pairs.

GREENSHANK *Tringa nebularia*

This long-legged wader with a long bill engages in a spectacular courtship display flight in spring, making erratic, undulating swoops from a great height, accompanied by a ringing, melodic song.

Greenshanks generally have a fast, level flight, but in courtship the male climbs high and follows a roller-coaster path down to the female on the ground. After each ascent, he then glides down and circles on bowed wings, singing. Sometimes the female joins her mate in aerial display, the pair swerving close together and diving steeply to zigzag in a low-level chase. In courtship, the male bows to the female on the ground, clicks his bill and sometimes leapfrogs over her.

The greenshank was badly harried in the past by egg collectors, who seemed to find a challenge in the task of tracking down the inconspicuous nest made by the female in a shallow scrape, with often only a boulder or a fallen branch as a landmark. But egg collecting is illegal now, and the bird is comparatively safe from people who intrude on the desolate expanses of boggy moorland in the Highlands, Skye and Outer Hebrides where it breeds. Threats today come from afforestation, especially in the major breeding areas of the Flow Country in Caithness and Sutherland, disturbance by humans, drying out of marshes and climate change. The Scottish populations are the most westerly of this species in the world.

Scattered arrival

These elegant waders are mainly summer visitors from Africa. On migration, they can be found all over Britain, by freshwater lakes and marshes as well as on estuaries and coastal wetlands. They are often seen singly but sometimes in small flocks. Once they arrive, they have a habit of perching on a rock, post or small tree if these are present in the open landscape. From there the male greenshank may deliver the same fluting song, a repeated 'ru-tu', that rings out during its display flight.

At dawn and dusk, the birds leave the vicinity of their nests and move to the shores of lochs to feed, mainly on water insects. In late summer and autumn, as they move south, they feed in marsh pools, estuaries and

A parent bird fiercely defends the young.

reservoirs. Often, the female leaves first, even before the young can fly, and the male and offspring follow a month or so later. A few greenshank stay for the winter and those that remain tend to gather along the western coasts of Ireland and Scotland with a few in the south of England. In the spring and autumn, numbers are swelled by passage migrants on their way to and from northern Europe.

As well as the song, the greenshank has two main calls – an excited 'chip-chip-chip' heard when the sexes change places on the eggs, and a loud 'chu-chu-chu' of alarm.

Identification
Long greenish legs; long grey-blue bill, slightly upturned; rump white, wings unmarked; upper parts ash-grey with dark markings; underparts white, with dark spots and bars in summer; sexes alike.

Nesting
Female makes scrape in ground, lines it with vegetation and sometimes hare droppings; lays early May–June; usually 4 eggs, buff, with dark blotches and spots; incubation about 24 days, by both parents; nestlings, tended by both parents, leave in a few hours, and begin to fly after about 27 days.

Feeding
Water insects and their larvae; worms and small fish; occasionally small frogs, more commonly tadpoles.

Size
30.5cm (12in)

| J | F | M | A | M | J |
| J | A | S | O | N | D |

Scottish Highlands and Hebrides; some winter in Ireland and south and west of Britain; widespread passage migrants in spring and autumn.

HEN HARRIER *Circus cyaneus*

A hen harrier can ride the wind with masterful ease and also perform vigorous and aerobatic manoeuvres. These skills are put to good use in the breeding season when the male passes food to his mate in mid-air.

While the female hen harrier is on the nest, the male will do all the hunting, calling to his mate after making a kill. She flies to meet him and the prey is delivered in one of three ways. The male may drop the food, in which case the female swoops to catch it in her talons, or the birds fly parallel to each other, both turning on their sides so that the male can pass the food across. Alternatively, the female turns on her back and flies upside down beneath the male,

accepting the food from his talons. Each pair has a favourite method of food exchange. Hen harriers are responsible parents, devoted to raising their young, which the male continues to do on his own if his mate is killed.

The hen harrier increased in numbers significantly in Scotland after the Second World War, and returned as a breeding bird to Wales. There are now more than 500 breeding pairs in Britain, but the increase has stalled and

Gradual movement

Most hen harriers spend the breeding season on the moors and in moorland valleys, but the birds are beginning to spread to heaths and sand-dunes. In winter many tend to remain where they are, except in very severe weather, although some move south, and others regularly visit coastal marshes and wetlands, where they are often joined by winter visitors from Europe.

In its low-level hunting flight, the hen harrier is like other harriers – it lazily beats its wings four or five times, glides with them half-raised, and then pounces to seize a mouse, a frog, a lapwing chick or the young or egg of some other ground-nesting bird. Hen harriers also chase small birds through the air but, in spite of their name, they are no real threat to hens.

In a spectacular courtship display, the male hen harrier flies steeply upwards, turns a somersault at the top of its climb, then plummets down with closed wings.

Identification

Male dove grey; female brown, with streaked underparts and black bars on wings; male distinguished from Montagu's harrier by white, not grey, rump and lack of black bars on wings.

Nesting

Female builds nest on ground, often in heather; lays late May–June; usually 4 eggs, white or pale blue; incubation about 28 days, by female only; nestlings, tended by both parents, leave after 6 weeks.

Feeding

Small ground-living animals; a few small birds caught on the wing.

Size

**Male: 43cm (17in)
Female: 51cm (20in)**

numbers remain tiny in England, despite suitable habitat being available to support many more pairs. Numbers are lower than they should be on many areas of moorland managed for grouse shooting. Despite the hen harrier's protected status, many are still shot or poisoned because, given the opportunity, they regularly take red grouse, often in large numbers. The dilemma about how to maintain and encourage both species is ongoing.

The female may roll over in mid-air to catch prey dropped by her mate.

J	F	M	A	M	J
J	A	S	O	N	D

Moors and young conifer plantations; widespread in winter, visiting heaths, farmland, wetlands and coastal marshes.

141

HOBBY
Falco subbuteo

Lightly built for a bird of prey, the hobby looks compact and streamlined at rest. In flight, it has few rivals for speed, grace and agility. Swooping to catch a swallow, it presents a breathtaking spectacle.

The scythe-shaped wings of the hobby carry it so rapidly on its hunting forays over downs or heaths that it can fly down a swift, or even catch a bat in flight. This handsome falcon is agile enough to twist and turn after a dragonfly, snatch the insect in its claws and hold it to its beak to eat, without pausing in flight. Hobbies seem to fly for sheer joy, tumbling, gliding and soaring, with marked changes of pace and direction, especially when hunting insects – chafers, moths, damselflies and beetles as well as dragonflies. They eat mainly insects, but during the breeding season they will take small birds that habitually fly in the open, away from cover, sometimes plucking them on the wing, although with bigger prey it is more usual to take the quarry to a branch or to the ground before plucking it.

Their mastery of the air plays an important part in courtship. The male advertises his presence by racing above the treetops in a zigzagging dash. Male and female circle together and the male 'stoops' at the female, as if preparing to attack her. After snatching a small bird, the male climbs high to dive on the female and pass the prey to her in the air at full speed.

Crow's nests

The birds usually breed in open country with scattered trees in which they may find the old nests of crows and sometimes sparrowhawks, or

The hobby has a distinctive streaky front, a dark crown and a thick black 'moustache'.

even squirrels' dreys, which they then adopt. Once the hobbies take over, they may remove some lining from the abandoned nest. These falcons never build their own nests from scratch. Their eggs are laid in June, and the hatching of the young hobbies a month later coincides with an abundance of unwary juvenile swallows, martins and other small birds on which they can be fed.

The hobby is a summer visitor, which makes it unusual because the other three falcons that breed in Britain – the kestrel, merlin and peregrine falcon – are resident. The birds arrive in April from their winter quarters in Africa and leave again in October. At one time more or less restricted to heathland, not much of which survives, hobbies were adaptable enough to spread to farmland and, although thinly dispersed, increasing numbers breed in England and Wales. Some estimates suggest as many as 2,000 breeding pairs are present during the summer.

The bird's odd English name comes from an old French word *hober*, meaning 'to leap about', and its scientific name, *subbuteo*, means 'smaller than buzzard'.

Identification
Slate-grey back; black 'moustache', creamy white breast and underparts streaked with black; red thighs; female similar to male, but slightly larger; in flight, scythe-like wings make it look like a large swift.

Nesting
Takes over abandoned nest high in tree, often a conifer; lays June; usually 3 eggs, white, heavily mottled with red-brown or yellow-brown; incubation about 28 days, chiefly by female; nestlings, fed by both parents, leave after 28–32 days.

Feeding
Grasshoppers, dragonflies and other winged insects; small birds; occasionally bats and larger birds.

Size
33cm (13in)

J F M **A M J**
J A S O N D

Farmland and heath, mainly in central and southern England but spreading.

MOUNTAIN, MOOR & HEATH

LINNET *Carduelis cannabina*

The sweet, twittering song of the linnet is one of summer's pleasures. The birds even sing in chorus. Its musical notes made the cock linnet a favourite cage-bird of Victorian and Edwardian England.

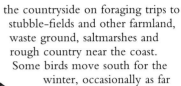

Today the fashion for putting linnets in cages has long passed, and the handsome red-breasted male pours out its medley of notes in the wild. Usually it finds a song-post on a bush or a fence, but sometimes a linnet will sing as it flies, bounding up and down through the air. The usual flight-note is a high-pitched chittering and there is also a 'tsoo-eet' anxiety note. The cock sings again in its courtship ceremony, uttering a series of low, sweet notes as it droops its wings, spreads its tail and rapidly shakes its feathers.

These attractive little finches are gregarious birds, widespread across Britain. Most breed along the east coast from Kent to Aberdeenshire, and they are scarce in upland regions and northwest Scotland. Linnets often gather in loose colonies, preferring places with plenty of low bushes where they can build their nests. They frequent gorse-covered commons and heaths and scrub-covered downland, but sometimes move into parks or big gardens, or use farmland hedges. The association with gorse gave rise to the linnet's old names of 'gorse thatcher' and 'furze linnet'.

Seed eaters

Cuckoos occasionally lay their eggs in linnets' nests, but the young cuckoos usually starve because of the specialised diet – chiefly seeds – on which linnet nestlings are fed. The name linnet is the English version of the French *linette*, which comes from the bird's fondness for the seeds of flax (*Linum usitatissimum*). Its scientific name *cannabina* comes from the hemp plant (*Cannabis sativa*), whose seeds it also eats along with a wide range of thistle and weed-seeds.

When the breeding season is over, linnets tend to mix with other finches in winter-feeding flocks, sometimes hundreds strong, which roam

The linnet's tail is quite long and forked. Its wing and tail feathers are edged with white.

the countryside on foraging trips to stubble-fields and other farmland, waste ground, saltmarshes and rough country near the coast. Some birds move south for the winter, occasionally as far as western France and Spain, while winter visitors arrive in Britain from Scandinavia.

Over the past 30 years there has been a major decline in linnet numbers of more than 50 per cent, due to loss of habitat and the effects of agricultural intensification. Even though the rate of loss seems to have slowed recently, there is still cause for concern, and linnets remain red listed along with various other farmland birds.

Identification
Chestnut back; white wing-bar; forked tail has white sides; male has crimson crown and breast in summer.

Nesting
Female builds nest of grass and moss, lined with hair and wool, usually close to the ground in bush; lays April–July; usually 4–6 eggs, light blue with sparse purple-red blotches; incubation about 11 days, chiefly by female; young, fed by both parents, fly after about 12 days; two broods, sometimes three.

Feeding
Mainly weed-seeds; some insects, especially caterpillars, are fed to the young, and perhaps also eaten by adults.

Size
13.25cm (5¼in)

J	F	M	A	M	J
J	A	S	O	N	D

Open country with gorse and other dense bushes, farmland with thick hedges, young conifer plantations and large gardens; near coast in winter.

MOUNTAIN, MOOR & HEATH

Birds of the barren heights

Frozen for much of the year and with a climate that resembles that of the Arctic tundra, the rugged mountains of the Cairngorms are home to some of the most spectacular and unusual birds in Britain.

In February 2008 a hillwalker was braving the wintry heights of Britain's second-highest peak, Ben Macdui in the Cairngorms of northeast Scotland, when something caught his eye. Perched among the tumbled granite boulders just north of the summit was a snowy owl – a bird that is rarely seen south of the Arctic Circle. For the walker, it was an extraordinary encounter. Yet for the owl, the stony, windswept terrain of the high Cairngorms must have felt like home, for it is the nearest thing in Britain to an Arctic landscape.

During the last Ice Age much of Britain was covered by ice sheets fringed by barren tundra. As the ice retreated some 12,000 years ago, the scoured, rocky ground was colonised by tough pioneer plants that, by degrees, gave way to the richer vegetation of temperate broad-leaved woodlands, and eventually to farmland. But this transformation never reached the high Cairngorms – a great dissected plateau of crystalline granite that, over large areas, lies more than 1,000m (3,280ft) above sea level. This northern wilderness remains an icy outlier of the Arctic. On the heights the landscape is like that of Spitsbergen, with mossy heath, lichens and rare montane plants clinging to life among the frost-shattered boulders and screes. Below the rocky peaks, vast expanses of rainswept heather moorland and blanket bog are cut by sheltered glens that support remnants of the ancient pine woodland, which moved in after the glaciers melted. It is a truly primeval scene.

Highland specialities

This stupendous landscape is now Britain's largest National Park, covering an area of 1,400 sq miles. It provides a home for some of the UK's most threatened wildlife, including many birds. A few, like the snowy owl, are rare vagrants – here today and gone tomorrow – but others are more reliable.

A winter visit offers a glimpse of Ice-Age Britain but the best time to come is in spring and summer, when the mountain flora is in bloom and the birds are performing their courtship displays. Familiar breeding waders, such as curlews, oystercatchers and lapwings, fill the air with their evocative calls while on the higher slopes a few Highland specialities may be found. These include the dotterel, a small,

fine-billed plover that is remarkable because the female has brighter breeding plumage than the male and takes the lead in courtship. She performs a butterfly-like display flight while her mate looks on, and he is the one to incubate their eggs. Another more elusive bird is the ptarmigan, an upland grouse that lives almost entirely in the high arctic-alpine zone. It turns pure white in winter to match the snow, but in summer is equally well camouflaged in mottled grey and brown, making it almost invisible as it crouches motionless among the lichen-covered rocks. The ptarmigan shares this apparently hostile habitat with the snow bunting, another species that breeds mainly in the Arctic, but also nests here on the boulder-strewn slopes of this semi-tundra landscape.

The ptarmigan need their camouflage to conceal them from the golden eagles that regularly patrol the skies, soaring majestically over the rounded peaks with wings raised in a shallow 'V', the tips spread out like open fingers. Occasionally, an eagle will come to rest on a crag or tree, a truly memorable sight, before it launches itself skywards again. Ravens thrive here, too, and perform spectacular aerobatics in spring, rolling and tumbling through the air while uttering deep, resonant calls. Peregrines nest in the mountains, and prey upon the breeding waders and red grouse that live among the heather.

Strutting display

Farther downhill, where the heather gives way to ancient pine woodland, a very early start in spring may be rewarded by the sight of black grouse conducting their dawn courtship rituals. Gathering on communal display grounds (known as 'leks'), the glossy black males strut and posture, flaring their white tails and giving their loud bubbling 'rookooing' song in competitive display while the females look on. Deeper in the woods, the similar but much bigger and far more elusive capercaillie puts on an even more dramatic performance, often attacking rival males that interrupt its bizarre clicking, wheezing, cork-popping song. Sadly, this gamebird is becoming rarer, but the pinewoods of the Cairngorms are among the few places where there is a chance of seeing it. The ancient Scots pines also support much smaller Highland

species, such as the lively little crested tit and the Scottish crossbill – the only British bird that is unique to these islands.

This region is also renowned for a striking bird that has an almost global distribution, but is no less exciting for that. Loch Garten in the north of the National Park welcomed the first ospreys to breed in Britain since the species was declared extinct here in 1916. A pair has nested successfully on the loch almost every year since 1959, and no visit to the Cairngorms is complete without a pilgrimage to the osprey centre on the lake shores. The hide here offers stunning views of the nest through the telescopes provided, giving an intimate insight into the lives of these magnificent birds. With luck, it is also possible to witness one of the most dramatic hunting techniques of any raptor as an osprey flies out over the loch, pauses to hover, then dives headlong into the water to seize a fish in its long, curved talons – a fitting emblem of the savage beauty of the Highlands.

Occasionally, one of these majestic birds will come to rest on a crag or tree, a truly memorable sight, before it launches itself skyward.

GOLDEN EAGLE

MERLIN *Falco columbarius*

The diminutive merlin is a persistent hunter. Having chased another small bird to the point of exhaustion, it delivers the final strike and heads for a plucking post, its prey clasped firmly in its talons.

The male merlin, or jack, is Britain's smallest bird of prey. Although little bigger than a blackbird, weighing a mere 160g (5½oz), he does most of the hunting throughout the breeding season, sometimes flying down birds as big as himself through sheer persistence, although skylarks, stonechats, meadow pipits and twites are among his chief prey. When hunting, both male and female merlin will follow every twist and turn as the targetted bird tries to shake off its dogged pursuer in its desperate attempts to escape. Hunter and hunted often shoot low over the ground but at last the merlin may suddenly accelerate upwards in a powerful climb, towering above its fast-tiring prey before forcing the bird down to the ground where it can seize its meal, using its long talons.

The merlin often spots its prey while quartering the moors, flying low and fast with quick, shallow wing-beats, and occasionally hanging in the breeze, but it also watches for vulnerable birds from a perch. Its tactic then is a short-distance surprise attack. If the bird is alert enough to fly away in time, this method may still require a low-level chase, but sometimes the merlin will catch it on the ground or dive steeply on to it. Although usually solitary hunters, a pair of merlins may hunt in unison to tire out prey and force small birds to the ground.

Food delivery

With its prey safely clutched in its talons, the male flies towards its nest, uttering a shrill, chattering 'quik-ik-ik' call. At one of its plucking posts close to the nest, it often tears off the prey's head and then brings the body to the female, or occasionally signals to her to take it in mid-air.

Merlins vary their diet with small mammals, lizards and insects during their winter wanderings, which can take them from their upland

The merlin often takes its prey in level flight.

breeding grounds to lowland pastures, marshes or the sand and shingle of the coast, where they are joined by winter visitors from Iceland.

On upland moors they occasionally kill a few game-chicks, although not enough to justify the persecution they have suffered from gamekeepers. Merlins have declined over most of Britain in the last 80 years or so. The process appears to be continuing, but the reasons for it are unclear. Habitat loss, persecution and pesticide contamination may all be involved.

The merlin's name has no connection with the magician of King Arthur legends. It comes from an old French name for the species, *émerillon*.

Identification
Slate-blue back and tail; female larger than male with dark brown back and banded tail; both have heavily streaked underparts.

Nesting
Nests on ground or in old crow's nest; lays May–June; usually 4 eggs, cream, with heavy red-brown freckles; incubation about 30 days, by both parents; nestlings, tended by both parents, leave at 26 days.

Feeding
Small birds, usually meadow pipits, but also larger ones such as lapwings, redshank and other waders in winter; some small mammals and lizards; a few insects.

Size
Male: 26.75cm (10½in)
Female: 33cm (13in)

| J | F | M | A | M | J |
| J | A | S | O | N | D |

Moorlands and coasts; winters in lowlands, mainly on coastal saltmarshes and farmland.

NIGHTJAR *Caprimulgus europaeus*

On warm summer evenings, the nightjar fills the gathering dusk with its weird 'churring' song. When the moon is bright, it will give voice all through the night and greet the dawn with the same unearthly notes.

The strange, somewhat mechanical sound that gives the nightjar its name has been compared to a distant motorbike or some small machine. An old country name for the nightjar is 'wheel bird' because its song was thought to resemble a working spinning wheel. Rising and falling in intensity, there are abrupt changes of pitch in the otherwise unvarying, prolonged 'churr' when the bird turns its head from side to side.

The nightjar delivers its song to advertise its ownership of territory as well as to attract a mate but although the sound is unmistakable, the singing bird may often be difficult to locate. The male may be perched on a branch, squatting low on a stump or simply sitting on the ground.

During the day, nightjars lie motionless on the ground and, at a distance, the delicate markings on their feathers

In the nest, the parent bird, eggs and young are superbly camouflaged among sticks and dead leaves.

In flight, the nightjar's call is a soft but insistent 'coo-ic', and the male makes a sound like a whip-crack by flapping his wings together.

Nightjars arrive from Africa in mid-May to breed on heaths, commons and other places with bracken or gorse, as well as on the borders of woodland, returning to the same vicinity season after season. Their numbers have been decreasing in Britain for more than 50 years. On its evening flights to catch insects, the nightjar visits pastures where farm animals graze – a habit that earned the bird another of its old names, 'goatsucker', from a false belief that it milks goats with its huge mouth.

Identification
Night-flying bird with long, falcon-like wings and tail; grey-brown 'camouflage' plumage; mouth fringed with bristles; male has white spots near wing-tips and on tail, absent in female; distinctive 'churring' song.

Nesting
Nests in unlined scrape in the ground, often near dead wood; lays late May–July; 2 eggs, white, marbled with brown or grey; incubation about 18 days, chiefly by female; nestlings, fed by both parents, leave nest after about a week but stay nearby, fly after about 17 days; usually two broods.

Feeding
Insects, chiefly those caught in flight.

Size
26.75cm (10½in)

make them look like dead leaves. The mottled, subtly beautiful camouflage makes the bird virtually invisible against tree bark. There are often pieces of wood near the nightjar's nest – an unlined scrape in the ground – and these make the sitting bird even harder to see. Singing peaks at the start of the breeding season, and declines after the birds have paired up and eggs have been laid.

Remarkable transformation
At dusk the nightjar seems to shape-shift as it leaves its daytime hiding place among the bracken and heather, transforming itself into a slender, long-tailed bird, seen in silhouette. It takes to the air silently on long, soft-feathered wings, twisting and turning through the twilight as it follows flying insects and traps them in the huge, rose-pink gape of its short, weak bill. Tiny but prominent hairs fringe the bill to funnel the moths and beetles into the open mouth.

Heath, moors and open woodland, mainly in southern England and East Anglia.

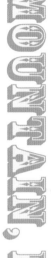

PEREGRINE *Falco peregrinus*

Large, forward-facing eyes give the peregrine falcon such keen vision it can spot prey from long distances. Unparalleled agility allows this supreme hunter to home in on its quarry at great speed.

Soaring way up above its hunting territory, the peregrine looks too remote to be menacing, but once it has singled out its prey – a gull, perhaps, or an unsuspecting feral pigeon – it arches through the sky in a breathtaking 'stoop', giving its target little chance of escape because this is the world's fastest living creature. Speeds of more than 90mph have been measured for the diving peregrine – some estimates quote 155mph – and the bird's talons strike the quarry with such force that they may break its head clean off its body. If the prey somehow manages to dodge the attack, the peregrine will not give up but often stoops again and again.

The peregrine's liking for particular prey is reflected in two of the old names for the bird, 'pigeon hawk' and 'duck hawk'. These form a major part of its diet, along with medium-sized birds, such as thrushes and starlings, but it takes others too, ranging in size from tiny goldcrests to herons and geese. On its favourite mountains and moorlands it takes grouse and waders, while along coastal cliffs it eats jackdaws and seabirds.

Setbacks overcome

Falconers have always prized these spectacular, efficient killers, but their reputation as hunters led to large numbers of peregrines being shot during the Second World War, because it was thought that they were a threat to carrier pigeons, used when radio silence was imposed on submarine-spotting planes.

The peregrine population was beginning to recover from this setback when it was hit by a worse one – the birds were either poisoned or made infertile by ingesting pesticides used on crops and eaten by their prey. In 1956 there were more than 650 pairs of peregrines in the British Isles. Six years later, only 68 breeding pairs were left, but since then the peregrine has staged a remarkable recovery. Now 1,400 pairs nest in the UK and 350 in Ireland, and several cities have been colonised by nesting pairs. These may be welcomed by the authorities because they survive by feeding largely on town pigeons.

Peregrines' natural, open-country habitats have cliffs and crags with rocky ledges on which they can nest, but they seem to regard various man-made structures as perfectly adequate substitutes – churches, high-rise buildings, viaducts, motorway bridges, electricity pylons have all been selected by nesting birds.

They mate for life, each spring performing spectacular aerial aerobatics, diving on one another and rolling in flight, displaying such precision that even a slight miscalculation could bring disaster. They often return year after year to the same eyrie. Some eyries have been in use for hundreds of years by successive dynasties of peregrines.

A courting male loops the loop after making a mock dive at the female.

Identification

Long wings, broad-based tail; anchor shape when gliding; grey above with paler rump, white below with dark bars; white throat against black cheeks and hood; juvenile streaked beneath. Flies with deep, rapid wing-beats and short glides.

Nesting

Nests in bare scrape on rock ledge or in abandoned nest of other species; usually lays April; usually 3 or 4 eggs, red-brown; incubation about 30 days, chiefly by female; nestlings, fed by both sexes, leave after 30–40 days.

Feeding

Birds on the wing; rabbits and other mammals.

Size

Male: 38cm (15in)
Female: 48.25cm (19in)

J F M A M J
J A S O N D

Nest on cliffs and crags on the coast and inland; some on tall buildings in urban areas. Winters on estuaries and other lowlands.

PTARMIGAN *Lagopus mutus*

In harsh weather the ptarmigan digs itself a snug, igloo-like burrow in which to shelter. It also changes colour with the seasons, its white winter plumage providing the perfect camouflage in snowy conditions.

Ptarmigan are birds of the high, barren mountain tops, seldom seen below 610m (2,000ft) and for the most part spending their lives above 1,000m (3,200ft). Early in the morning they move down the mountainsides to feed on the green shoots and fruits of the sparse vegetation above the tree line, but apart from hunger, the only force that can drive these hardy birds down into the sheltered corries is a full-scale blizzard. Otherwise, during the winter a pair, or family group, will dig out a tunnel where they can huddle together, completely enclosed by snow. Enough air penetrates the surface cover for them to breathe and the insulation provided in their

hideaway keeps them safe from hypothermia at a time when they are at their weakest, unable to find food easily.

In another adaptation to high-mountain living, the ptarmigan's colour undergoes several complex changes, from mottled brown in summer turning distinctly patchy in autumn to nearly all white in winter, so the bird always blends in with the background of lichen-covered rocks, scanty vegetation and varying degrees of snow. Its plumage is extremely dense and full feathering extends to the feet, which serve as miniature snowshoes. Any adaptations such as these help in the struggle for survival – a

struggle that begins even before the chicks hatch out in a nest that is sometimes only thinly lined with grass, and often protected from the upland gales by just a boulder. Hen ptarmigan have been observed using an injury-feigning display, crawling along the ground and thrashing their wings to distract predators from their eggs and chicks.

Uncertain future
When ski-lifts were first built in the Cairngorms, fears were voiced for the future of the ptarmigan, but these have proved to be largely unfounded. Worse problems are caused by sheep removing much bilberry and heather, both part of the bird's diet, but more likely to cause ptarmigan

to disappear entirely from Britain is the seemingly unstoppable effect of a warming climate – white plumage and no snow make ptarmigan an easy target for predators.

Male birds stake a claim to territory in March, flying up with croaking cries. They chase females in flight and on the ground, fanning their tails and drooping their wings. The ptarmigan's guttural calls and dry, cackling song give the bird its name. In Gaelic, *tarmachan* means 'croaker'. The initial 'p' was given to it in the 17th century for reasons long forgotten.

Identification
White wings and dark body in summer; female tawnier than male; pure white in winter except for black tail; male has black mark through eye.

Nesting
Female makes scrape near rocks; lays May or June; usually 5–9 eggs, creamy with dark markings; incubation about 25 days, by female only; chicks, tended by both parents, leave soon after hatching, fly after 10 days.

Feeding
Mainly fruit, shoots and leaves of crowberry, bilberry, heather and other mountain plants; a few insects, mainly crane-flies.

Size
35.5cm (14in)

Moulting birds show a variety of intermediate plumages in autumn.

Although in Arctic Eurasia and North America it occurs in lowland tundra, in Britain it is restricted to the highest Scottish mountain tops.

RAVEN *Corvus corax*

Large and black as night, the raven has a formidable beak which it uses to feast on carrion. Yet despite its reputation as a menacing bird of ill-omen, it often indulges in playful antics in flight.

The largest member of the crow family, the raven is the world's biggest perching bird, almost equal in size to a buzzard, to which it bears a slight resemblance when viewed in flight from a distance. But when performing its aerial acrobatics, it is unmistakable.

Ravens fly with characteristic deep wing beats and spend more time gliding, twisting and turning than any other member of the crow family. While descending in a shallow glide, a raven will often flip over 180° on to its back, and then flip back up the right way, an action that may be repeated three or four times in quick succession. Occasionally, it indulges in a full roll, turning in a complete arc. Such unusual behaviour has been interpreted by some ornithologists as a way of rapidly losing height. However, since the raven typically continues in a smooth glide after these exuberant manoeuvres, other observers believe that the bird is just playing. That idea is reinforced by other playful behaviour, including hanging upside down from branches and sliding down snowy slopes.

Ritual gestures

Ravens are skilled in synchronised flying and pairs revelling in these antics in early spring, twisting and turning almost wing tip to wing tip, are perhaps incorporating them in courtship rituals. Ceremonies on the ground between male and female, who mate for life, include bowing, neck stretching and ruffling the throat feathers. In the mating display, the male spreads his wings and tail, and crouches with neck stretched up but bill pointed down. Sometimes he jumps into the air, or preens the female's face with his large and powerful bill.

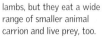
If available, the raven will feed on dead sheep and lambs, but they eat a wide range of smaller animal carrion and live prey, too.

Ravens are the vultures of sheep country, patrolling in pairs or family groups in search of carrion – or a sickly sheep or deer, waiting to die. They will eat almost anything, from insects and shellfish to grain and acorns. Once they were common scavengers in the streets of London, but they were gradually driven northward and westward to the hills and sea cliffs.

In flight, the raven utters a range of calls from a distinctive croaking 'pruk-pruk-pruk', which echoes for some distance, and a hollow-sounding, resonant 'kronk, kronk', to softer, higher pitched sounds that can be heard only at close range.

The nest, a substantial cup of sticks and other local materials, lined with sheep's wool or hair, is usually built on an inaccessible ledge, but in some districts ravens nest in trees.

Identification
Glossy black plumage; massive bill; end of tail wedge-shaped; sexes alike.

Nesting
Both sexes build nest of sticks cemented with mud and moss, on ledge or in crevice; lays February–April; usually 4–6 eggs, pale green or blue with dark markings; incubation about 19 days, by female only; nestlings, fed by both parents, leave after about 6 weeks.

Feeding
Chiefly carrion and small animals; also seeds, fruit, grain, fish; eggs and young of other birds.

Size
63.5cm (25in)

J	F	M	A	M	J
J	A	S	O	N	D

Mainly uplands and coastal areas in north and west, and in Ireland. Recent small expansion in numbers and range.

MOUNTAIN, MOOR & HEATH

RED GROUSE *Lagopus lagopus*

The red grouse rarely strays far from its home territory. When a flock is disturbed, the birds explode into rapid flight with whirring wings and rattling calls, but they soon glide down to hide in the heather.

The upland moors of Britain can be uncannily quiet places until the silence is broken by a loud chorus of harsh 'qurrack-rack-rack' calls of alarm as a group of red grouse make their escape, often flying up from practically under walkers' feet. However, the birds never go far. Remarkably sedentary, males often travel no farther than about a mile during their entire lifetime, although females are usually a little more adventurous.

In Britain, only the ptarmigan – a fellow member of the grouse family – has adapted to life in harsher surroundings. Although red grouse do live at sea level in a few places, mostly these hardy birds inhabit upland moorland, living above

The main causes of reduced grouse populations, though, are the lack of good moorland management combined with wet summers. Numbers now – around 155,000 breeding pairs in Britain plus up to 2,500 pairs in Ireland – are probably roughly half those of the 1920s.

The wings have no bar.

In winter on the high, bleak moors, grouse may have to keep treading with their feet for long spells to avoid being buried in drifting snow. Snowstorms are still common in April, when the female is laying, but even if the eggs are badly frosted, grouse chicks rarely fail to hatch – as long as their parents stay on guard against that moorland egg-thief, the hooded crow. Red grouse are also preyed upon by hen harriers, a protected species. Unfortunately, hen harriers are often illegally destroyed in order to safeguard the grouse. The shooting season for grouse lasts from 12 August to 10 December.

As native birds red grouse are unique to Britain and Ireland, but they are closely related to the willow grouse of Norway and are regarded as a race of the same species.

Identification
Dark wings and tail; male's body dark red-brown; female's browner, more barred.

Nesting
Female makes scrape in the ground, lined with grass or heather; lays April or May; usually 4–9 eggs, creamy white, almost obscured by dark chocolate blotches; incubation about 23 days, by female only; chicks, tended by both parents for about 6 weeks, leave soon after hatching, fly after about 13 days.

Feeding
Mostly ling heather; also fruits and shoots of cranberry.

Size
Male: 38cm (15in)
Female: 34.25cm (13½in)

the tree line among the ling heather on which they rely for food, eating different parts of the plant from winter until its seeds fall in autumn. Unlike other gamebirds, red grouse are not reared and released for shooting, but wild populations are encouraged by intensive keepering, involving the systematic burning of patches of heather to produce young shoots, on which they also feed.

Territorial behaviour
The cock birds mark out their territory in a dramatic display, leaping into the air with spread wings and descending steeply again while extending their necks and feet, and fanning their tails. They challenge rival cocks with their barking calls, 'go-bak, go-bak-bak-bak-bak'. Birds that cannot establish a well-heathered territory often fall victim to disease, caused by a tiny parasitic worm, or are taken by predators, such as foxes.

| J | F | M | A | M | J |
| J | A | S | O | N | D |

Heather moors mostly in northern England and eastern Scotland; also in Wales and Ireland; only small numbers in southwest England.

MOUNTAIN, MOOR & HEATH

RED KITE *Milvus milvus*

A whole ragbag of paper and fabric, even soft toys, may catch the red kite's attention when it builds its nest. If an item can provide a cosy nest lining for its young, the red kite will take it.

Handkerchiefs, socks, gloves, paper and hosiery are among the linings found in the red kite's nest, alongside the usual wool, moss and hair. This pronounced habit is not a recent phenomenon – Shakespeare acknowledged it when he warned in 'The Winter's Tale': 'When the kite builds, look to lesser linen.'

Red kites were widespread over Britain until the 18th century, and were common scavengers on the filthy streets of medieval and Elizabethan London, encouraged as street cleaners, but then became persecuted until they became one of Britain's rarest breeding birds, restricted to wild parts of central Wales. Careful protection led to numbers very slowly increasing in that area, so that now much larger numbers breed there, partly sustained by artificial feeding. Since 1992, kites have been reintroduced into several parts of England, Scotland and Northern Ireland, greatly expanding their numbers and range. They prefer woodland for nesting, building bulky, untidy structures high in deciduous trees, often adding sticks and twigs to old crows' or buzzards' nests. For hunting, they like rolling, open country, arable farmland and moorland fringes.

Mastery of the air

Kites are magnificent fliers, circling tirelessly for hours over wooded valleys on their long, slender wings, usually bent at the 'wrist', and steering with their long, forked tails. Their effortless flight long ago added a word to the English language – the ornamental kites flown by children and adults alike, along with those used for military and other purposes, all get their name from these birds.

As red kites fly, they scan the earth for small mammals, alighting on a nearby perch before making the kill with a sudden pounce to the ground. However, despite being efficient hunters, they mostly eat carrion, often holding back to observe the scene before flying down to a carcass. Some birds visit abattoirs and rubbish tips as well as homing in on dead sheep and other mammals. Although red kites are not generally aggressive towards other birds of prey, they are adept at snatching food from them in flight. At kite-feeding stations in Wales, hunks of meat are put out for the birds, helping them through hard winters. The downside of their scavenging habits is that many red kites are dying as a result of eating poisoned bait, put out to kill foxes and other predators.

Pairs of kites perform aerobatics in their courtship ceremony, and they have a diving display flight, in common with many birds of prey. Their call is a shrill, mewing 'weeou-weeou-weeou'.

The long wings are often held at an angle.

Identification
Rich, bright brown plumage with streaked, white head; slender body; narrow wings, sharply bent backwards in flight; deeply forked tail; female slightly duller.

Nesting
Both sexes build nest of sticks and earth in tree, often on an old nest of a crow; lays April or May; usually 2 or 3 eggs, white, with red-brown speckles; incubation about 30 days, by female only; nestlings, tended by both parents, leave after 50–55 days.

Feeding
Carrion, especially sheep; small mammals, rabbits, fledgling rooks and gulls; sometimes worms and frogs.

Size
Male: 56cm (22in)
Female: 61cm (24in)

J	F	M	A	M	J
J	A	S	O	N	D

Woodland hills in Wales, Scotland, northern and central England; hunts over moorland, in winter over bogs and other open country.

RING OUZEL
Turdus torquatus

For a thrush, this summer visitor acts out of character, breeding in wild upland regions instead of the lowland areas preferred by its cousin, the blackbird. Another difference is the telltale white crescent on the ring ouzel's chest.

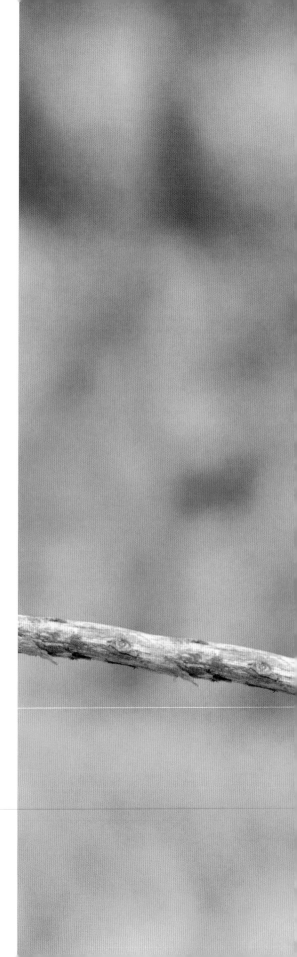

The ring ouzel has many old names, including 'heath throstle', 'tor ouzel' and 'mountain colley', most of which reflect the places where it chooses to live, but the most well-known alternative is 'mountain blackbird', and there is no doubt that these close relatives do look alike. As well as its white chest band, points of difference are that the ring ouzel has longer wings and tail, silvery edges to its flight feathers and is more streamlined – and the two birds are quite different in character. Blackbirds are garden birds, bold and often tame, but ring ouzels are birds of mountain and moorland, shy and difficult to approach. They are most often seen perching on distant rocks or flying away.

There may be particular difficulty in distinguishing a ring ouzel from a part-albino blackbird, which may have white on its breast, but there is little danger of confusing the two species during the breeding season, because nesting ouzels are rare below 300m (1,000ft). The overlap between them comes when ring ouzels travel between their breeding territories in the uplands of Scotland and northern England and their winter quarters in North Africa, and stop in the south to rest and feed. In spring and autumn, British breeders may be joined by passage migrants on their way to and from Scandinavia. The birds form loose flocks that gather on areas of short natural grassland near the coast, or on downland, usually with low, dense cover nearby for hiding in if disturbed when feeding, or for taking shelter in bad weather conditions.

Departing migrants feed in groups.

Secluded nests

When nesting, ouzels seek out remote gullies, abandoned quarries and steep hillsides. The nest is built on or close to the ground, often near a moorland stream or track in mature heather or occasionally under bracken, but sometimes they nest below ground level in entrances to pot holes or old mine shafts, and occasionally on the fringes of forestry plantations.

The contact call is a clear, piping 'pee-u', and their alarm call is a harsh 'tac-tac-tac'. The song is a simple affair with repeated phrases consisting of a few melancholy fluting or piping notes with a distinct pause between phrases. On still days, in the relative silence of the mountains, the song carries a long way.

Like other thrushes, ring ouzels eat animal and vegetable food in roughly equal quantities. In spring and summer they find a plentiful supply of insects, small snails and earthworms in short grassland. In autumn they turn to wild fruit, especially when on migration.

Numbers have recently declined almost everywhere, which is probably the result of a changing climate.

Identification
Male sooty black with broad white crescent on breast; pale wing-patch; female browner, with smaller, duller half-collar.

Nesting
Both sexes build untidy grass cup nest on ground or on crag, disused building or bush, often with a base of heather stems; lays mid April–June; usually 4 eggs, pale blue-green with blotches of red-brown; incubation 14 days, mostly by female; nestlings, tended by both parents, leave after 14 days.

Feeding
Insects and their larvae; earthworms; occasionally snails and small lizards in summer; wild fruit – bilberries, crowberries, rowan berries, haws, sloes – in autumn.

Size
24cm (9½in)

| J | F | M | A | M | J |
| J | A | S | O | N | D |

Mountains and moors, mainly in west and north. Occurs far more widely on migration, especially on chalk downland and coastal grassland.

SHORT-EARED OWL *Asio flammeus*

The short-eared owl reverses a family trait by hunting in daylight. When resting, it can see all round by swivelling its head and its glaring yellow eyes deter many a potential intruder.

Although one of the scarcer of Britain's owls, the short-eared owl is the easiest to spot because it hunts over open, treeless country in broad daylight as well as at dusk. It systematically quarters the ground, slowly and silently, alternating a few deep wing beats with long glides, listening for telltale rustles in the grass below. The 'ears' that give the owl its name are, in fact, merely small tufts of feathers, with no function as organs of hearing. Its real ears are hidden beneath its facial feathers. The owl's mottled plumage gives it equally good cover while it rests on the ground or in a tree. Often its bright yellow eyes are the only indication of its presence.

At sunset and dusk in April and May, the short-eared owl patrols high over its territory in a display flight. It circles and hovers, giving its low, booming song, and glides on outspread wings. Then it suddenly twists its wings under its body so that the tips meet behind its tail, and rapidly claps them together a number of times. As it claps its wings, the bird plunges like a stone, dropping a few metres before resuming its slow flight. Unusually among owls, the birds nest in a shallow scrape on the ground, sheltered by tall grass, reeds, heather and scrub. When short-tailed voles, the short-eared owl's favourite prey, are plentiful, clutches are bigger than usual, up to 14 eggs. The owlets, vulnerable to the predations of crows and foxes, grow quickly.

Favourite food

It has been calculated that a single short-eared owl may eat as many as 2,000 voles in four months. A good supply of these rodents is the main factor controlling the bird's distribution. Periodically, vole plagues break out in hilly districts – sometimes with devastating effects on grass crops – and then short-eared owls rapidly move in to breed. If there are enough voles, the owls will raise two broods. The

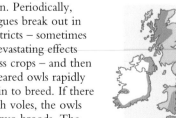

This owl nests on the ground.

spread of plantations of conifers, an ideal habitat for voles, helped the short-eared owl to increase and extend its range southward to moorland in Yorkshire and North Wales, but this process seems to have gone into reverse. It does, however, breed regularly in East Anglia.

In winter the owls tend to move south, where voles may be easier to find, and are joined by migrants from northern Europe, especially along the east coast of England. Some of these stay while others are just passing through on their way farther south. Some go as far as central Africa. In years when breeding has been successful and numbers have increased, short-eared owls may be seen on coastal marshes and on rough grassland and dunes in central and southern England and south Wales.

Identification
Buff-brown plumage with streaked breast; black patches under long, rounded wings; sexes alike.

Nesting
Nest is a depression in the ground, lined with vegetation; lays April; usually 4–8 eggs, white, almost spherical; incubation about 26 days, by female only; nestlings, fed by female on food brought by male, leave after about 15 days, fly about 11 days later; sometimes two broods.

Feeding
Chiefly short-tailed voles and other small mammals; small birds; insects.

Size
Male: 35.5cm (14in)
Female: 42cm (16½in)

J	F	M	A	M	J
J	A	S	O	N	D

Open country, mainly in northern England and Scotland; more widespread in winter.

SNIPE *Gallinago gallinago*

For most of the year the snipe is a secretive bird, but in spring it throws off its habitual caution and engages in courtship displays, filling the air with a strange, throbbing hum produced by its tail.

The 'song' of the snipe – a resonant, quavering humming, which has earned it the country name of 'heather bleater' – has nothing to do with its voice. In the early morning and at dusk, the male rises high in the sky, circles widely and then dives with its tail fanned out so that the stiff outer tail feathers project at right angles to the body. As the bird plunges through the air at an angle of 45°, air flowing over the projecting feathers makes them vibrate, producing a far-carrying hum, referred to as 'drumming'. In the early part of the 20th century, during fierce debates about what caused the sound, one ornithologist proved the point by fixing tail-feathers from a snipe on either side of a cork and whirling them round on a string, reproducing the hum.

The snipe may 'drum' at any time of year, but the sound is usually produced as part of the bird's courtship behaviour, and heard

The chicks, dark in colour, remain close to the grassy nest.

regularly from late March to the middle of June. The snipe also delivers a monotonously repetitive 'chipp-er, chipp-er, chipp-er' territorial song, both on the wing and when perched on a prominent fence-post.

Long bill

The snipe's long straight bill has a flexible tip and the bird uses it for probing in soft, wet mud for worms. Its bill makes up a quarter of the bird's total length and is the longest in proportion to its overall size of any British species. Sometimes a snipe may be spotted feeding quietly at the edge of a pool,

but often the bird is not seen until it has been flushed. At the last minute it bursts up with a loud harsh 'creech' of alarm. Jinking and swerving, it zigzags rapidly away, diving back down into cover at a safe distance. The snipe is still shot, but in nothing like the numbers of the 19th century and earlier when it was a popular table bird. Shooting is not the reason for the dramatic decline of the resident population. Residents have gone from most of the lowlands and this can be put down to drainage or afforestation of many of the open fens, bogs and wet grasslands that snipe need for breeding. In autumn and winter, snipe sometimes move from their boggy moorland haunts to feed along the shore, and their numbers are swollen by northern migrants.

Parties of snipe, called 'wisps', carry out manoeuvres in the air, and parent birds have been seen carrying their young, but this is rare.

Identification
Brown streaked and patterned plumage; long straight bill; boldly striped head; zigzag flight; sexes alike.

Nesting
Nests in hollow lined with grasses, in tussock of rushes, grass or sedge, usually near water; lays April–August; 4 eggs, pear-shaped, olive-grey or olive-brown, heavily marked with dark sepia; incubation about 20 days, by female only; chicks, tended by both parents, leave the nest in a few hours, fly after about 21 days.

Feeding
Chiefly worms, also water-beetles, beetles, caddis larvae, grubs of flies, snails, woodlice; some seeds of marsh plants.

Size
26.75cm (10½in)

J F M A M J
J A S O N D

Boggy areas with good cover; recent major decline in lowland residents, but up to a million northern breeders winter in Britain.

SNOW BUNTING *Plectrophenax nivalis*

The hardy snow bunting may be found high in the inhospitable Scottish mountains. Some choose to remain close to their breeding sites throughout even the coldest winter, while others move to the coast.

Snow buntings are at the southern edge of their breeding range in Britain. Essentially Arctic birds that breed on rocky coasts, high mountains and tundra, a few choose to nest among the mist-shrouded peaks of the Scottish Highlands. About 70 years ago they were more widespread in the region, but in recent years probably no more than 25 breeding pairs have been present in Britain at any one time, nearly all of them in the Cairngorms. They are among Britain's rarest breeding species, and climate change may reduce numbers even further.

Some remain close to the breeding sites all year, but many females and young leave the mountains to spend the colder months on the coast, farther south and east, and they are joined by thousands of visitors from Scandinavia, Finland and Iceland. Flocks of snow buntings can be seen from autumn until spring, searching for seeds of coarse grass on sand dunes and in other rough open country near the coast. On the mainland they usually feed in small parties, but a flock some 2,000 strong has been recorded on Fair Isle. They often follow the tideline, searching among the seaweed for any seeds that may have drifted in, and sometimes appear to be playing leapfrog, the birds at the back of the group fluttering up and landing at the front.

Startling flight

The flash of white wings when snow buntings are flushed in winter – which gave rise to the bird's old country name of 'snowflake' – can come as a surprise to anybody who has been watching them feed, because their white markings are obscured by brown when they are on the ground. When the flock takes to the air, the birds give a soft, rippling contact call. Their song is loud and clear, a fluty 'turee-turee-turee-turiwee'. The Scottish breeders return to the Highlands in spring, where they feed on insects carried on air currents and trapped in the snowfields, as well as on grass and sedge

seeds. Increasingly, they scavenge scraps left by human visitors, especially around the car parks and ski lifts of the Cairngorm resorts. For nesting, though, they favour the wildest places, tucking the nest away in a cranny between rocks. The male, striking in his snow white and coal black breeding plumage, has a display flight in which he hovers almost like a skylark, singing vigorously. Egg-laying may be delayed by late snowfalls.

The female, like the male in winter, is brown and white.

Identification
In winter, both sexes are buff-brown above, with white underparts; more white shows on male; in summer, male has black on back and centre of tail, rest of plumage is pure white, bill orange.

Nesting
Female builds cup nest of dry grasses, lichen and moss, lined with hair and feathers, in rock crevice; lays late May–June; 4–6 eggs, yellow-white, sometimes with green or blue tinge, with red-brown spots and blotches; incubation about 13 days, by female only; nestlings, tended by both parents, leave after about 11 days; sometimes two broods.

Feeding
Seeds of grass, rushes and weeds; crane-flies and other flying insects in summer; occasionally grain, sandhoppers and beetles.

Size
16.5cm (6½in)

J	F	M	A	M	J
J	A	S	O	N	D

Breeds in Scottish Highlands almost exclusively in the Cairngorms; in winter coastal areas of north and east, including winter visitors.

WHEATEAR *Oenanthe oenanthe*

A perching bird that spends much of its time on the ground, the wheatear is the first of the summer migrants to arrive. It takes up residence in early March, following a gruelling journey from Africa.

When wheatears fly in from their winter quarters south of the Sahara, not all of them choose to stay. Some are just passing through on their way farther north, but those that are staying spread out mainly among the stony uplands of northern and western Britain, where they are well camouflaged among the rocks. Often a flash of white from the boldly marked tail is the only thing that gives the bird away. It is from its tail that the wheatear takes its name.

Wheatears hunt for insects in a ploughed field.

'Wheatear' is nothing to do with ears of wheat but is derived from two Old English words, 'hwit' meaning white and 'aers' meaning backside. The bird's old country name is 'white arse'.

On reaching their nesting grounds, the birds begin a curious dancing courtship display. Male and female face one another in a shallow hollow and the male starts leaping into the air with feathers puffed-out. He jumps out of the hollow on to the bank, and then may jump from one bank to the other, in rapid rhythm. Then he throws himself down in front of the female, with wings and tail spread out and head stretched along the ground.

Scratchy voice

The wheatear is a restless, ground-loving bird, perching low down on a rock or fence-post to deliver its squeaky, warbling song, although after a display on the ground, it will perform a dancing song flight, and it has been observed hovering like a hawk and diving back to earth. Sometimes it sings while hovering. Calls include a harsh 'weet-chack'. When feeding, the wheatear chases insects on the ground, bobbing its head and hopping. At other times it bobs its whole body, as well as flicking its wings and pumping its tail up and down.

Drystone walls and rabbit burrows are among the wheatear's favourite nesting sites. It looks for dark, rocky crevices or holes on open moorland, bare hillsides and heaths. It has even been known to nest in old tin cans and drainage pipes. Southern lowland heaths and downs were once part of its breeding range, and it used to nest by the coast among sand-dunes, but much less

so following the introduction of myxomatosis and the consequent reduction in the rabbit population and their burrows.

The wheatears that pass through on their way to nest in Iceland and Greenland are somewhat bigger and more brightly coloured than the British breeders. They belong to a different race.

Thousands of wheatears used to be trapped each year as they rested on the south coast on migration, and were served up as delicacies on Victorian dinner-tables.

Identification

Noticeable white rump; male in summer has blue-grey back, black mask and wings, buff underparts; in winter has brown back, mask and wings; female similar to male in winter plumage.

Nesting

Nest of grass and moss, lined with feathers and hair, built chiefly by female; lays late April–June; usually 6 eggs, pale blue, sometimes with red-brown spots; incubation about 14 days, mainly by female; nestlings, fed by both parents, leave after about 14 days; sometimes two broods.

Feeding

Insects and larvae; some spiders, centipedes and snails.

Size

14.5cm (5¾in)

J F **M A M J**
J A S O N D

Upland pastures with drystone walls or rabbit burrows for nesting; moorland, heathland and coastal grassland; more widespread on migration.

MOUNTAIN, MOOR & HEATH

WOODLARK *Lullula arborea*

A beautiful, fluting song is the mark of the woodlark in spring. It delivers the melody from any convenient perch to claim its territory, and also while climbing slowly skywards on broad, rounded wings.

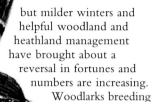

The woodlark's distinctive song may not be as spirited as the skylark's, but it makes up in sweetness for what it lacks in power. The bird's generic name *Lullula* is related to the song, which includes a series of liquid 'lu-lu-lu' notes interspersed among soft, repeated, almost yodelling phrases, varying in pitch and pace. It also has a melodious 'tit-loo-eet' flight or alarm call.

The song is given from the ground, from a perch or song-post overlooking its territory, or in flight. The woodlark's song-flight is almost as spectacular as the skylark's, although the woodlark doesn't fly quite so high. It begins to sing when it is a metre or so off the ground, at first repeating one or two notes six or seven times. Then it pauses, as if to get its breath for a series of musical phrases. As it sings, the bird spirals high in the air above its territory, circles down until it is about 30m (100ft) from the ground, then drops to earth. The song, sometimes given at night, is heard mainly from early March to the middle of June.

Woodlarks nest in almost any kind of grassy country that has a few shrubs and some scattered trees. They prefer sandy heathlands, limestone slopes, parkland and the borders of woods, but have also taken to forestry plantations with cleared areas.

Shrinking territories

A series of severe winters since the early 1950s hit the birds hard. They used to breed regularly as far north as Yorkshire and North Wales, and were widespread all over southern England, but now they are almost entirely limited to East Anglia and the southwest. The New Forest and Breckland are among their favoured territories. The species is rarely seen in Wales, and no longer breeds there. The decline was probably due to loss of habitat as well as the weather, but milder winters and helpful woodland and heathland management have brought about a reversal in fortunes and numbers are increasing. Woodlarks breeding upcountry tend to move south to Hampshire, Surrey and Devon for the winter and some fly as far as the warmer parts of Europe. Those that remain in Britain sometimes join up in wandering flocks to feed, and some wintering flocks have been seen in East Anglia. Seeds are its favourite food then. During the breeding season it forages on the ground for insects and spiders on which to feed its young.

Identification
Streaked brown plumage with white eye-stripes meeting across nape; small black and white mark on forewing; distinguished from skylark by smaller size, very short tail without white sides, lower crest and different song; sexes alike.

Nesting
Both sexes build cup nest of grass and moss, lined with grass and hair, in depression in the ground; lays late March–July; usually 3 or 4 eggs, pale grey with fine red-brown or olive mottling; incubation 13–15 days, by female only; nestlings, fed by both sexes, leave after 11 or 12 days, fly some days later; usually two broods, sometimes three.

Feeding
Mainly insects; some spiders; seeds in autumn.

Size
15.25cm (6in)

The woodlark has a small crest and an extremely short tail with white tips.

| J | F | M | A | M | J |
| J | A | S | O | N | D |

Wooded areas and heaths with trees and scrub, mainly in southwest England and East Anglia.

Wetland

Whether they are glittering upland streams, lazy lowland rivers or expanses of reeds and scrub, wetlands can provide many memorable encounters with birds, from flocks of migrant Bewick's swans to the electric flash of a diving kingfisher.

BEWICK'S SWAN *Cygnus columbianus*

Every Bewick's swan can be recognised by the pattern on its bill. The yellow and black markings, like human fingerprints, are peculiar to each bird, a phenomenon first noticed by naturalist Sir Peter Scott.

Bewick's swans were among naturalist and artist Sir Peter Scott's favourite birds. He began studying them in 1964, when they were first attracted to Slimbridge in Gloucestershire, where he lived. (Sir Peter founded the Wildfowl & Wetlands Trust at Slimbridge, and his former house is now WWT headquarters.) He drew each swan's bill pattern, gave the bird a name and monitored its behaviour from year to year, effectively starting a research project that continues to this day. The swans are ringed and, with international cooperation, each individual's social and breeding habits and life history can be recorded. This project is made easier by the birds' faithfulness to both their winter and summer quarters.

Sadly, numbers are decreasing. Around 9,000 Bewick's swans winter in East Anglia, especially on fenland, and about 300 at Slimbridge. Each October, they fly in from northern Europe and Russia, often in company with the larger whooper swan, congregating on flooded grasslands to

For a swan, the Bewick has a short neck.

fatten up after the rigours of breeding. In the early spring, they leave again for their breeding grounds in the tundra.

One of three

The Bewick's swan is the smallest, and the rarest, of the three British swans, the other two being the whooper and the mute. It tends to carry its neck more stiffly erect, instead of in the mute swan's pronounced curve, and it has a softer, higher pitched voice than the whooper. It usually gives a 'hoo' or 'ho' note, or makes a honking sound. When flying in their V-shaped skeins, Bewick's swans call to keep in touch with one another, making a musical, babbling like the yelping of a pack of small dogs. With its relatively short neck and rounded head, it is more goose-like than the other two species.

Until 1830, Bewick's and whooper swans were referred to collectively as 'wild swans', probably because they look similar and arrive and leave at more or less the same time. Nineteenth-century scientist William Yarrell named the Bewick's swan after Thomas Bewick, a renowned engraver and illustrator of birds. The telescope that Thomas Bewick used to observe the swans is still kept at Slimbridge. The whooper swan's name comes from its call – a powerful, trumpeting 'whoop-a'.

Identification
White; long bill slightly concave with black and yellow markings; sexes alike.

Nesting
On islets; build large mound of moss and lichen or dried plants, with depression for eggs; lays June; 3–5 eggs, creamy white; no reliable data on incubation; cygnets, tended by both parents, fly at about 6 weeks.

Feeding
Seeds, water plants.

Size
122cm (48in)

J F M A M J
J A S O N D

Wet meadows mainly in eastern and western England and Ireland.

BITTERN *Botaurus stellaris*

The extraordinary booming song of the bittern is unmistakable as it reverberates across vast expanses of marshland and fens. Even more remarkable, research has shown that no two birds sound alike.

The boom of the bittern resembles something between a lowing cow and a distant foghorn. Small differences between individual calls have been detected, and since older, stronger males seem to utter louder sounds, it may be that females are able to discern the age and vigour of the calling male – although even calls that are not quite so loud can still travel up to 3 miles in clear, fenland air.

The male calls from the same place at any time of day, but especially at dawn and dusk, advertising his presence to rival males as well as potential mates. Male bitterns are highly aggressive in defence of their territories in the breeding season, fighting viciously. Several may take to the air at once, lunging at each other with their formidable bills, and birds have been found dead from stab wounds.

Two hundred years ago the distinctive sound of bitterns was not uncommon in East Anglia, but with the draining of marshes the birds were gradually pressed back into the fens, and even there they were extinct by 1850. Fifty years later, their foghorn song was heard again on the Broads, with increasing frequency, but not until 1911 was breeding actually proved, at Sutton Broad. They had started to spread out when a renewed decline brought the population of booming males down to 11. Then, early in the 21st century, extensive conservation efforts brought another recovery and numbers are back up to more than 75 booming males. In winter, a small number of bitterns arrive from Europe and the birds may be seen in more open marshy areas of southern England.

Skulking habits

The bittern is a secretive, solitary bird and, when unaware of being seen, it looks rather like a large domestic hen, hunched up with its long neck drawn in. If it suspects danger, it may freeze, with neck and beak stretched vertically. The streaked plumage provides excellent camouflage among wind-blown reeds, and the bittern may even sway slightly from side to side in time with

A bittern climbs reeds by grasping them in clumps.

the vegetation, making it virtually invisible. If a predator approaches the nest or takes a bittern unawares, the bird will adopt a defensive posture, crouching with the elongated feathers of the foreneck and crest ruffled, wings outspread and bill raised, ready to rush forward in attack, stabbing with its bill.

Bitterns are almost entirely confined to dense swamps, fens and reed-beds, although they may fly between feeding areas. In flight the bittern draws its head back and looks somewhat owl-like. Booming is not the bittern's only sound. At dusk it produces a harsh flight-call, 'kow' or 'kwah'.

Identification
Buff plumage is mottled, streaked and barred with dark brown and black; green feet and legs; sexes alike.

Nesting
Female builds untidy pile of sedges and other material, usually in water or on thick water vegetation; lays April–May; 4–6 eggs, olive; incubation about 25 days, by female; nestlings, fed by female, leave in 2–3 weeks, fly after about 8 weeks.

Feeding
Frogs and small fish; water-voles, water-beetles, water-boatmen, dragonfly nymphs; some small birds and nestlings; sometimes water-weed.

Size
76.25cm (30in)

| J | F | M | A | M | J |
| J | A | S | O | N | D |

Large reed-beds, mainly in eastern England; in winter visits smaller reed-beds, marshes and even ditches.

BLACK-TAILED GODWIT
Limosa limosa

An elegant, long-legged wader, the black-tailed godwit ventures into quite deep water. It uses its long, straight bill to probe in the wet mud, repeatedly stabbing the ground and narrowly missing its toes.

Remarkably long legs enable the black-tailed godwit to wade farther out into the shallows than most other waders, and its extremely long, almost-straight bill allows it to probe deeper in the sand and mud for prey, especially worms.

Early in the 19th century, the black-tailed godwit was lost to Britain as a breeding bird. Large numbers were netted to be served up as table delicacies, and the remaining birds were driven away by the draining of the fens, so that by the 1830s they had ceased to nest in these islands. Today, because of protection, the black-tail's prospects are promising. Since 1952 they have become established at protected sites on the Ouse and Nene Washes, East Anglia, and pairs have nested in recent years in several other parts of Britain, including Orkney and Shetland. These northern birds are from the slightly smaller Icelandic race of the species.

Despite this progress, the black-tailed godwit remains a very rare breeding bird in Britain, mainly because of its need for a particular nesting habitat – damp grassland and marshy lowland districts. Many more black-tails may be seen outside the breeding season because the bird has become a frequent passage migrant and winter visitor. Flocks of both the European and Icelandic races of black-tails may gather on estuaries, mudflats and sandy shores, and to a lesser extent near fresh water.

Call and display
The flight call is a loud 'wicka-wicka-wicka', but over the breeding grounds two other calls may be heard, 'pee-oo-ee' and a greenshank-like 'wik-ik-ik'. The song, which sounds like a repeated 'crweetuu', is most often heard as part of the display performance. The male, resplendent in bright, breeding plumage, first rises steeply with rapid wing beats, then flies in slow motion with tail spread out, calling loudly all the while, before gliding silently downwards and finally side-slipping to the ground.

The name 'godwit' probably comes from its loud call and is nothing to do with references to 'God knows', as has been suggested. The 'black-tail' refers to the broad black tail band, which is prominent in flight, as are its broad white wing-bars. In early spring, late summer and winter, as the birds travel to and from roost sites, their dark and white wing patterns have a mesmerising, flickering effect as flocks perform impressive coordinated manoeuvres. The black-tail often lands with a twisting dive.

Winter plumage is mainly brown-grey.

Identification
In winter, brown-grey above, light below; in summer, head and breast red or chestnut; broad black band on end of pure white tail; long legs; straight bill; broad white wing-bar shows in flight; sexes alike.

Nesting
Both sexes make scrape in ground, usually well hidden in thick grass, padded with dead grass and lined with leaves; lays May; 4 eggs, light green to brown, blotched and spotted with brown; incubation 24 days, by both parents; chicks, tended by both parents, leave nest after a few hours, fly after about 4 weeks.

Feeding
Insects, including beetles, grasshoppers, dragonflies, mayflies; shellfish, snails, slugs and earthworms.

Size
40.5cm (16in)

J	F	M	A	M	J
J	A	S	O	N	D

Breeds in seasonally flooded grassy lowlands. In winter mainly on muddy estuaries and coastal grassland.

WETLANDS

BLACK-THROATED DIVER

Gavia arctica

A wailing cry resonating across a Scottish loch is one of the most haunting sounds of spring. This is the unmistakable call of a black-throated diver, asserting ownership of its territory.

Along with its slightly smaller red-throated cousin, the black-throated diver is renowned for its voice. During spring and summer, as well as an eerie wail and hoot, a variety of shorter, equally atmospheric calls and croaks indicate the presence of divers, and they give a barking 'kwuk-kwuk-kwuk' flight note. At other times, they are generally silent in flight. A special cry is uttered when paired birds fly off, but before pairing up there is a good deal of chasing about on the water, and the female may turn somersaults as she leads the male in this sexual chase.

Both birds are handsome in their breeding plumage – ruby eyes set in a soft, dove grey head, velvety smooth, contrasting with the black throat and striking black and white pattern down the side of the

These divers have shallow wing beats.

neck, under the throat and along the back. The pattern is lost in winter, leaving a sharp line between the black and white of head and neck.

Powerful swimmers

A black-throated diver has been known to swim for 400m (1,312ft) underwater before coming up for air. Its lower legs are flattened and can be rotated to give extra propulsive power, and all four toes are webbed (ducks have no webbing on the hind toe). A price these birds pay for being such good swimmers is that on land they are extremely clumsy, since their legs are set so far back on their bodies. In fact, they rarely visit land except to nest, and even then they choose somewhere very close to the waterside to lay their eggs. This has its drawbacks – one of the main causes of breeding failure is the nest being flooded. They are also vulnerable to disturbance.

Black-throated divers have a superficial resemblance to cormorants and shags, but they can be identified by their manner of swimming – a black-throated diver holds its head and bill straight instead of tilted upwards.

About 170 breeding pairs of black-throated divers are to be found in Britain, and most of them are confined to the larger freshwater lochs of the Highlands and some Scottish islands although, since the 1950s, they have also nested on Arran and occasionally elsewhere in southwestern Scotland. In winter, they are much more widespread, although still not common. Most move to sheltered coasts where they are joined by birds from northern Europe, and many may appear on the east coast of England. Their flight is direct and fast.

Identification

Chequered black and white on back, black throat and striped neck in summer; these become white in winter; distinguished from winter red-throated diver by straight bill, more extensive darker grey on head and neck and blacker back.

Nesting

No proper nest; eggs laid on the ground, very close to water, and exceptionally on a heap of water-weed; lays May–June; 2 eggs, pale green or brown, sparsely marked with black; incubation about 28 days, by one or both parents; chicks, tended by both parents, leave shortly after hatching, fly in about 9 weeks.

Feeding

Trout, perch, roach, herrings, sprats, crabs, prawns, mussels.

Size

68.5cm (27in)

J F M A M J
J A S O N D

Scottish Highlands and islands in summer; on offshore waters around most coasts in winter, with a few on inland reservoirs and lakes.

Secret life of the fens

Hidden away beyond the busy boating thoroughfares of the Broads are some of the most rewarding wild wetlands in Britain, home to many elusive and extraordinary waterside birds.

Few bird calls are as unusual and evocative as the booming of a bittern. It is not just the extreme rarity of the sound – only breeding males boom and just 82 were counted as doing so in 2009 – but also its strangeness that makes it so memorable. As the deep notes reverberate over a reed-bed on a misty spring morning, they seem more likely to emanate from a distant foghorn than a bird. The sound is redolent of remote, marshy fens, with swaying reeds extending to flat horizons beneath big skies – the marginal world of the wetlands.

Long ago great tracts of East Anglia were like this. The fens to the southeast of the Wash were a vast watery wilderness, teeming with fish and ringing with bird calls. They are now mostly drained farmland, with fields of dark peaty soil where the reeds once grew, but head east to the Broads and the landscape, in places, still retains the atmosphere of the wild wetlands. Ironically, it was created artificially. The deep fenland peat was dug for fuel in the Middle Ages and the excavations flooded, creating a string of lakes, or broads, linked by rivers and flanked by extensive reed-beds, marshes and wet alder or willow carr. For centuries these were havens for wildlife, despite increasingly busy waterway traffic that now seems to dominate the scene. However, while 13 of the broads are generally open to navigation, and a further three have navigable channels, there are 63 broads altogether, which leaves a lot of fenland off-limits to boaters, and largely undisturbed – an area that now has a status equivalent to that of a national park.

Elusive prizes

This lush, tranquil area has many quiet corners but the best sites for wildlife are the nature reserves at Strumpshaw Fen – renowned for its swallowtail butterflies – Carlton Marshes, Surlingham Church Marsh and Hickling Broad. These are strongholds for freshwater wetland birds, such as coots and moorhens, and their less familiar relative the water rail – normally so secretive that the only clues to its presence are its strangely pig-like squeals and grunts. Little grebes bob and dive on the water, along with wildfowl, such as garganey, gadwall and shoveler.

In spring the air is full of the territorial songs of warblers, often hidden among the reeds and waterside scrub but briefly visible as they flit from perch to perch. This is especially true of Cetti's warbler, which announces itself with brief, yet astonishingly loud outbursts of rapid-fire liquid notes, defying discovery in the dense cover of a willow or alder.

Most elusive of all is the bird that draws so many to these reed-beds – the bittern. Although a type of heron, and hence closely related to the elegant grey herons and little egrets that stalk so conspicuously through the shallows, the bittern only rarely emerges from cover, usually at dusk. By day it hides among the reeds, perfectly camouflaged by its streaky brown plumage and its habit of pointing its bill skyward to mimic the vertical stems. Another inhabitant of reed-beds is the little bearded tit, which flits low over the reeds on whirring wings, and clambers nimbly through the feathery stems giving its metallic, twanging calls. Like the bittern, the bearded tit is a challenge to locate. The magnificent marsh harriers, however, are commonly seen as they sail over reed-beds on raised wings in search of prey, such as moorhen chicks, and often perch on prominent vantage points as if inviting admiration.

Winter visitors

The reed-beds and fens are glorious in summer, but they are equally exciting in winter when icy reflections illuminate the fresh breeding plumage of the wildfowl, and water rails emerge warily from their frozen hiding places to search for scraps, while migrant and wintering hen harriers often cruise low over the marshes. A visit to Buckenham or Cantley Marshes at this time is certain to be rewarded by the sight of taiga bean geese. These northern grey geese overwinter here, along with other wildfowl. They are joined by many waders, including lapwing, redshank, snipe and golden plover. From an elevated watchpoint at Hickling Broad, you can watch rare cranes flying in to their winter roost, as well as roosting harriers.

Another good site for winter waders is the tidal estuary of Breydon Water, just south of Great Yarmouth. This is a different type of wetland, with saltmarsh vegetation fringing the gleaming mudflats and a tang of seaweed in the air. Here, and especially in the northeast corner, waders retreating before the rising tide roost high on the shore in massed flocks. These include curlews, dunlins, knots, black-tailed godwits and oystercatchers. Short-eared owls quarter the fringing marshlands at low level, searching for voles among the rough grass, and occasionally a high-flying peregrine sends a shiver of fear through the roosting flocks so they burst into the air in a dazzling confusion of flashing wings, wheeling and swirling overhead until, as their panic subsides, they settle back to wait for the tide to turn. At such moments it's easy to forget the icy winter wind and just marvel at the sheer glory of birds.

185

DIPPER *Cinclus cinclus*

The only songbird that is truly aquatic, the dipper can stroll along a riverbed in calm weather, completely submerged. In rougher conditions, it spreads its wings and tail, and appears almost to fly underwater.

The idea that the dipper can defy the laws of specific gravity and walk along the river bottom was once ridiculed by some respected naturalists, but those who had seen it happen and stuck to the evidence of their eyes have been proved right. Experiments have demonstrated that when the bird walks upstream with its head down looking for food, its back humped and wings beating rapidly, the force of a fast current against its slanting back keeps it on the bottom. Occasionally, it will change the angle at which it holds its wings and bob back up to the surface for air – or to return to a rock to eat a tasty morsel it has found. Sometimes it even swims like a duck, despite not having webbed feet.

The dipper has evolved several adaptations so that it can find food underwater, including membranes that it can draw across the nostrils and eyes. It also has particularly strong legs, and feet equipped with powerful muscles and sharp, curved claws with which to grip rocks and stones. Very soft body feathers cover a dense layer of down for insulation in cold water, and the dipper has a preen gland larger than most other small birds. The extra oil is necessary to ensure the feathers are waterproofed.

Taking the plunge

The dipper, looking like a plump wren, enters the water by wading or diving. Often it will perch for some time on a rock or stone in midstream, bobbing its body and curtseying, as if hinged on its legs, and blinking its white upper eyelids. Sometimes it dips its head in the water to look for spots to visit before plunging in. While perched, it sings loudly and lyrically, the sound

Underwater, the dipper walks with back slanted and head down.

resembling and mingling with the splash of tumbling water but audible above it. Its most common call-note is 'zit-zit-zit', and there is also a metallic 'clink-clink'.

The dipper is usually confined to fast-running streams in hilly districts in the north and west, but can sometimes be seen on shores of lakes in the hills, and in winter, when some immigrants arrive from the Continent, also by sea lochs. It is rarely seen far from water. Highly territorial, the dipper defends its stretch of water as well as the banks alongside it, and, except in the breeding season, is not usually seen with others of the species.

Courtship display includes posturing to show off the white breast, bowing and wing-quivering. Its flight is rapid and direct, its short wings whirring.

Identification
Dark brown plumage with white breast and band of rust on upper belly; highly characteristic bobbing or dipping action; sexes alike.

Nesting
Both sexes build substantial domed nest, mainly of moss, lined with dead leaves; nest nearly always on ledge or in cavity close to water; frequently on bridges, sometimes under a waterfall; lays March–early May; 4 or 5 eggs, white; incubation about 17 days, by female only; nestlings, fed by both parents, fly after about 23 days; two broods.

Feeding
Water-beetles, water-boatmen, caddis larvae and nymphs of dragonflies and mayflies; worms and tadpoles; minnows and other small fish.

Size
17.75cm (7in)

Fast streams and rivers, sometimes lakes, mostly in uplands of north and west; sometimes on slower lowland rivers in winter.

GREAT CRESTED GREBE

Podiceps cristatus

In spring both males and females display their striking head plumes to great effect in an elaborate courtship dance. This display often involves head-shaking, diving and the offering of water plants to each other.

Inland lakes and reservoirs provide the setting for the courtship of the great crested grebe. Ceremonies begin in midwinter – especially from January onwards, when the birds start forming pairs and taking up territories – and continue for weeks or even months. Pairs stay together for the breeding season. The sexes play interchangeable roles in these elaborate rituals of posture and display, which can be divided into four sections, each containing different stylised movements. Head-shaking is the most common ceremony, performed while the birds face each other. In another ritual, known as 'the penguin dance', the birds dive to collect weed, then swim towards one another, suddenly rising breast to breast from the water, vigorously paddling with their feet and swaying their bills, plus weed, from side to side. The grebe's courtship ceremonies were studied intensively by the renowned biologist Sir Julian Huxley from as early as 1912, and his writings on the subject are among the classics of bird-watching literature.

During the dance, the birds make good use of their head ornaments, or tippets. These consist of a frill of black-tipped chestnut feathers hanging down on each side of the head and linked by similarly coloured nape feathers. The tippets and the black head crest can be raised and lowered at will.

Shared parenting

Great crested grebes nest in loose colonies. Male and female change places on the nest every three hours or so,

and after the chicks have hatched they are often carried on the back of one parent while the other brings food. Grebes habitually eat their own feathers and feed them to their young. The reason for this strange behaviour is thought to be that the feathers prevent fish bones piercing the stomach and digestive tract.

During the 19th century, great crested grebes were all but exterminated in Britain, because their feathers were in demand by the fashion industry. Grebe feathers – sometimes the entire plumage – were used to decorate women's hats, and by around 1860 there were believed to be no more than 42 pairs left in the whole of England.

Their relative abundance nowadays – more than 12,000 adults are present in Britain and Ireland in the breeding season – is one of the triumphs of the bird protection movement. The increase in flooded gravel pits and other man-made water habitats in the south during the past 40 to 50 years has helped their recovery – grebes nest exclusively on inland stretches of freshwater, including slow-flowing rivers. In winter, they may also be seen on estuaries and coastal waters.

Identification
Double-horned crest and chestnut 'frills' about the head in breeding season; long white neck, but this may not show when bird is hunched up and resting; sexes alike.

Nesting
Both sexes build pile of weeds in water, either floating or grounded; floating nest is anchored to nearby plants; lays April–July; 3–5 eggs, white, but soon discoloured by water-weeds; incubation about 28 days, by both parents; chicks, tended by both parents, leave soon after hatching, dive at 6 weeks and are independent at 9–10 weeks; sometimes two broods.

Feeding
Small fish; molluscs; algae, weed and other vegetable matter.

Size
48.25cm (19in)

| J | F | M | A | M | J |
| J | A | S | O | N | D |

Large shallow lakes, reservoirs and flooded gravel pits, with fringing vegetation and some on slow-flowing rivers, except in far north; on coasts in winter.

WETLANDS

GREY HERON *Ardea cinerea*

A remarkably flexible neck is a distinctive feature of the grey heron. Long and thin, it curves into a sunken 'S' shape while the bird is resting, but is fully stretched when the heron is fishing.

Like a tall grey sentinel, the heron stands motionless in the shallows, long neck extended, poised to wade forward and strike with its dagger-like bill at a fish, frog or water vole. An elongated sixth vertebra in its neck, which can be locked and released, acts like a coiled spring so that the heron can strike with astonishing speed and power. Binocular vision gives it great accuracy. When the heron is at rest, however, it draws its neck right in so that its head is hunched on to its back, making the bird look somewhat smaller than it actually is. It also retracts its neck when flying, which it does with lazy beats of its great broad wings. The grey heron has a wingspan of nearly 2m (6ft).

Grey herons will range more than 12 miles for food. Sometimes they raid garden ponds for goldfish, and they may visit cornfields, searching for small rodents. Small fish are swallowed whole, head first, and larger ones are stabbed repeatedly, then taken to the bank to have the flesh picked from their bones. The sight of a grey heron taking a large eel is memorable, with the eel writhing about wildly as the heron tries to keep it grasped firmly enough to disable, stab and kill it.

Treetop nests

Grey herons nest in colonies, known as heronries, building near the top of deciduous trees, often more than 20m (66ft) above the ground. Occasionally, they nest in parks. A small heronry has been established in Regent's Park, London, since 1968, while one of the biggest in Britain is located at Walthamstow Reservoirs, with up to 100 or more pairs. Once a heronry has been established, birds will return to the same site, year after year.

Courtship is preceded by a dance ceremony in which the male stretches his neck up and then lowers it over his back, with the bill pointing upwards. When there are

The male performs a ritual courtship dance.

eggs or nestlings to care for, one parent stays on guard against predators while the other is away feeding.

The common breeding heron of Britain is the grey heron, as distinct from the purple heron, which is a rare visitor from the Continent. The breeding population is fairly stable at 14,000 pairs, with a temporary drop after severe weather. When lakes and rivers freeze, grey herons may struggle to find enough food and many head for the coast. Numbers are swelled by winter visitors from Norway and northern and eastern Europe.

Grey herons have a wide and raucous vocabulary. The common call is a harsh 'krornk'.

Identification
Grey upper parts; dark grey flight feathers; long, wispy black crest; bushy breastplate and yellow bill (redder in spring); usually flies with legs trailing and neck drawn in; sexes alike.

Nesting
Nests in colonies, usually in trees, but also locally in reed-beds or on sea cliffs; female arranges platform of sticks or reeds brought by male; lays February–May; 3–5 eggs, light blue; incubation about 25 days, by both parents; young, fed by both parents, leave after 7–8 weeks.

Feeding
Fish, water voles, beetles, frogs, moles and rats.

Size
91.5cm (36in)

J	F	M	A	M	J
J	A	S	O	N	D

Widespread on rivers, lakes, estuaries and seashores. Most abundant in lowlands where there is unpolluted water and trees for nesting.

WETLANDS

GREY WAGTAIL *Motacilla cinerea*

This graceful bird's slender tail is seldom still. Whether the wagtail is walking beside a stream or perched on a boulder, it pumps its tail vigorously up and down and, when agitated, splays it like a fan.

The grey wagtail's constantly moving tail is as long as its body. In fact, its tail is the longest of all the wagtails found in Britain, the other two being the pied and the yellow, to which it is superficially similar. In spite of its name, the grey is one of the most colourful of them. Its bright yellow underparts contrast boldly with its blue-grey back and black tail whatever the time of year.

The grey wagtail has a marked preference for being near water – especially rushing water, giving rise to its old country name of 'water wagtail', and in hilly country it is often seen in company with dippers.

It is the most graceful of the wagtails in its movements as it flits along mountain streams, pausing to walk across boulders and hop over smaller rocks, searching for waterside or aquatic insects. It often flies up to perch on branches overhanging the stream, its tail still swinging up and down, and makes longer flights with deep bounds and sudden bursts of acceleration.

Birds may roost together in winter.

Feeding tactics

Grey wagtails often dart up into the air from a boulder or other perch to snatch a flying insect or chase it, zigzagging to intercept it. They also chase insects into the shallows, wading in to lunge after the prey with their bills below the water. Another tactic is to hover in front of foliage while snatching insects from the surface of a leaf.

In winter, the grey wagtail moves to lowland streams and sometimes coastal marshes. It may be found around cress beds, sewage farms and small lakes, but it is seldom far from a weir or some other tumbling water. It

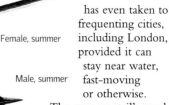

Female, summer

Male, summer

has even taken to frequenting cities, including London, provided it can stay near water, fast-moving or otherwise.

The grey wagtail's usual call is very like the pied wagtail's double-noted 'tschizzik', but is more metallic and staccato, and sometimes only a single 'tsik'. The song, a shrill 'tsee-tee-tee', is not often heard. The male has a variety of courtship displays. In one, a slow-motion flight, the tail is fanned. In another, the bird runs towards the female on the ground and takes up a posture presenting his black throat. Males are often very aggressive towards rivals.

While still most common in the hilly areas of the north and west, the grey wagtail has for many years been increasing in eastern and southern England.

Identification

Blue-grey above, yellow below, including tail feathers; long black tail with white sides; male's throat is black in summer, white in winter; female's slightly more buff.

Nesting

Female builds cup nest of twigs, moss and grass, lined with hair, usually in hole or on ledge close to water; sometimes uses the old nest of a dipper or other bird; lays April–June; usually 5 eggs, buff, faintly speckled with grey-brown; incubation 12 or 13 days, chiefly by female; nestlings, fed by both parents, fly after 12 days; sometimes two broods.

Feeding

Mostly insects, including flies, small beetles, dragonfly nymphs, freshwater snails, small fish; on coast, sandhoppers and small molluscs.

Size

20.25cm (8in) including 10.25cm (4in) tail

J F M A M J
J A S O N D

Widespread, but most abundant in northern and western uplands except in winter when more common in south-west Britain.

WETLANDS

KINGFISHER *Alcedo atthis*

The brilliant, iridescent plumage for which the kingfisher is renowned provides surprisingly good camouflage while the bird sits motionless, its sapphire colouring blending in with reflections on the water.

This most brilliantly coloured of British birds can be remarkably hard to see except in flight. Only the size of a plump sparrow, its rusty orange underparts hide it well against sandy or mud banks, and among twigs and branches, while it sits still, waiting to spot a fish. From above, the blue-green plumage blends in with rippling reflections on the water.

The kingfisher is largely confined to the banks of rivers and streams because of its fishy diet, but it also feeds on lakes and large ponds and – especially in hard weather – on the seashore. It takes off suddenly and returns to cover as quickly as possible. The kingfisher's bright colouring may be a defence adaptation, warning predators to leave it alone because its flesh is foul-tasting.

Kingfishers are liable to starve to death in hard winters, when their food supply is cut off by frozen waters. After the winter of 1962–3, their numbers fell drastically throughout the British Isles. Along upper reaches of the Thames in 1961 there was one pair of breeding kingfishers to every 1¾ miles, but in 1964 only one pair to every 20 miles. In Scotland, partly as a result of mild winters, but also in some areas because of improvements in water quality, kingfishers have recently increased in numbers and spread northwards.

Fishing technique

The bird fishes with a shallow dive from a perch or from a hovering position, and beats its catch on a branch before bolting it down, head first. A fish swallowed tail first would choke the bird as its fins and scales opened, so the kingfisher carries a fish by its tail only when the fish is to be presented to another bird. This ritual is an important part of courtship and takes place after both birds have tunnelled out a burrow for the nest. The male bringing fish to the female cements the pair-bond.

To start with, the chicks are reptilian in appearance, encased in spiky feather sheaths and with long bills. Their feathers open out when they are three weeks old. By then, an awful stench emanates from the nest tunnel as regurgitated parts of the fish build up, and a 'whitewash' slime of disgorged fishbones flows out.

Kingfishers may be noisy in spring and autumn when they are defending nesting and wintering territories. The call is a penetrating whistle, either a single 'chreee' or a double 'chee-keee', sometimes extended into a trilling sound.

The nest is excavated in a canal or river bank.

Identification
Brilliant blue or green (depending on light) above, orange-chestnut below, white throat and patch on each side of the neck; female has red base to lower part of bill.

Nesting
Both sexes dig out tunnel about 60–90cm (2–3ft) long, often in canal bank; lined thinly with fishbones; lays April–August; 6 or 7 eggs, glossy white, almost round; incubation 19–21 days, by both sexes; nestlings, fed by both sexes, fly after 23–27 days; two broods.

Feeding
Mainly small fish such as sticklebacks and minnows; also water-beetles, dragonfly nymphs and other water life.

Size
16.5cm (6½in)

J	F	M	A	M	J
J	A	S	O	N	D

Along slow-moving rivers, canals, streams and lakes. Most numerous in lowland central and southern England.

MANDARIN DUCK *Aix galericulata*

The exotic plumage of the male mandarin duck – an eye-catching combination of orange, maroon, green, chestnut, black and white – makes it an unmistakable sight on the lakes of southern England.

'Once seen never forgotten' is a phrase that certainly applies to the male of this beautiful native of the Far East. His large multicoloured head is topped with a drooping crest and conspicuous side 'whiskers', like a ruff. He has a puffed up breast and large erectile wing 'sails' at the rear. The female's colouring is much subtler and, by comparison, drab.

Mandarins were first brought to Britain to be kept in captivity in 1745, but the first breeding success was not recorded until 1834 at London Zoo. In the 1920s mandarins were released in an attempt to encourage breeding populations to become established in London's parks, and these, well supplemented by escapees from various collections, were enough for the duck to settle itself in the wild. There are now an estimated 7,000 mandarin ducks living in south and central England, more than half of them in Windsor Great Park and Virginia Water, with a few having scattered as far as Scotland and Northern Ireland. Mandarins prefer to live on lakes, ponds and rivers of slow-moving water, with well-vegetated islands and undisturbed tree-lined banks.

Green wing patches are apparent in flight.

Essential trees
The mandarin is one of a small group of ducks called perching or tree ducks, due to their habit of perching on the branches of overhanging trees and on partly submerged trunks or branches. The mandarin feeds by dabbling its bill in the water, but it seldom upends. It is a rapid flier, moving deftly among trees, and it takes off just as easily from land as it does from water. It feeds mainly on aquatic insects and vegetation. In the autumn and winter it particularly likes nuts, including acorns and beech mast. It also eats snails.

Generally monogamous, mandarins tend to stay together for several breeding seasons, although the male may look for another female while his mate is incubating the eggs. Mandarins usually nest in tree holes up to 10m (33ft) high, but sometimes the female may choose a shallow depression on the ground, concealed in thick vegetation. Nest-boxes are often used. Occasionally, a female will lay eggs in another bird's nest, and a quarter of completed clutches are not incubated. Within 24 hours of hatching, the ducklings are encouraged to parachute down to the ground by the female's soft calling, and follow her to the water.

Males have a courtship whistle while females may make a soft, croaky flight call or a harsh, coot-like 'kett', often in flight, but mandarins are usually fairly silent birds. They often suffer in hard, cold winters, when freezing conditions cause food shortages.

Identification
Large head, short neck, long tail; male has green and chestnut crown and crest, white stripe from bill to nape, orange ruff, maroon breast edged with black and white stripes, chestnut-orange wing 'sails'; red bill; female has a greyish head with whitish 'spectacles' and small grey crest; upper parts olive brown, upper breast and flanks brown with white spots.

Nesting
In tree hole or nest-box, occasionally on the ground; lays late March–end April; 9–12 eggs, cream; incubation 28–33 days by female; ducklings leap from nest hole within 24 hours of hatching, fledge in 40–45 days.

Feeding
Aquatic insects; vegetation and seeds; acorns, walnuts, chestnuts, beech mast; stubble-field grain; snails.

Size
41–49cm (16–19in)

| J | F | M | A | M | J |
| J | A | S | O | N | D |

Lakes, ponds and slow-moving rivers fringed with trees and shrubs. Most in southern and central England but expanding elsewhere.

WETLANDS

MARSH HARRIER *Circus aeruginosus*

Traditionally a bird of reed-beds, the marsh harrier has adapted to nest on arable land and hunt over the surrounding countryside. Some have abandoned their annual migration and spend the winter in East Anglia.

Adaptations in behaviour, as well as concerted efforts at conservation, have helped this long-winged raptor's recovery from just one pair in 1971 to more than 200 by the early 21st century. Although once widespread, marsh harriers stopped nesting in Britain regularly around 100 years ago, mainly because of the draining of the fens. They returned to Norfolk in the late 1920s, and slowly spread until by 1958 there were 15 nests. After that there was a serious decline – due perhaps to the side effects of pesticides – to a low point of near extinction, followed by the current resurgence. Despite this

great success story, the marsh harrier is still one of Britain's rarest breeding species.

For many years, the RSPB's nature reserve at Minsmere in Suffolk was the marsh harrier's only nesting place in Britain, but now birds are found farther south, too, and a few nest as far north as lowland Scotland. Most breed on nature reserves

Female (right) has cream shoulders and head. The juvenile (left) has a pale head but some are all dark.

pass, flying on her back with legs and talons extended. In hunting flight, the buzzard–sized marsh harrier is extremely graceful and buoyant, gliding along, wings held aloft in a shallow 'V' shape. The tips of the primary feathers are spread like fingers, to prevent stalling at slow speed, and when the harrier spots its prey, it folds its long wings and drops suddenly, snatching up its meal with its formidable talons.

While most British marsh harriers are summer visitors, arriving in spring from North Africa, some prefer not to undertake the arduous flight, and these birds gather each evening in communal roosts in the reed-beds of East Anglia.

Identification
Mainly dark brown; male has tawny, brown-streaked breast, large blue-grey wing patches and grey tail; female has pale crown and throat; male in flight shows broad grey band on wings.

Nesting
Female builds substantial pile of aquatic vegetation, lined with grass, always on the ground among thick growth of marsh plants; lays late April–June; 4 or 5 eggs, very pale blue; incubation about 38 days, mainly by female; young, fed mainly by female, leave nest in 35–40 days, fly a week or two later.

Feeding
Water voles; moorhens, coots, starlings and other birds; rabbits; eggs and young; frogs and grass snakes.

Size
53.25cm (21in)

with reed-beds, although they have also taken to arable farmland, especially fields of oilseed rape and winter wheat. Pairs are highly sensitive to disturbances at their nesting site.

Low-flying hunter
The marsh harrier quarters its hunting grounds from just a few metres above the reeds, looking for the ripple that will betray a water vole below, or sending a party of coots scuttling for cover. Over grassland, it hunts rabbits, pheasants and small songbirds. Starlings are its favourite when it has young chicks to feed. The chicks do not all hatch at once, so there is a hierarchy among them. In years when the food supply is limited, only the oldest and biggest will survive.

In courtship, the male performs a spectacular soaring flight, diving and somersaulting in descent for as much as 60m (200ft). The call is a shrill 'kwee-a'. The female may call loudly for food when she is incubating, and sometimes flies up to take it from the male in an aerial

| J | F | M | A | M | J |
| J | A | S | O | N | D |

Reed-beds, marshes and nearby arable fields mainly in eastern England; on migration in drier, open habitats; some winter in East Anglia.

WETLANDS

MUTE SWAN *Cygnus olor*

A serene appearance belies the mute swan's aggressive tendencies, especially when breeding and in defence of territory. Even its name is deceptive since it hisses and snorts loudly when angry.

Mute swans are by no means silent – they grunt and hiss when annoyed, and some produce a weak trumpeting, while the young have a high-pitched whistle. In flight, the powerful beating of their wings makes a loud, rhythmic thrumming sound known as 'wing music'. But the legendary 'swan song' – the music said to be made by a dying swan – is a myth, with no foundation in reality.

The fact that the mute swan flies at all is remarkable. It is the biggest British bird and the third heaviest flying bird in the world, the other two being Africa's Kori bustard and the great bustard of Europe, Africa and Asia. After a laborious take-off from water, the swan tends to fly at full speed, because of its weight, and the throbbing of its wings can be heard up to 1¼ miles away.

Legend says that Richard the Lionheart brought back the first mute swans from Cyprus after the Third Crusade, but they were probably breeding wild in England long before that. They gradually became semi-domesticated because of

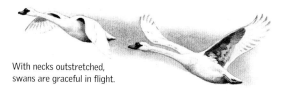

With necks outstretched, swans are graceful in flight.

their value as ornamental birds and as a luxury food. For centuries the Crown controlled the ownership of swans through royal swanherds and courts called 'swanmotes'. Privately owned swans were pinioned, meaning their wings were clipped, and branded or nicked in the skin of the upper bill as a mark of ownership. In the reign of Elizabeth I, 900 distinct swanmarks were recognised.

Swan-upping

The custom of marking is preserved in the swan-upping ceremony on the Thames every July, when rings are placed on cygnets' legs by the bargemaster of the Dyers' Company (one leg is ringed) or the swanmarker of the Vintners' Company (both legs are ringed). An unmarked bird belongs to the Queen, as seigneur of the swans. There was a similar ceremony on the rivers Yare and Wensum near Norwich. In the past 100 years, mute swans have been allowed to escape and are now common wild breeding birds. Abbotsbury Swannery in Hampshire is the world's only managed colony of mute swans.

Mute swans mate for life and are highly territorial. When a pair's space is invaded, the male, or cob, reacts by swimming with his neck arched in a swept-back 'S', his neck feathers fluffed out and his wings raised to make him seem even bigger. This display, known as 'busking', is used to attract a potential mate, as well as to intimidate rivals and intruders.

Identification
White plumage; orange bill with black base and knob (less prominent in female); long neck, usually carried in a curve; sexes alike; cygnets' grey-brown plumage gradually changes to all white during second year.

Nesting
On ground near water; male brings sticks and reeds, which female arranges in a huge pile; lays March–May; usually 5–7 eggs, grey-green; incubation about 36 days, by both parents; cygnets, tended by both parents, leave nest after 1 or 2 days, fly after about 4 months.

Feeding
Chiefly water vegetation; some small frogs, fish and insects.

Size
153cm (60in)

J F M A M J
J A S O N D

Breeds by lakes, slow-flowing rivers, canals and estuaries. Widespread in Britain and Ireland, except extreme north.

WETLANDS

201

OSPREY *Pandion haliaetus*

Essentially a land bird, the osprey has perfected a dramatic hunting technique that involves plunging into the water, seizing a big fish and hauling it up into the air in an exhibition of gravity-defying power.

Most birds of prey that hunt fish try to avoid immersion in water. Soaked feathers make it practically impossible for a big bird to take off again, especially when carrying a heavy fish. The osprey, however, specialises in diving from a great height, often submerging its whole body, and relying on the sheer power of its wings to pull itself and its prey free from the water and back up into the air. Just before the bird hits the water, it throws its feet forwards and folds its wings back and up so that it slices through the surface with maximum efficiency. A number of little sharp spines, or spicules, cover its foot pad and toes and these help the osprey to keep a firm grip on its slippery, struggling prey, which it hooks initially with its long, curved, razor-sharp talons.

The osprey's keen eyesight not only allows it to locate prey under the water in most weather conditions, but also to judge the depth at which the fish are swimming.

Guarded site

In the mid 1950s a pair of these large, brown-and-white birds set up their nest in a tree near Loch Garten, Highland – ospreys were back in Britain after an absence of almost 50 years. Their return captured the public's imagination, and more than a million people have visited the Loch Garten site to see the birds – through a telescope at a discreet distance. The nesting area, now a bird reserve, is guarded by the RSPB. The need for a close guard was underlined in 1958, when the nest was robbed.

The number of ospreys in Scotland has increased to more than 100 pairs, and recently a few pairs have nested in England, notably at Rutland Water in Leicestershire, and also in north Wales.

The nest is added to each year, becoming bigger and bigger.

The osprey, known colloquially as the fish hawk, is normally seen near lakes, broads and estuaries outside the breeding season. It lives almost entirely on fish, and one reason that it was harried out of the country is that it competes with fishermen for trout. Fish remains found at Loch Garten have all proved to be pike or trout but Welsh nesters also take grey mullet.

A hunting osprey has a rather slow, flapping flight, but it also soars and hovers. Its shrill, cheeping cry is like the call of a young gamebird. In early spring, before the female arrives at the eyrie, the male performs spectacular flights, climbing as high as 300m (1,000ft), hovering briefly with tail outspread and then plunging earthwards.

Identification
Upper parts dark brown, contrasting with white underparts speckled with brown; dark brown band on side of head; long wings distinctly angled in flight; sexes alike.

Nesting
Both sexes build bulky pile of sticks, in tree or on ground near loch; lays late April–early May; usually 3 eggs, white, heavily blotched with red-brown; incubation about 35 days, mainly by female; young, fed by female, fly in 7–8 weeks.

Feeding
Almost entirely fish, mainly pike and trout.

Size
56cm (22in)

Lakes, reservoirs and large rivers, breeding almost entirely in Scotland though spreading to England and North Wales; more widespread in winter.

RUFF *Philomachus pugnax*

The transformation of the male ruff from mottled brown wader to Elizabethan dandy is an astonishing phenomenon, made all the more so by its rarity – and the fact that the colours differ between birds.

Courting male ruffs present an extraordinary sight. Their huge and exotic ruff feathers and ear-tufts may be shades of purple-brown, black, chestnut, yellow or white, and no two males have exactly the same pattern. The extravagant plumage is used to overawe rivals and impress females as they gather at traditional sites, known as 'leks' or 'hills'. The same site may be used for many years.

The courtship displays are as violent as they are colourful. Each dominant male, known as an 'independent' or 'resident', has a defined territory, or court, in the lek, which he defends aggressively. The males rush at one another with ruffs fluffed out, threatening and sometimes coming to blows, rising off the ground and aiming kicks at each other's heads – and all without uttering a sound. After a fight, the males crouch with bills on the ground, ruffs spread out and ear-tufts raised, waiting for the females, or reeves, to make their choice. The reeves, which are distinctly smaller than the males, pick their way between the crouched ruffs and select one for mating by preening his ruff. Mating may take place on the display ground, or the paired birds may fly off together. Both sexes are promiscuous, and males take no part in raising the young.

In winter (left) the male looks similar to the female but in summer (right) his thickened neck shows in flight.

Alternative strategies

Other males, known as 'satellites', do not fight over territory but they often secure matings while the established males are threatening one another. They are tolerated probably because, in their conspicuous white plumage, they attract more reeves to the display ground.

Recent research has discovered another category of male. These are small and mimic females. They wait until a female shows readiness to mate by crouching, then sneak in without being noticed by residents, because of their appearance, and mate quickly before residents get a chance. These males have been dubbed 'faeders', from an Old English word for fathers, by the Dutch researchers who discovered the strategy. Ruffs breed more commonly in Holland than they do in Britain.

Ruffs once used to breed quite commonly in this country, but their popularity as table delicacies and the draining of marshlands meant that by the middle of the 19th century they had almost entirely stopped breeding in Britain. They come to Britain now mainly as passage migrants in autumn and spring, but since 1963 very small numbers have bred in East Anglia and occasionally elsewhere, and some may be seen in winter along the Norfolk coast and at Rutland Water.

Identification

Male in summer has huge ruff around neck, and ear-tufts; smaller female (reeve) is generally grey with boldly patterned back; in winter sexes are similar; oval white patches on each side of dark tail in all plumages.

Nesting

Reeve alone builds nest, usually hidden in a hollow, and lines it with dried grass; lays May; usually 4 eggs, variable in colour from pale brown to pale blue with dark blotches; incubation about 21 days, by reeve only; chicks, tended by reeve only, leave soon after hatching and become independent in a few days.

Feeding

Chiefly insects, with some worms, molluscs and plant seeds.

Size

Male: 28cm (11in)
Female: 23cm (9in)

J	F	M	A	M	J
J	A	S	O	N	D

Freshwater marshes mostly in south; mainly passage migrant; a few breed occasionally and some winter in eastern England.

SAND MARTIN *Riparia riparia*

Despite its small size, the sand martin bores a long tunnel in an earth or sand bank, then excavates a nesting chamber at the end of it, using its tiny bill and feet to scrabble away the detritus.

Sand martins nest in colonies and a whole collection of nest entrances making a dotted pattern in a sand bank was once a common sight. Both sexes dig out a tunnel roughly 60–90cm (2–3ft) long in the sandy soil, scooping out a small chamber at the end for the nest, to be lined with a heap of grass, leaves and feathers.

The smallest of Britain's three swallows, sand martins are the earliest to arrive. Interweaving flocks fly in at the end of March, gathering over lakes, rivers and reservoirs to recuperate and feed on gnats. Later, they seek the nesting sites of previous years in steep river banks and cliffs, and even in railway cuttings and road embankments, so long as an area of water is nearby. The birds head for watery locations because they feed on the flying insects that breed there. As well as natural fresh water, flooded sand and gravel pits make ideal hunting grounds. Nature reserves often provide artificial sites, hoping to attract the birds. They need

The sand martin digs out a nest tunnel using its feet.

a bank at least 2m (6ft) high, with a vertical face, in order to provide some protection from ground predators, such as foxes.

Comings and goings at the colony are abrupt. At one moment the spot seems almost deserted, with perhaps only a young bird, showing its white chin, peering from a hole. The next moment the air is clamorous with wings and chattering as birds dip and swing up to their nest entrances. Birds already clinging on to the steep bank side or cliff face keep up the singing chatter at those flying up. Then just as suddenly the main body of birds takes off and disperses.

Easily identified

There should be little danger of confusing the sand martin with a swallow or a house martin. The sand martin's brown breast band is distinctive, its tail is the least forked of the three and it lacks the house martin's white rump. Its calls, a rasping 'chrrrrp' and a sharper 'brrt' of alarm, are drier, harsher and more rattling than those of the other two species.

The sand martin hardly ever comes to the ground, but often rests on overhead wires and roofs. Large flocks roost in reed-beds and osiers outside the nesting season. These locations are often patrolled by sparrowhawks and sometimes hobbies, which take the birds as they fly in at sunset. Communal roosting in Britain does not last long. In September most sand martins leave. Dramatic population crashes occurred in 1969 and 1984 due to drought conditions in their African winter quarters, but conservation measures have aided successful breeding in Britain and the population has stabilised.

Identification
Plain brown above, white below; brown band across the breast; tail short and slightly forked; sexes alike.

Nesting
Both sexes bore tunnel, about 60–90cm (2–3ft) long, in sandy banks, cliffs or gravel-pits; grass and feathers gathered in flight for lining nest chamber; lays May–August; 4 or 5 eggs, white; incubation about 14 days, by both parents; young, fed by both parents, fly after about 19 days; normally two broods.

Feeding
Mosquitoes, other small flies, beetles, mayflies and other insects, usually caught over water.

Size
12cm (4¾in)

J F **M A M J**
J A S O N D

Widespread where there are sandy banks for nesting, usually by rivers or in sand or gravel pits.

WETLANDS

SHOVELER *Anas clypeata*

Unlike other surface-feeding ducks, the shoveler rarely upends to find food, preferring to scoop up water from which it can glean nutritious morsels. The huge bill is twice as wide at the tip as it is at the base.

The heavy bill that gives the shoveler its name is specially adapted for feeding on the surface of ponds and lakes. All dabbling ducks have a series of comb-like projections at the sides of the bill, called 'lamellae', and in the shoveler the system is at its most efficient. The lamellae are longer and closer together than those of other ducks so that when they intermesh they form a very fine sieve, capable of filtering the tiniest of food particles, including freshwater plankton. The shoveler sits low in the water

The drake chases his mate, issuing a throaty 'took-took' call. The duck has a double quack, but at other times shovelers are quiet birds.

The ducklings start to develop the large bill while they are still very young.

Shovelers are found in varying numbers over most of Britain, most frequently in East Anglia, but their distribution is patchy and they are scarce breeders. The main reason for this is probably a shortage of suitable breeding sites. For breeding, they prefer marshes, damp meadows and sewage farms, with plenty of cover, although they sometimes breed beside more open lakes, provided that shallow muddy water is available where they can feed.

In winter most British breeders move south to the Mediterranean but large numbers arrive from northern and eastern Europe and Russia, favouring flood plains but spreading out to almost any kind of inland shallow water. Britain's winter population of more than 15,000 individuals amounts to around a fifth of all those found in northwestern Europe.

Identification
Both sexes have huge bill and pale blue patch on forewings; drake has dark green head, white breast and chestnut sides; duck has speckled brown underparts; in eclipse plumage (May–December) drake is much like duck, but darker.

Nesting
Duck lines deep hollow in dry ground with grass and down; surrounding grass stems sometimes form a 'tent'; lays April–May; usually 8–12 eggs, buff or green; incubation about 24 days, by duck only; ducklings, tended by duck, leave soon after hatching, fly after 40 days.

Feeding
Animal and vegetable food in equal amounts – freshwater insects and shellfish mixed with seeds, buds and leaves of water plants.

Size
51cm (20in)

and as it paddles quickly through the shallows, it thrusts its spoon-like bill forward, sometimes submerging just the tip and sometimes the whole bill. By this means, it scoops up tiny plants and animals, and filters out what it doesn't want. It feeds in the same way in thin mud.

Group feeding is not unusual. The ducks swim round in a tight circle, one stirring up food particles for the one behind to collect. Although shovelers tend not to search for food under the water, they may dive if alarmed.

Frequent fliers
Shovelers are clumsy on land, and their bills give them a top-heavy look, but they are active fliers, although they also look unbalanced in the air – with big head and enormous bill stretched out in front, short tail behind and small wings set quite a way back on the body. In the spring, duck and drake circle their territory in a courtship flight.

| J | F | M | A | M | J |
| J | A | S | O | N | D |

Shallow, richly vegetated waters in lowland areas. Most numerous in eastern England; more widespread in winter in lowland Britain and Ireland.

WETLANDS

WATER RAIL *Rallus aquaticus*

The discordant voice of the water rail often betrays this secretive bird's presence among reeds and sedges. The call most often heard starts as a grunt and ends with a sound like a pig squealing with fear.

The water rail's peculiar repertoire of cries and screams includes a variety of grunts, groans, whistles, squeaks, hisses and a sharp 'kik-kik-kik' call. These often alarming noises are delivered by both sexes throughout the year, but especially in the breeding season, and go by the old country name of 'sharming'. Often a pair will duet, with the male uttering lower, slower notes followed by the female's higher, faster calls.

In the marshes, fens and swamps where it breeds, the water rail darts nervously from one piece of dense cover to another, with its long red bill lowered, giving rise to its old name of 'skittycock'. The bird's small size and its ability to compress itself laterally – so that from in front or behind it appears very narrow – enable it to slip through the densest of vegetation unnoticed. It has a high-stepping walk, with long legs and toes adapted for walking on floating vegetation, and as it moves along it often flicks up its tail in alarm, showing the white feathers underneath. It will even swim for short distances, if necessary.

The water rail's flights often last for just a few seconds – if disturbed, the bird may flutter off feebly with its long legs dangling, soon landing in suitable cover.

Winter feeding

In hard weather water rails become bolder, moving into the open to feed in unfrozen spots. If alarmed, they will stand motionless, allowing time for a close look at them. If food is hard to find, they will attack any frogs they may come across, as well as small mammals, such as water voles. A water rail is even fast and agile enough to snatch small birds, such as wrens, in flight.

First, the water rail paralyses its prey with repeated blows to the back of the head to sever the spinal cord, using its whole body like a hammer by rotating stiffly at the ankles. Then it stabs the quarry with its long bill. Water rails will also feed on the corpses of vertebrates that have succumbed to the cold or starvation.

The female is duller than the male, and chicks are black.

Courtship includes the feeding of the female by the male. The female may get up from the nest and eggs to walk round the male, rubbing her bill against his while making soft crooning noises.

Water rails remain in Britain throughout the year. The population grows in September, when birds fly in from the Continent and Iceland. Water rails are extremely difficult birds to count and may be more widespread than estimates suggest.

Identification
Long red bill; slate-grey breast, face and throat; flanks barred, upper parts dark brown with black streaks; white under tail; distinctive voice; female duller than male.

Nesting
Both sexes build nest of dead reeds near lake or river or on marshy ground; nest raised above water level and hidden from above; lays April–July; usually 6–11 eggs, buff with grey or brown blotches; incubation about 20 days, by both parents; nestlings, tended by both parents, leave soon after hatching, fly after about 7 weeks; two broods.

Feeding
Insects, spiders, freshwater shrimps, worms; perhaps small fish; the roots of grasses and watercress, seeds and berries; occasionally amphibians, small birds, mammals and carrion.

Size
28cm (11in)

J	F	M	A	M	J
J	A	S	O	N	D

Reed-beds and marshes, particularly in East Anglia and Ireland; not in northwest Scotland.

WETLANDS

211

Coast

The frontier zone of the seashore is a paradise for birds. In summer rocky cliffs are packed with noisy breeding colonies of gannets and other seabirds, while in winter millions of waders swarm across estuaries to feast on animal life hidden in the mud.

ARCTIC SKUA *Stercorarius parasiticus*

No other seabird's prey is safe from this pirate. The Arctic skua's highly developed feeding techniques include dive-bombing other birds, and frightening them into disgorging their latest catch.

When a seabird is attacked it will often vomit up its last meal, so reducing its weight for a quick escape. Skuas take advantage of this behaviour, hurtling down on gulls, terns and kittiwakes and bullying them until they disgorge the fish they've just eaten. As well as finding food by this form of extortion, Arctic skuas are experienced nest robbers. Normally, they hunt singly – and they can terrorise birds far larger than themselves – but occasionally male and female go hunting together. They make an efficient team, with one bird matching itself against, say, a pair of common gulls while its mate robs their nest of either eggs or nestlings.

The Arctic skua is predominantly brown, but there are two main colour variants – a dark form and a light form – and intermediates between them are often seen. All adult Arctic skuas are easily recognisable by their two central tail feathers, which extend in short, straight spikes beyond the rest of the tail. These birds are close relatives of gulls but have a more rakish, streamlined build, and long, pointed almost falcon-like wings. They are far more powerful, and graceful, in flight than gulls, twisting and turning as they relentlessly pursue other seabirds until a fish is given up.

Northern fastness

The Arctic skua's main breeding grounds are on the tundra of northern Europe, and as a breeding bird in Britain it is confined to Scotland, mostly Orkney and Shetland, but numbers are falling due to lack of food. Like other skuas, it nests on windswept moors often some distance inland, and not on sea-cliffs. The colonies are noisy. Wailing 'ka-aaow' and gruff 'tuk-tuk' calls are associated with a spectacular display flight, and dry 'tick-a-tick' calls with attacking an intruder. The Arctic skua is boldly aggressive in defence of its nesting site, and will fearlessly

dive-bomb humans as well as sheep, cattle, ponies and dogs. In contrast, during the winter, which Arctic skuas spend at sea, the birds are silent.

In spring and autumn, migrating Arctic skuas are seen all along the coasts of Britain and Ireland, especially on southern estuaries where terns and gulls are plentiful and the skua can give full rein to its scavenging ploy. An old, and mistaken, notion that skuas chase other birds in order to catch and eat their faeces gave rise to their scientific name *Stercorarius*, which comes from the Latin for 'dung'.

Identification
Dark brown upper parts, underparts vary from light brown to dark brown, with intermediate forms; all mature birds have two central tail feathers that form a distinctive point; sexes alike.

Nesting
Usually nests in colonies on moors and other rough land; both sexes make scrape, sparsely lined with dry grass or other local material; lays June; usually 2 eggs, olive-green to brown with dark markings; incubation 25–28 days, by both parents; chicks, tended by both parents, leave shortly after hatching, fly after about 5 weeks.

Feeding
Fish disgorged by other birds; small mammals; eggs and chicks; insects and their larvae; carrion; berries.

Size
45.75cm (18in)

J F M **A M J** **J A S O** N D

Northern Scotland and Scottish islands; passage migrants along coasts, often closer to shore than other skuas.

Immature birds are brownish.

ARCTIC TERN *Sterna paradisaea*

Twice yearly, this champion migrant undertakes an incredible journey, flying from one end of the globe to the other. The round trip may cover a distance as great as the circumference of the Earth.

This elegant tern, weighing not much more than a blackbird, nests from Britain northwards to the Arctic, and winters more than 9,000 miles away in Antarctic seas. Some individuals may live for 29 years or more, so in the course of a lifetime travel over half a million miles. Since it breeds in the north, during the Arctic summer when daylight is continuous, and spends the other half of the year in the south in similar conditions, the Arctic tern probably experiences more hours of daylight than any other animal.

Despite recent declines in breeding success, due in no small part to the overfishing and change in habits of its main food – sand-eels – the Arctic tern remains among the most numerous breeding terns in Britain. The birds take up residence north of a diagonal line drawn from Anglesey to Northumberland, but mostly on Scottish islands, and virtually none breed away from the coast, choosing sand or shingle beaches, rocky islands and saltmarshes as nesting locations.

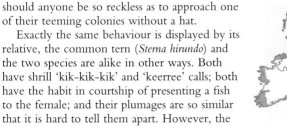

Watchful guardian
Arctic terns may breed in mixed colonies, with eiders for instance. They are intensely aggressive in defence of their breeding sites, and their zero tolerance of intruders provides good protection for other species' nests and young. The Arctic tern is well known for dive-bombing intruders, with harsh cries of 'keeyah' and striking out with its bill. It has been known to draw blood from a human's head, should anyone be so reckless as to approach one of their teeming colonies without a hat.

Exactly the same behaviour is displayed by its relative, the common tern (*Sterna hirundo*) and the two species are alike in other ways. Both have shrill 'kik-kik-kik' and 'keerree' calls; both have the habit in courtship of presenting a fish to the female; and their plumages are so similar that it is hard to tell them apart. However, the

Arctic tern's underwings are translucent apart from a narrow dark trailing edge around the wing-tips, which are more sharply tapered than the common tern's. The Arctic also has shorter legs and a wholly red bill. It is not as direct as the common tern when fishing, pausing several times on its descent, and making a last-minute plunge at a fish.

Terns are often known locally as 'sea swallows', and in spring Arctic terns may be seen at inland reservoirs on their way north. In the autumn they are more likely to be seen around the coast as they head back south.

Other birds, such as eiders, often nest in Arctic tern colonies, protected by the terns' aggressive reaction to intruders.

Identification
White, with black crown and nape; red bill; young birds and winter adults have a white forehead; sexes alike.

Nesting
Scrape in ground, made by female, next to tuft of grass or rushes, often lined with shells, grass or splinters of wood; lays mid May–June; 2 or 3 eggs, buff, green or blue-white, usually with heavy brown markings; incubation about 23 days, by both parents; nestlings, tended by both parents, leave after a few days, fly after about 3–4 weeks.

Feeding
Small fish, especially sand-eels; sometimes insects.

Size
38cm (15in)

J F M **A M J** **J A S O** N D

Mainly Scottish islands and coast; a few on coasts of north Wales and Ireland; inland on spring migration, coasts on autumn migration.

AVOCET
Recurvirostra avosetta

Striking black and white plumage, coupled with a long, upcurved bill, makes the avocet instantly recognisable. This, and its return as a breeding bird after a long absence, has lead to its adoption as the symbol of the RSPB.

The return of avocets to nest in Britain is one of the success stories of bird protection. Two hundred years ago they were plentiful, but fen drainage reduced their numbers. The birds that were left were shot for feathers to make fishing flies, and their eggs stolen to make puddings. The last breeding colony, at Salthouse in Norfolk, was wiped out by 1825.

Then, after the Second World War, a few pairs, probably dislodged from their Dutch breeding grounds by wartime flooding of the polder regions, began to nest on Minsmere and Havergate Island in Suffolk. The RSPB secured both sites as reserves, the colonies flourished and avocets began to spread elsewhere. Now more than 800 pairs breed at several colonies in East Anglia and southeast England, the odd pair nest inland and a few breed in northwest England. They are mostly to be found on nature reserves or other protected sites.

Mating behaviour follows a set pattern. A pair cement their bond with a ceremony that involves vigorous preening and splashing, and the female stretching her head and neck along the surface of the water. After mating has taken place, the pair cross bills, the male stretches a wing across his mate's back and they walk forward together. Then they run away from each other.

In one formal display, pairs bow simultaneously in a close circle.

Strange ritual

In another ceremony, known as 'grouping', the purpose of which is not clearly understood, several pairs bow low to each other, sometimes forming a circle, with their bills towards the centre and almost touching. They often move in unison and stamp their feet, and ritual fighting may follow. The male and female of the pair keep close to one another all the while.

The avocet is mainly a summer visitor to East Anglia. It winters on the Tamar and Exe estuaries in Devon, at Poole harbour in Dorset and Pagham harbour in Sussex. Some British breeders join moulting flocks in Holland in the late summer, and then either return to traditional wintering sites in southern and southwestern England, or travel farther afield to western Europe. Some even go as far as Africa.

Like the spoonbill, the avocet uses its curved, upturned beak in a side-to-side action to sweep the shallows for small sea creatures. It can swim quite well, having small webs between its toes, and often upends like a dabbling duck to reach prey. One of its old names, 'yelper', seems inappropriate for so elegant a bird, but is understandable because the bird yelps loudly if an intruder approaches its nest or young. In calmer moments it calls 'klooit' and has a soft, grunting note in flight.

Identification
Bold black and white plumage; long, slender, upcurved bill; long, leaden-blue legs project behind tail in flight; sexes alike.

Nesting
Nests in colonies near water, on tussocks or sandbanks; nest is often a substantial pile of dead vegetation; lays late April–May; usually 4 eggs, pale buff, spotted with grey and dark brown; incubation about 23 days, by both parents; chicks, tended by both parents, leave in few hours, fly after about 6 weeks.

Feeding
Shrimps; water insects and their larvae.

Size
43cm (17in)

J F M A M J
J A S O N D

Coastal lagoons in east and southeast England; winters in larger numbers mainly in south and southwest England.

219

BARNACLE GOOSE *Branta leucopsis*

The barnacle goose is precise in the places it chooses to live. All those that spend the winter on Scotland's Solway Firth breed in Spitsbergen, while those from Ireland and the Western Isles breed in Greenland.

The breeding grounds of the barnacle goose are in Spitsbergen, Greenland and Novaya Zemlya in Arctic Russia. As winter approaches, the Spitsbergen birds head for the saltmarshes of the Solway Firth, where 29,000 plus arrive; the Greenland birds fly to the Hebrides where they graze on improved grassland and machair, the short turf found behind sand-dunes. These birds, together with those that find their way to Orkney and Ireland, number about 65,000. The Russian birds go to Holland, but some overshoot, turning up in Kent and Norfolk.

The location of the barnacle goose's breeding grounds was a mystery for centuries and over time a myth grew that gave rise to its name. In medieval times, people believed that the goose did not come from an egg, like other birds, but was generated from the curiously shaped goose barnacles, which

Wings are flicked alternately in mating display.

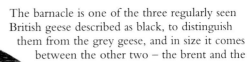

are still washed ashore in clusters, attached to driftwood. To a fanciful eye, some of these barnacles could resemble a goose. So persistent was the myth that less than 100 years ago, when the mystery had been solved, barnacle geese were still eaten during Lent in parts of Ireland, in the belief that they were more fish than fowl.

Local name

An old Scottish name for these birds is 'rood goose' and Dumfries has an annual Rood Fair that more or less coincides with the birds' arrival.

The barnacle is one of the three regularly seen British geese described as black, to distinguish them from the grey geese, and in size it comes between the other two – the brent and the Canada goose. The smaller brent has an all-black head and no wing-bars, and the Canada goose is browner than the barnacle, with less white on its face. The barnacle's striking black-and-white head makes it stand out from white-fronts and other grey geese.

Barnacle geese fly in straggling lines or ragged groups. Gregarious birds, they are more terrestrial than other geese and rarely settle on the sea. They are quite noisy, giving a barking cry that, in concert from a large flock, sounds like a pack of yelping dogs. Family groups appear to bicker among themselves. Each bird produces a subtly different sound, depending on how wide it opens its bill, and each one makes the same sound every time it calls, which may enable the birds to identify one another.

Identification

White face and black head; neck and upper breast black; lower breast and flanks whitish; back lavender-grey; wings strongly barred; black tail, bill and legs; sexes alike.

Nesting

Nests in colonies on rock ledges, and sometimes on islands; nest depression is lined with down and lichen; lays late May–June; usually 3–5 eggs, grey-white and soon stained; incubation about 28 days, by female only; goslings, tended by both parents, leave nest after a few days, fly after several months.

Feeding

Almost entirely grass.

Size

58.5–68.5cm (23–27in)

J	F	M	A	M	J
J	A	S	O	N	D

On coastal lowlands, feeding on arable farmland, marshes and estuaries. Most winter in Ireland, the Hebrides (especially Islay) and the Solway Firth.

COAST

221

CHOUGH *Pyrrhocorax pyrrhocorax*

A specialist feeder, the chough has a bright red, downcurved and sharply pointed bill, unlike that of any other British crow. It is perfectly adapted for probing short grass in search of insects.

The chough needs turf to be cropped short by grazing sheep, cattle or rabbits, so that it can use its slender bill to probe the soil and animal dung for the insects, larvae and invertebrates on which it feeds. Sadly, modern agricultural methods have made this kind of grassland increasingly scarce, so much so that nowadays the chough is a rare bird in Britain. It breeds mainly on sea-cliffs in Wales, Ireland and, after a long absence, Cornwall.

It was once much more widespread. The pioneering 18th-century naturalist Gilbert White saw choughs on the Sussex cliffs. In Cornwall the bird was once so common that it was called the Cornish chough and it is incorporated in the county's traditional crest. It also appears on the coat-of-arms of Flintshire, in North Wales. Jackdaws have been blamed for invading the choughs' territory and driving them out, but it seems more likely that the jackdaws moved in after the choughs disappeared. The main reason for the chough's decline is that it is such a specialist feeder.

Skilful fliers

In flight, choughs are spectacular performers, appearing to revel in showing off their aerial skills. They harness the wind with seemingly effortless ease, soaring in the updraught at the edge of cliffs, flamboyantly wheeling around coastal headlands and swooping from ledge to ledge, often diving acrobatically at breakneck speed with wings almost closed, or turning over on their backs in the air. Few other big birds can make such tight turns or manoeuvres.

Wing tips are upturned in soaring flight, with primary flight feathers separated into 'fingers'.

Their calls include distinctive, ringing 'chow' and 'chi-yaaa' notes, and their name, pronounced 'chuff', was originally pronounced 'chow' to reflect the birds' commonest call. This is how the name was spoken in Shakespeare's

day, but at that time it was probably referring to the jackdaw. The scientific name *Pyrrhocorax*, meaning 'fire raven', was used in ancient times by Pliny, and at one time the chough was thought to bring fire, although there is no evidence for it.

Choughs are sociable birds outside the breeding season, gathering in flocks of as many as 100 to roost on ledges, crevices and caves along sea-cliffs and, sometimes, mountain crags. They are often seen on coastal fields in company with jackdaws and rooks.

A communal courtship ceremony, in which members of the flock strut and flap their wings together, has been recorded. In other courtship ceremonies, the male caresses the female's bill and preens her head feathers, often feeding her.

Identification
Black plumage with green and blue gloss; curved red bill; red legs; sexes alike.

Nesting
Both sexes build nest of sticks, lined with wool and hair, in crevice or hole in cliff-face – often in sea-cave, sometimes inland in building or abandoned mineshaft; usually lays April–May; usually 3–6 eggs, white with green or cream tint and grey-brown blotches; incubation about 18 days, by female only; nestlings, fed by both parents, leave after about 45 days.

Feeding
Chiefly insects and larvae; worms, spiders and sometimes lizards.

Size
38cm (15in)

J	F	M	A	M	J
J	A	S	O	N	D

Coasts of Cornwall, Wales, Isle of Man, Inner Hebrides and Ireland, and inland Wales. Small numbers inland in mountains of North Wales.

EIDER *Somateria mollissima*

If a large black-and-white duck patters across the waves in a laboured take-off, and then launches into an unexpectedly confident flight, it is likely to be a drake eider. Lines of eiders often fly low over the water.

It takes a lot of effort for this bulky, long-bodied duck to achieve lift-off but, once airborne, it flies strongly on its short, broad wings. Flocks travel in long, irregular lines just above the waves. These ducks spend their whole life in and around the sea, in all its moods. They even fall asleep on rocks that are wet with spray, and may take to the water in the middle of a storm, bobbing up among waves that look big enough to crush them. In winter, they mostly move far out to sea, but may return to inshore mussel beds to feed, and large flocks of non-breeding birds, believed to come from Holland, are seen off the coasts of southern England at all seasons. Their calls, a crooning 'ah-oo' from the male and a harsher note from the female, may be heard on a calm day. Eiders breed on flat, rocky and sandy shores, from the Arctic to the British Isles. Their breeding range in Britain reaches Coquet Island off Northumberland on the east coast, Walney Island off Cumbria on the west coast, and parts of Ireland.

The female plucks down from her breast to line the nest she and her mate build close to the line of high tide. She incubates alone and will sit for days without moving. When at last she leaves, she rearranges the down to cover the eggs. In parts of the Arctic and sub-Arctic, although not in Britain, this down forms the basis of an important industry – the eider's nesting colonies are 'farmed', and the nests are robbed of their fine dark lining to make into quilts ('eiderdowns') and pillows.

Safety first
As with other species
in which the colouring of male
and female differ markedly, the duck's barred
brown plumage camouflages her on the nest.
Even so, these highly social birds breed in often
large colonies for safety, densely packed in a
small area, and nests can suffer very high rates of
predation by gulls, crows and foxes – in some
cases resulting in almost complete breeding
failure. A particularly vulnerable time is when
the very pretty downy black ducklings have to
leave the shelter of their brooding mother and
the colony, and make a dash for the sea. Then
they are especially at risk from marauding gulls.

To combat this, eiders have a crèche strategy
– many ducklings from a large number of broods
are assembled under the watchful eye of a few
females, while the others go off to feed.
This makes it harder for predators
to single out a target, and the
adults give early warning at the
first sight of danger. This is
such an effective system
that some females in
charge of crèches
'kidnap' ducklings
from another brood,
and keep these
unfortunate 'hostages' on
the edge of the crèche
and their own offspring
in the centre.

Bill tossing and neck
jerking are features
of the male eider's
courtship display.

Identification
Drake is white above, black below; duck is
brown, except for white on wing; forehead has
no bulge, joins bill almost in a straight line.

Nesting
Both sexes build nest of grass and seaweed,
always on the ground; female lines nest with
feathers and down; lays May–June; 4–6 eggs,
light green; incubation about 30 days, by
female only; ducklings, tended by female, leave
immediately, fly after about 2 months.

Feeding
Molluscs, including mussels, whelks, cockles;
crustacea, including small crabs; very little
vegetable matter.

Size
61cm (24in)

| J | F | M | A | M | J |
| J | A | S | O | N | D |

Rocky coasts in Scotland,
northern Ireland, northwest
and northeast England. In
winter most numerous on east
coast, but some further south.

COAST

FULMAR *Fulmarus glacialis*

The fulmar's ability to eject a foul-smelling fluid a fair distance with impressive accuracy keeps predators and rivals at bay. However, this talent makes bird ringing a risky business since chicks inherit the skill.

As an unusual method of discouraging unwanted attention, projectile spitting seems to be particularly effective. The fulmar stores oil from the marine creatures that form the bulk of its diet in its stomach, and shoots it out when provoked. In chicks, this ammunition takes the form of a greyish, lumpy substance – it's orange in adults – and the smell is truly dreadful. Any clothes hit by the oil retain the odour, despite repeated washing, and really have to be thrown away. Any bird attempting to take a chick, or an adult, is liable to have its feathers clogged with the substance, and this has proved to be so much of a problem for peregrine falcons that they have been driven away from some of the fulmar's breeding areas along rocky coastlines. Shetland is an example. In Iceland and on St Kilda, the fulmar used to be called 'foula maa', meaning 'foul gull'. Fulmars themselves have a superb sense of smell. Enlarged tube-like nostrils on top of the bill allow them to detect food and breeding colonies from a great distance.

Success story

One hundred years ago, fulmars barely had a toehold in Britain. They bred on the most westerly of the Outer Hebrides, St Kilda. Then, at the beginning of the 20th century, they colonised Foula in the Shetlands, and so began a spectacular advance that has been restricted only by the coastline. There are now at least 500 colonies, with a total British and Irish population of more than 600,000 pairs of breeding birds, on suitable cliffs all around the coast. There is some argument about the reason for this population explosion, but most ornithologists link it with an increase in the amount of offal being discarded by trawlers, providing a ready food supply for the birds.

Like shearwaters, petrels and albatrosses, to which it is related, the fulmar is a bird of the open sea. It has the effortless gliding flight typical of shearwaters, but occasionally flaps its wings like a gull and rises higher than most of the shearwaters. Colonies are generally occupied throughout the year, although the attendance of individual pairs is sporadic outside the breeding season. In May, the female lays a single egg in a hollow in turf or on a bare rock. Fulmars will look over a possible site for several years before settling there.

Fulmars have an exceptionally long period of immaturity, and on average do not start breeding until they are nine years of age. They are also long lived, sometimes surviving for 30 years or more.

Identification
Pale grey back, wings and tail; white head and underparts; tubular nostrils show at close range; stiff-winged flight; sexes alike.

Nesting
Scrape in turf on cliffs, or depression in rock; nest sometimes lined with a few pebbles; lays May; 1 egg, white; incubation about 52 or 53 days, by both parents; nestling, fed by both parents, leaves after about 53 days.

Feeding
Fish, whale or seal offal; also fish and crustacea.

Size
47cm (18½in)

Courting pairs squat on cliff ledges.

J F M A M J
J A S O N D

Breeds on most coastal cliffs (especially in north and west) and sometimes coastal buildings; in winter, most stay out at sea, but some visit colonies.

COAST

GANNET *Morus bassanus*

Large webbed feet may seem like a disadvantage in a packed colony, but the gannet puts them to good use, placing one over the other and both feet over its single egg in an ingenious incubation strategy.

Two-thirds of the world's gannets are hatched on the cliff ledges of around 20 UK gannetries. One of the largest, after a huge increase, is on the Bass Rock in the Firth of Forth. The gannet's specific scientific name, *bassanus*, reflects this long association. A visitor noted in 1518: 'Near to Gleghornie, in the ocean, at a distance of two leagues, is the Bass Rock, wherein is an impregnable stronghold. Round about it is seen a multitude of great ducks that live on fish.' Now, more than 490 years later, the 'great

The gannet's long narrow wings are swept back when diving.

ducks' are still there – 50,000 pairs of them, packed closely together in a noisy, squabbling mass. For most of the year, gannets are silent birds, but they make up for this in the breeding season. The screeching roar of a gannet colony –

is nothing short of breathtaking. The birds cruise into the wind and, when a shoal of fish is spotted, they dive-bomb their quarry from as high as 30m (100ft). Using their long wings – which can span 2m (6ft) – and big feet to manoeuvre into position, they hurtle down in a dazzling white shower, hitting the water at speeds in excess of 62mph and sending up tall jets of spray.

Gannets travel long distances in search of fish for their young – by the time of fledging the chick weighs more than its parents – but outside the breeding season, they seldom return to shore. Flying far across the North Atlantic, they wheel against the wind on barely moving wings, resting in the waves when they must, and heading landwards only when instinct calls them back to their lonely fortresses to breed.

Identification

White plumage with black wing-tips; buff-yellow wash on back of head; cigar-shaped body; pale blue bill with black lines; immatures dark brown with white cheeks, resemble adults by fourth year; sexes alike.

Nesting

Both sexes gather pile of seaweed and flotsam, on cliff ledge or flat ground; lays March–June; 1 egg, white; incubation about 44 days, by both parents; nestling, fed by both parents, flies and makes own way to sea after 90 days.

Feeding
Fish, offal.

Size
91.5cm (36in)

the biggest in the world is on St Kilda, the most remote island in the Outer Hebrides – has few equals in nature.

Gannets return to the same nest and the same mate each year, renewing the pair bond with ceremonial courtship displays, involving fencing with their bills. In another display, known as 'sky pointing', the gannet stands with its head and neck stretched so that its bill points directly up at the sky. This posture warns its mate that it is about to leave the nest – one parent always stays with the egg or chick to defend it from aggressive neighbours.

Plunge dive

The gannet's fishing technique is spectacular – wings folded back, dagger-shaped bill an extension of its streamlined body, it forms a living arrowhead, piercing the surface of the sea. To watch a feeding flock in frenzied action

J F M A M J
J A S O N D

Breeds on coastal cliffs or rocky islands, mainly in north and west. Seen offshore throughout year, and some are at colonies as early as January.

GREAT BLACK-BACKED GULL
Larus marinus

Ruthless in its quest for food, the heavyweight great black-backed gull is equipped to win most fights for food. An inventive predator, it has been known to drop small mammals into water to drown them.

This is the world's largest gull, weighing twice as much as a herring gull or lesser black-backed gull. Its jet-black wings span up to 1.5m (5ft), and with its great weight and formidable hooked beak, it is the likely victor in any dispute with other gulls – and it can be a ferocious killer in seabird colonies, tearing its prey inside out. Eider ducklings that stray from their parents are among its favourite quarry. It can gulp them down in a single mouthful. Burrow-nesting species, such as puffins and Manx shearwaters, are especially vulnerable – the great black-back feeds them to its young. Land birds flying over the sea on migration are generally too tired to take on the unequal struggle and are easily knocked down. These great gulls even attack sickly lambs, while landfill rubbish tips have a magnetic attraction.

Erstwhile trophies
Victorians used to shoot great black-backs and put them on display as trophies. Partly because it ceased to be a target for marksmen, as it was at the end of the 19th century, and partly because it will eat almost any animal food, alive or dead, the great black-backed gull recovered from virtual extinction. This comeback is also due to an increase in the amount of edible offal left unburnt at fish docks and other places.

It breeds widely all round the British Isles, except on the east coast of England and the southeast coasts of both England and Scotland. However, unlike most of its close relations, the great black-back does not breed far away from the coast anywhere in the British Isles. Rocky cliffs and offshore islands are its domain, although outside the breeding season it has become

considerably more common inland than used to be the case, and flocks sometimes form in winter.

Its voice is like the herring gull's 'kyow-kyow-kyow', but much deeper and more raucous. The great black-back also has a chuckling 'uk-uk-uk' call, which it utters especially when humans invade its breeding territory. In defence of its eggs and young the great black-back swoops low over intruders.

In its first summer, the great black-back's heavy black bill stands out from its pale head and underparts.

Identification
Black back, white underparts; dark markings on head in winter; immatures brown above, pale below; sexes alike.

Nesting
Nests in small groups, on ground, rocky stack or cliff ledge; both sexes build substantial nest of heather, seaweed and other local materials; lays April–May; usually 3 eggs, olive or light brown with dark spots; incubation about 27 days, by both parents; young, fed by both parents, leave after 2–3 weeks, fly after 7–8 weeks.

Feeding
Almost any kind of animal food, including dead fish, offal, carrion and other birds; small vegetable element.

Size
68.5cm (27in)

J	F	M	A	M	J
J	A	S	O	N	D

Mainly rocky coasts in west of Britain and Ireland; very few breed in east, almost all in northeast Scotland; more widespread in winter.

KITTIWAKE *Rissa tridactyla*

On a precipitous ledge high above the sea, the kittiwake, unlike other gulls, constructs an elaborate, cup-shaped nest, anchoring it in place with mud – a sensible precaution given its precarious position.

The kittiwake differs from other British gulls in building a more secure cup-shaped nest on its chosen breeding site, which is always some form of narrow ledge, often not much more than a slight projection. The birds choose ridges on cliff-faces, shelves on seaside piers or bridges, or even windowsills. The kittiwake's claws are longer and sharper than those of other gulls, giving it a more secure footing. From the moment of hatching, its young display an impressive ability to remain firmly rooted to the spot – a vital skill, given their perilous situation. Secure in their cup, they stay in the nest for more than six weeks until they can fly – to leave earlier would mean falling to their deaths.

At its breeding colonies the air is filled with deafening cries of 'kitt-ee-wayke', from which the bird takes its name. This note features largely in mutual bowing and bill-rubbing courtship ceremonies. The strident calls were once supposed to be the ghostly cries of souls lost at sea.

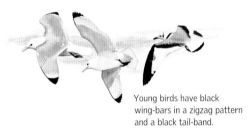

Young birds have black wing-bars in a zigzag pattern and a black tail-band.

Sea rover
Alone among the gulls breeding in Britain, the kittiwake is faithful to the sea. Other gulls have taken advantage of man-made food supplies, flocking to rubbish dumps, sewage outfalls and food markets, but the kittiwake roams the sea for much of the year, following the movements of fish and ships. Juveniles may spend the autumn and winter near harbours, but adults rarely go to land except to breed.

Buoyant and graceful in flight, the kittiwake copes superbly with gales, bounding along in huge arcs, almost shearing the waves at the low point of each dip. At such times, its flight is more akin to the action of unrelated shearwaters and fulmars than it is to that of other gulls. Also like fulmars, kittiwakes use air currents around nesting colonies, manoeuvring to land exactly on or by their nests with amazing precision.

Once pursued for food, sport and the millinery trade, kittiwakes are no longer subjected to this hunting, and numbers increased substantially during the 20th century. However, even some of the largest colonies have recently failed to produce any young. The reason is a reduction of their food supply, and the population is plummeting dramatically.

Identification
White with black wing-tips; uniform grey head and nape in winter; black legs and yellow bill; immatures have dark stripes on wings; dark markings on head in winter; sexes alike.

Nesting
Nests in colonies, usually on narrow cliff ledges or inside sea caves; both sexes build cup-shaped nest of seaweed, moss and other local materials; lays May–June; 1–3 eggs, pale blue-grey to buff-brown with dark blotches and spots; incubation 26–28 days, by both parents; young, fed by both parents, leave after 40–45 days.

Feeding
Almost entirely fish and fish offal.

Size
40.5cm (16in)

J F M A M J
J A S O N D

Coastal cliffs all around Britain except southeast and parts of eastern England; scarcer in Ireland; most winter well out to sea; rare inland.

Seabird spectacle

On the western tip of South Wales, the coast and islands of Pembrokeshire provide astounding views of birds that spend most of their lives out on the open ocean, returning to land only to breed.

The rocky western shores of the British Isles are among the most exhilarating wild places in Europe, with dramatic cliff-top paths giving splendid views of rugged headlands and sheltered coves, and out across the glittering, white-crested sea. For any wildlife watcher, these paths also provide access to a very special treat – the busy breeding colonies of ocean birds that build up on cliffs, stacks and islands each spring. A big colony at the height of the breeding season is a real spectacle – a teeming seabird city with birds constantly flying in and out, squabbling with rivals, displaying to mates, defending their territory and harassing potential enemies. The sights, sounds and even the smells are unforgettable.

The Pembrokeshire Coast National Park in South Wales is the only British national park that is primarily coastal. It was designated

mainly because its landscapes and seascapes are stunningly beautiful, but it is also a vital breeding habitat for seabirds. A coastal path follows every rocky inlet and promontory, offering intimate views of breeding sites on the cliffs and isolated rock formations, as well as long-range sightings of offshore migrants later in the year. Boat trips are available to take visitors to nearby islands that are internationally renowned for their seabird colonies.

Long view

More than 180 miles long, the coastal path extends all the way around Pembrokeshire from near Cardigan in the north to beyond Tenby in the south. The best sections for seabirds are Strumble Head near Fishguard and the jutting headlands in the extreme west that enclose St Brides Bay. Strumble Head is well known

> These extraordinary birds can be watched at close quarters as they return from hunting trips, their big, gaudy bills packed with silvery sandeels for their young.
>
> PUFFIN

as a seawatching site – a place where anyone armed with a good telescope can expect to see a wide variety of ocean birds. Autumn is the best time, when large numbers of shearwaters, petrels and skuas pass offshore, especially during southwesterly gales just after dawn. This is birdwatching in the raw, exposed to the full force of the elements, and although an old wartime observation post offers shelter, it is definitely an activity for the dedicated.

Ramsey Island near the headland beyond St David's offers another bracing experience, but with wider appeal. Here the tidal streams squeezing between the island and St David's Head create one of the most powerful tidal races on the British coast, with whirlpools, steep crashing waves and frothing white water. Boats from nearby St Justinians take adventurous souls right through this maelstrom, but also – less alarmingly – around the island itself, which in spring and summer has spectacular cliff colonies of breeding seabirds, such as fulmars, kittiwakes, guillemots and razorbills.

The whole island is owned by the RSPB, and although daily numbers are limited, visitors are permitted to land to explore. Ramsey is particularly well known for the choughs that forage for insects on its fields and breed on

the cliffs. These elegant, red-billed, red-legged crows perform the most glorious, exultant aerobatics in the buffeting wind, accompanied by wild, high-pitched 'chow' and 'chi-yaaa' calls that echo off the cliff faces.

Island delight

South of St Brides Bay lies another group of island reserves that offer close encounters with remarkable birds. Some 7 miles offshore, Grassholm (RSPB) has one of the largest gannet colonies in the world, and boat trips around the island are guaranteed to provide stunning views of these sleek, gleaming white seabirds both on their nests and as they dive headlong into the sea to catch fish. Nearer land, the waters around Skokholm (Wildlife Trust) are alive with seabirds during the breeding season. For most people, however, the prime destination on this coast is the inshore island of Skomer, another Wildlife Trust reserve.

Just a short boat trip from nearby Martin's Haven, Skomer offers most of the wildlife attractions of the Pembrokeshire coast concentrated in a single square mile. In spring and summer its cliff faces attract masses of breeding kittiwakes, fulmars and guillemots, and they occupy every tiny ledge, with a few razorbills nearer the water. The cliff tops are riddled with burrows – many dug by rabbits but now occupied by puffins. Surprisingly approachable, these extraordinary birds can be watched at close quarters as they strut and quarrel among the burrows, or return from hunting trips with their big, gaudy bills packed with silvery sandeels for their young. From the cliffs you can peer down into the clear waters and see the puffins seeming to fly underwater in pursuit of prey, then burst up on whirring wings to head for home. They fly all around the boats like airborne clockwork toys.

Choughs nest on Skomer and are often to be seen soaring and tumbling on the upcurrents of air by the cliffs. Short-eared owls hunt by day over the island, and there is a good chance of seeing a peregrine or raven. For the most memorable experience, though, it is necessary to take advantage of the farmhouse accommodation on offer, because the shearwaters and storm petrels that occupy many of the nesting burrows on the island come to land only after dark. Skomer supports the world's largest colony of Manx shearwaters, with more than 100,000 pairs, and their nocturnal return is accompanied by an eerie cacophony of coos, howls and screams that, in the dark, could easily be mistaken for some manifestation of the supernatural. This is nature at its wildest and most alien.

KNOT *Calidris canutus*

A distant eddy of smoke or squall of rain drifting out over an estuary may, in fact, be a flock of knots performing elaborate aerobatics. The flock appears dark and then light as the birds swirl in perfect unison.

These winter visitors provide a dynamic spectacle when they perform their group manoeuvres – sensational coordinated displays during which dense clouds of birds wheel together over the water, grey upper parts to the fore as they tilt one way, and pale rumps and tails making the mass silvery as they turn again. As the flocks come in to roost, the incoming tide reduces the space available on mudflats or sandbanks, but the knots are undeterred, the later birds having no hesitation in alighting on the heads or backs of others.

Early naturalists were baffled by the knot – no one had any idea where these thousands of birds in tightly packed flocks came from and where they returned to once winter was over. Even the knot's name is old and obscure. One theory was that, in the middle of the 18th century, when the Swedish naturalist Linnaeus was classifying all the living creatures then known, the knot was thought of as a little King Cnut, the 11th century Viking monarch who stood on the shore to show that even a king cannot order the tide to go back, and this idea was reflected in the Latin name, *canutus*. However, that explanation is more fanciful than probable. The name may come from the birds' low-pitched cry 'knut, knut', which when uttered by a closely packed flock becomes a continuous low twitter. Knots also produce another, mellower note – a higher-pitched, whistle-like 'twit-twit'.

The juvenile knot has pale-edged feathers on upper parts and a pale apricot tinge below.

Winter flight

It has now been established that migrating knots sometimes make vast journeys, quitting their bare breeding grounds far north of the Arctic Circle to stream south in their hordes

as far as southern Africa, Patagonia, New Zealand and Australia. They begin to arrive in Britain, chiefly on eastern and northwestern coasts and along the coasts of northern and eastern Ireland, in late summer and continue into October, the young arriving first.

Although non-breeders may remain in Britain all year, the main groups start to return to their northern breeding grounds the following April and May, by which time some birds will have grown their full, brick-red breeding plumage. On migration, the flocks keep up a collective chatter. Once they reach the Taimyr peninsula of northern Siberia, or islands still further north, the male performs a circling song-flight and engages in courtship chases. Then, after a brief, energetic summer without night, the flocks gather for their trip south and the cycle begins again.

Identification
Grey above, paler below in winter; mottled black and chestnut above, russet below in summer; grey tail; light rump and wing-bar show in flight; dumpy, short neck; sexes alike.

Nesting
Nests in stony Arctic tundra, in hollow lined with lichen; lays June–July; usually 4 eggs, grey-green to olive-buff, with dark markings; incubation probably 3 weeks, by both parents; chicks, tended chiefly by male, leave nest when dry, fly after about 4 weeks.

Feeding
In winter – small crabs and other crustacea, worms, small molluscs, insects; in summer – insects, spiders, molluscs, plant buds and other vegetable matter.

Size
25.5cm (10in)

J F M A M J
J A S O N D

Coastal mudflats and sandy beaches, especially on estuaries.

LONG-TAILED DUCK *Clangula hyemalis*

Extremely long central tail feathers that can be manipulated at will mark out this sea duck. Just as memorable are its wild, yodelling cries, which have been likened to the distant skirl of bagpipes.

For most of the year, the drake's tail feathers measure up to 13cm (5in) long, and can be held aloft, level or even submerged. The female's tail is always short and pointed, and from July to September, when the birds are moulting, the drake's tail is not in evidence. The long-tailed male was once known to wildfowlers as 'sea pheasant' because of his tail, which is not fully grown until the third year. He shared this name with the pintail, the only other duck with an elongated tail seen in British waters. The long-tail has a low, rolling flight.

In Scotland, where most British long-tails are to be found, the duck is known as 'coal and candlelight', a name supposed to echo the cry it makes, but the pitfalls of translating a bird's call into

The flight features shallow upstrokes and deep downbeats.

human speech are nowhere better illustrated than in the case of the long-tailed duck. Its loud, ringing 'coal and candlelight' has also been written down as 'ow-ow-owdl-ow', 'cah-cah-coralwee', a simple 'calloo' and, probably nearest of all to the actual sound, 'ardelow-ar-ardelow'. However it's written, the call is far-carrying and evocative – comparisons have been made to the baying of hounds and the sound of bagpipes – and since the ducks are garrulous, it can be heard wherever they may be for most of the year.

Late arrivals

Flocks of long-tails appear around British coasts much later than other sea ducks. A few of them fly in from late September or October, but larger numbers arrive between late December and early January. The biggest flocks – each numbering more than 1,000 birds – are to be found in the Moray Firth and Orkney, but they also gather in large numbers in waters around the Hebrides, the Firth of Forth and Shetland. Usually, they keep well out to sea – even in bad weather – diving 27m (90ft) deep or more, and staying down for at least a minute at a time.

By May, most long-tailed ducks have left Britain for their breeding grounds, mainly on the lake islands of northern Scandinavia. Sometimes a few non-breeding birds will stay in the north of Scotland, and some may even nest there although this is by no means certain.

Long-tails are among the most numerous of all duck species worldwide, and are probably the most numerous of all Arctic breeding ducks and all sea ducks.

Identification
Drake has long pointed tail, dark brown upper parts and breast, white flanks and belly; head and neck, mainly white in winter, brown in summer except for white on side of face; duck has short tail, sides of head white, brown upper parts and white underparts; both have short bill and dark wings without bars.

Nesting
Very rarely breeds in Britain; nests always in hollow in ground, near water; lays late May; 6–9 eggs, olive or buff; incubation about 3½ weeks, by duck; ducklings, tended by duck only, leave nest immediately, fly after about 5 weeks.

Feeding
Small molluscs; crabs and shrimps; some vegetable matter.

Size
58.5cm (23in)

J	F	M	A	M	J
J	A	S	O	N	D

Winters off coasts of northern Ireland, Scotland and eastern England. Most numerous in northern Scotland, Shetland and Orkney.

COAST

239

MANX SHEARWATER *Puffinus puffinus*

The remarkable homing ability of the Manx shearwater contributes to its reputation as one of nature's most adept travellers. This summer visitor is more at home swooping above the waves than it is on land.

A Manx shearwater, taken from its breeding site on the Welsh island of Skokholm and released in Massachusetts, well away from its normal range, found its way back to its mate and chick in 12 days. This experiment proved what ornithologists already suspected – that the birds have a phenomenal homing ability.

Many of the Manx shearwaters seen around the coast of Britain in summer go halfway across the world in winter, to the South Atlantic. They cover vast distances in an almost effortless gliding flight, sometimes swooping so low that the tips of their long, narrow wings actually shear the waves. On land, by contrast, they are awkward birds, able to move only with an ungainly shuffle, but they never go ashore, except to breed.

The Manx shearwater is the most common shearwater and the only one to breed in Britain. The birds mostly breed on grassy islands along the western seaboard, where they are safe from rats and other ground predators. Ninety per cent of the world's population nests off Britain and Ireland and the majority inhabit just three locations – the two Pembrokeshire islands of Skomer and Skokholm, and the island of Rhum in Scotland. The colony on Rhum is unusual because it is located inland and on top of a mountain. The Skomer colony numbers some 95,000 pairs. Despite its name, very few Manx shearwaters are to be found on the Isle of Man.

Night music

At sea, the birds are normally silent, but at night on their breeding grounds they set up an extraordinary noise. They nest in burrows, often taking over rabbit warrens, and in the hour before midnight, particularly when there is no moon, the shearwaters produce an unearthly chorus as their mates fly in from fishing expeditions. The burrows, honeycombing the ground, throb with an eerie range of strangled cooing noises.

For two months after the single chick has hatched, one parent remains with it while the other travels long distances to find food, returning with a full crop – a pouch in its throat for carrying fish. When the time comes to fly south, both parents desert their offspring, leaving it unattended in the burrow. After some eight or nine days, the young shearwater leaves, too, making its own way south.

The bird's puzzling scientific name *Puffinus puffinus* came about because the word 'puffin' was originally given to the portly chick of the Manx shearwater, but it was later transferred to the adult and young of the puffin.

Identification
Upper parts, crown and nape black; chin, throat and underparts white; sexes alike.

Nesting
Both sexes excavate burrow in turf, usually at least 1m (3ft) deep; often takes over rabbit burrow; lays April–May; 1 egg, white; incubation 47–55 days, by both parents; nestling, tended by both parents, fledges in 62–76 days.

Feeding
Small fish, such as herring, sprats and pilchards.

Size
35.5cm (14in)

The chick, which has dense down at first, stays in the burrow until its flight feathers have grown.

J	F	M	A	M	J
J	A	S	O	N	D

Breeds on remote headlands and isolated grassy islands off west coasts of Britain and Ireland; winters far out in north-west Atlantic.

COAST

PUFFIN *Fratercula arctica*

This portly bird's bill of many colours is its most outstanding feature, and the puffin puts it to good use as a weapon, digging tool and courtship aid – and for carrying large numbers of fish crossways.

The puffin's wide, triangular bill – comical in the eyes of some observers – has given rise to such popular names as 'sea parrot' and 'bottlenose'. It makes the puffin unmistakable, and is used to send signals to neighbours, rivals and mates. In threat displays, puffins thrust out their bills in a gesture that may be the prelude to a fight. They toss their heads, hiding their bills, when they want to make peace. In courtship, pairs knock their bills together, left and right alternately, shaking their heads to and fro, in a ritual known as 'billing'. On turf-covered sea-cliffs, which are their main breeding sites, puffins hack into the soil – or even into soft rock – with their bills to make nesting burrows, shovelling away the loose earth with their webbed feet.

Some pairs on the Isle of May and elsewhere use rabbit burrows to avoid having to dig their own tunnels. If a rabbit is still in residence, the puffins chase it away. Although lighter, a puffin is usually more than a match for a rabbit. Should the birds attempt the same ploy with a Manx shearwater, however, the puffins come off second best to the shearwater's powerful, hooked bill.

The puffin spreads its webbed feet to act as 'brakes' when landing.

The puffin sometimes collects grass and feathers to line its nest, plucking pieces of vegetation until it has a heap of materials clasped in its bill. Then it shuffles back to its nest-hole with its finds.

Summer colour

The puffin's bill is at its brightest in summer, when the birds go ashore to breed. It changes in winter, when they live on the sea, losing its horny sheath and exposing the duller colours beneath. Puffins usually winter in sea areas a little south of their breeding grounds, but they are sometimes seen on deeper water. The bird's plump body provides momentum as it dives into the waves and it swims surprisingly well. The short wings that make its whirring flight seem so laboured turn into powerful flippers in the water, helping the puffin perform fast rolls and turns in pursuit of fish. Its large orange feet serve as stabilisers and rudders.

By carrying the fish it catches crossways in its bill, impaled on backward facing spines on the roof of its mouth, the puffin can carry many fish at once – 62 have been recorded. They are often neatly arranged, heads and tails alternating, and this is probably the result of the puffin turning its head from side to side as it takes one fish at a time from a shoal in which the fish are all swimming in one direction.

Puffins have declined in Britain, particularly in the south. Between the Scillies and the Isle of Wight, colonies of thousands once held sway, but no more than a few dozen remain there now.

Identification
Huge bill, blue, yellow and red in summer; mainly yellow and horn-coloured in winter; black upper parts and white underparts; sexes alike.

Nesting
Both sexes dig burrow in turf or under boulders, or occupy abandoned rabbit burrow; nest may be lined with vegetation and feathers; lays May; 1 egg, white with faint brown markings; incubation about 6 weeks, mainly by female; nestling is fed by parents in burrow for about 6 weeks, then deserted and left hungry; after several days' fast, it crawls out and flutters down to the sea by night.

Feeding
Marine organisms, including molluscs and small fish.

Size
30.5cm (12in)

| J | F | M | A | M | J |
| J | A | S | O | N | D |

Cliffs and islands mainly in north and west; seen elsewhere on migration; winters far out at sea.

RED-BREASTED MERGANSER
Mergus serrator

A slim, flat-backed duck paddling along with an untidy double crest on display is likely to be the red-breasted merganser. It uses a snorkelling technique, submerging its head to get an accurate fix on a target fish.

In common with its close relative the goosander, which is a bigger bird, the red-breasted merganser searches for fish by submerging its head to locate its prey first so that it doesn't waste energy on diving and chasing. Sometimes red-breasted mergansers hunt cooperatively, herding the fish by diving in a line or encircling them, so they can't escape easily.

The red-breasted merganser is a sawbilled duck, equipped with tooth-like serrations on its long, thin bill, so that wriggling fish cannot slip away. Two rows of sharp barbs on the upper surface of its tongue also help anchor the slippery prey. The

drake is easily recognised by the ragged crest on his head, which is dark green but looks almost black from a distance. The female's crest is wispier and her head is rusty brown. Only the drake has a chestnut breast, spotted black.

Although this handsome duck is now a protected species throughout Britain, thanks to the Wildlife

The female has a single black line on the white wing-patch while the male has two.

mergansers walk on land without difficulty and in winter are sometimes seen standing on shingle bars.

The bird's courtship displays include much bowing and gesturing with head and bill. The drake will stretch its head and neck, showing its red gape, raising its crest, arching its wings and pattering along the water in a cloud of spray. Sometimes, it will give voice with a kind of rattling purr. The female makes a muffled croak or harsher 'krrr'. Red-breasted mergansers are ground nesting and sometimes choose to build in gull colonies, to take advantage of the early warning of possible danger, and the protection from it, that the gulls provide.

Identification
Drake has dark green head with double crest, chestnut breast, grey and white back; duck browner than goosander, with fuzzy crest, blurred white throat, brownish-grey body; both sexes have red bill.

Nesting
Duck makes lining of leaves and down in hollow in ground, well screened by thick vegetation; lays May–early July; 7–12 eggs, olive-buff, sometimes with blue tinge; eggs covered with down when duck leaves nest; incubation about 28 days, by duck only; ducklings, tended by duck, leave shortly after hatching, fly after about 5 weeks.

Feeding
Small fish, eels, crabs, shrimps; worms and insects.

Size
58.5cm (23in)

and Countryside Act 1981, licences to kill it are issued freely in Scotland under the same act, despite the fact that salmon and trout – the two fish that matter most to anglers in Scotland – do not form a large part of its diet. Conservationists point out that red-breasted mergansers take as many predatory coarse fish, and so help game fish to survive.

Heading south
Despite this, red-breasted mergansers are widespread in Scotland. Breeding birds are found on many rivers and lochs and in low-lying coastal areas. They are also common in Ireland and in the past 30 years have colonised northwest England and north and central Wales. Given a chance, they may well spread further south as breeders.

In winter, red-breasted mergansers prefer salt water to freshwater, and visit estuaries all round the coasts of the British Isles. Flocks several hundred strong occur regularly on some estuaries in Scotland. Visitors from Iceland and Scandinavia increase numbers. Red-breasted

J F M A M J
J A S O N D

Freshwater and sheltered bays and estuaries in Scotland, northwest England, Wales and Ireland; usually coastal waters in winter.

245

SANDERLING *Calidris alba*

Gregarious waders, sanderlings gather in flocks along the shore. With heads down, the birds scurry seawards after a receding wave, and then race back as the next breaker rolls in, like a bunch of clockwork toys.

Groups of sanderlings, mingling with other waders along the tideline, can be picked out at a distance by their restless manner of feeding, deftly retreating from the incoming surge to avoid being washed off their feet, then almost instantly advancing to snap up shrimps, sandhoppers and any other prey that has been uncovered by the waves. They may pause now and then in their high-speed chase to dab at the remains of a stranded fish or jellyfish. Their ability to run so fast across a flat beach is helped by their lacking a hind toe, unlike other sandpipers. Away from the tidal area of the shore, around pools and quieter water, sanderlings feed somewhat less frenetically, and they are so tame – or so intent on feeding – that a human can get quite close before they run off, and even then they will not go far. They seem reluctant to fly, but when they do, they rise

Plumage darkens in spring and summer.

with a hubbub of shrill 'twick-twick' calls, and their flight is swift, direct and generally low over the water. A white wing-bar, which shows as they fly, is more conspicuous than the dunlin's, and the tail is dark at the centre and white at the sides.

Brisk travellers

Sanderlings are fairly numerous in winter, but in summer most fly to the Arctic to breed. These small, energetic waders are able to migrate long distances and in spring and autumn numbers are swelled by passage migrants – birds travelling from the Arctic as far as South Africa and back, stopping off in Britain to rest and feed. In winter, sanderlings are probably the world's most widespread wader. Those that breed in eastern Siberia, Alaska and Arctic Canada reach South America, southern Asia and Australia.

A few non-breeding birds may stay in Britain all year, but sanderlings have never been recorded as breeding in the British Isles. In his display flight at the breeding grounds, the male rises in the air then descends steeply, giving a loud, rather harsh churring 'song'.

Sandy shores are the sanderling's usual winter habitat, but it occasionally feeds on mud-banks, and sometimes turns up on freshwater margins inland, especially on migration. The birds gather in large, tightly packed flocks to roost.

Identification

Pale grey and white in summer, with distinctive black 'shoulder' spot; in summer, upper parts are brown with darker streaks; straight bill; can be told from ringed plover by longer bill and lack of breast band, and from dunlin by more conspicuous white wing-bar; sexes alike.

Nesting

Does not breed in Britain; nest is scrape in ground, usually unlined; lays late June; 4 eggs, pear-shaped, olive-green with dark brown spots and blotches; incubation about 24 days, by female only; chicks, tended by both parents, leave nest after a few hours.

Feeding

Small crustacea, including shrimps; marine molluscs and worms; remains of fish or jellyfish.

Size

20.25cm (8in)

J	F	M	A	M	J
J	A	S	O	N	D

Sandy coasts, mudflats and estuaries in winter; small numbers in summer; passage migrants in spring and autumn.

247

STORM PETREL *Hydrobates pelagicus*

This little bird spends most of its life far out at sea, gliding above the waves, and even 'walking' on water. On calm days it patters across the ocean's surface, wings raised, dipping its head to pick up food.

The oceans of the world are home to petrels. They are small birds – the smallest has a head and body about the size of a sparrow's and the largest is about starling sized, although they have longer wings. The storm petrel is the second smallest of all seabirds, weighing only 23–29g (1oz). Only the Least storm petrel, which breeds off California and Mexico, is smaller.

Storm Petrels have an unusual method of feeding. They hover just above the surface, legs dangling, peering down, even pattering along while periodically stretching down to pick up surface food with their bills. The name 'petrel' is said to have been derived from the biblical episode in which St Peter walked on the water.

The storm petrel was once known to sailors as 'Mother Carey's chicken' and thought to be the harbinger of bad weather whereas in fact storm petrels follow ships to feed on plankton, offal and oil churned up by the ship's passage. In the absence of ships, they use their remarkably acute sense of smell to help them locate food.

However, storm petrels are certainly renowned for their ability to cope with rough sea conditions. They go ashore only to breed or when driven by storms, but it takes a storm of extraordinary fury to get the better of these birds. They shelter from Atlantic gales by keeping to the troughs of waves and avoiding the crests. Should a severe storm blow a storm petrel inland, it makes an incongruous sight as it rests exhausted on a lake or reservoir, or even on a road.

Safety in numbers

On land, storm petrels stick together, breeding in colonies on rocky islands. They find sheltered cavities in which to lay their eggs – among boulders, in rocky crevices or in abandoned rabbit burrows. While the sitting bird remains tucked away, its mate goes back to sea, returning after dark. Only the birds' strange nocturnal crooning or purring 'songs' indicate where they are. Loud and continuous, the song is interspersed with loud hiccups and squeaking sounds. It was described memorably by the naturalist Charles Oldham as sounding 'like a fairy being sick'.

The storm petrel has colonies in the Scillies, on Skokholm and Skomer off the Pembroke coast, and on many islands off the west and north coasts of Scotland and the west and southwest coasts of Ireland. The world's 20 or so species of storm petrel are classified in a separate family from the larger petrels and shearwaters.

Identification

Sooty plumage and white rump (superficially similar to house martin), long wings, square tail; weaving flight near water; follows ships; sexes alike.

Nesting

Digs burrow, or nests in abandoned rabbit burrow, or crevice among stones; usually lays June; 1 egg, white with faint brown spots; incubation about 44 days by both parents; nestling, fed by both parents, leaves after 7–8½ weeks.

Feeding

Chiefly plankton, fish and floating oil; also seaweed.

Size

15.25cm (6in)

J	F	M	A	M	J
J	A	S	O	N	D

Breed on remote islands off Scotland and mainly western coasts of England, Wales and Ireland, but mostly remains at sea.

249

TURNSTONE *Arenaria interpres*

As well as stones, any flotsam washed up by the tide may be overturned by these stocky waders in search of food. The birds sometimes work together to flip especially heavy weights.

The turnstone lives up to its name by making good use of its stout bill and strong legs. The bill is short, straight and laterally compressed with a sharp, flattened chisel-like tip, and its short legs have little spines beneath the toes and sharply curved claws to give it a strong footing as it goes about its business.

Stones are not the only objects moved about by turnstones as they search the shore for food – seaweed, pebbles, shells, driftwood, dead fish, anything that might conceal insects or small shellfish may be turned over or levered aside by their probing bills. They are quite capable of shifting a weight of at least 96g (3½oz), which is just under their own weight in winter. If they come across anything heavier, several birds work together, even excavating the ground around the object until they can flip it over.

In winter, the turnstone has a dark brown breast and back, and a less clear-cut pattern of markings than in summer.

Autumn arrivals

Turnstones are common winter visitors from Russia and Scandinavia, and also appear in Britain as passage migrants in spring and autumn, when a few birds may turn up inland on freshwater. These birds are generally breeders from northeast Canada and Greenland, but the greatest numbers gather on rocky and stony beaches, where seaweed harbours a rich supply of food. Turnstones are unfussy eaters, and have been known to consume garlic, dogfood and even soap, along with the more usual sandhoppers. They eat carrion, too, searching along the tideline in small feeding parties, often in the company of other waders. On one occasion, turnstones were found feeding on a human corpse washed up on the beach in Anglesey.

On the shore, in winter plumage, their mottled backs provide good camouflage against the stones, pebbles and seaweed. The first sight of a flock may be as they fly up, showing the black and white pattern of their wings. They are noisy birds for their size, twittering 'kit-kit-kit' when disturbed, or crying a clear 'kecoo-kecoo'.

In summer almost all of the turnstones return north to breed in the Arctic. They nest on rocky islands, often close to bigger birds, such as gulls and skuas, which would take their eggs if the turnstones did not keep a constant watch. In breeding plumage, their upperparts are bright chestnut, rather than tortoiseshell, giving rise to their full name of 'ruddy turnstone'. A few non-breeders stay in Britain, especially on the north and west coasts.

Identification
In winter, upper parts are black-brown, underparts white except for a broad dark breastband; in summer, upper parts appear tortoiseshell, head is whiter; bill short and black; legs orange; sexes alike.

Nesting
Does not breed in Britain; nest is either on bare rock or by tussock, sometimes scantily lined with vegetation; lays May–June; 4 eggs, green with brown markings; incubation about 21 days, mainly by female; chicks, tended by both sexes, leave nest within a few hours.

Feeding
Sandhoppers, shellfish, insects; young fish and remains of fish; bread and carrion have been recorded.

Size
23cm (9in)

J F M A M J
J A S O N D

Almost all shores in winter, especially rocky and pebbly stretches covered with seaweed; small numbers in summer; passage migrants.

WHITE-TAILED EAGLE

Haliaeetus albicilla

The white-tailed eagle's size, emphasised by its enormous, plank-like wings, makes 'a flying barn door' an apt description. Its front-heavy appearance is accentuated by a huge, hooked bill and short tail.

Bigger than a golden eagle, to which it is not related, the white-tailed eagle is the largest bird of prey in northern Europe. Its great, broad wings have a span of 190-244cm (6.25-8ft). Its active flight, with a long series of shallow wing beats alternating with brief glides, differs from a golden eagle's, which is typically made up of a few deep wing beats alternating with a long glide. It often soars for long periods at great heights. Especially impressive are its dramatic courtship displays. These include a breathtaking performance, in which a pair cartwheel down from a great height, talons locked together with one bird above and one on its back beneath, spinning down fast and pulling out at the very last minute, not far above the rocks or crashing waves.

During the breeding season, the birds are very noisy, giving loud yelping cries, and the pair often perform a duet.

Scottish wanderer

The white-tailed eagle once bred extensively in Scotland, Ireland and northwest England but by 1916 it was gone, unable to contend with persecution and human disturbance. The only sightings were of the odd birds that strayed from their Scandinavian breeding grounds. However, a successful reintroduction programme, started on the Hebridean island of Rhum in 1975, is gradually having some effect on numbers and now 45 breeding pairs are established in Scotland, birds are being introduced in eastern Scotland, and a further reintroduction programme is being considered for eastern England. The white-tailed eagles that are occasionally seen in eastern and southern England are rare winter visitors from Europe.

The bird's scientific name, *Haliaeetus*, comes from the Greek for sea, *hals*, and eagle, *aetos*, giving rise to its alternative name of sea eagle. A bird of rocky coasts, it also frequents estuaries

and inland waters where it can hunt for food. It is a formidable predator, taking large ducks and even geese as well as its more usual fish. It is a scavenger, too, much more so than the golden eagle. Rotting fish stranded on the shore and carrion form part of its diet, and it will seize prey from other birds, notably ospreys, if the opportunity arises. Sickly lambs may be targeted, but farm livestock is usually only eaten as carrion. However, its perceived threat to farmers' livelihoods was one of the reasons for its persecution.

In winter, white-tailed eagles wander all over Scotland, but tend to roost communally in tall trees, usually in mature woodland, or on rocky crags.

The eagle soars on broad, flat, square-ended wings.

Identification

Heavily built with big head; brown plumage, head and neck paler; very large, hooked bill; long, broad wings, fingered at the tips; short, wedge-shaped tail, white in adults, dark brown with white centres to feathers in juveniles; sexes alike.

Nesting

Both sexes build massive construction of sticks on sea-cliff or in tall tree, added to annually; lays March or April; 1–3 eggs, white; incubation 36–42 days, mainly by female; nestlings fed by both parents, fly in 10–12 weeks.

Feeding

Fish, seabirds, mammals, carrion.

Size

75-92 cm (30-36 in)

J	F	M	A	M	J
J	A	S	O	N	D

Western Isles and Highlands; rare winter migrant to eastern and southern England.

Index

Page numbers in bold refer to main entries

A

Accipiter
  A. gentilis **92-3**, 96
  A. nisus 96, **118-19**, 207
Aegithalos caudatus **106-7**
Aix galericulata 31, **196-7**
Alauda arvensis 31, **64-5**, 66
Alcedo atthis **194-5**
Anas clypeata 184, **208-9**
Apus apus 31, **34-5**, 71
Aquila chrysaetos **134-5**, 146, 147
Arctic skua **214-15**
Arctic tern **216-17**
Ardea cinerea 185, **190-1**
Arenaria interpres **250-1**
Asio
  A. flammeus 97, **164-5**, 185, 235
  A. otus **104-5**
avocet **218-19**

B

barn owl **44-5**, 66, 67
barnacle goose **220-1**
barred warbler 31
bearded tit 185
Bewick's swan **176-7**
bittern **178-9**, 184, 185
blackbird **10-11**, 31, 37, 162
blackcap **78-9**
black grouse **128-9**, 146
black-headed gull 136
black-tailed godwit **180-1**, 185
black-throated diver **182-3**
blue tit **12-13**
Bombycilla garrulus **38-9**
Botaurus stellaris **178-9**, 184, 185
brambling **80-1**
Branta leucopsis **220-1**
brent goose 221
bullfinch **82-3**
Burhinus oedicnemus **68-9**
buzzard 96

C

Cairngorms 146-7
Calidris
  C. alba **246-7**
  C. canutus 185, **236-7**

Canada goose 221
capercaille **84-5**, 146
Caprimulgus europaeus 96-7, **150-1**
Carduelis
  C. cannabina **144-5**
  C. carduelis 14-15
  C. spinus 31, 96, **116-17**
Certhia familiaris 13, 31, 96, **120-1**
Cetti's warbler 185
chaffinch 11, 37
Charadrius morinellus **132-3**, 146
chiffchaff 124
chough **222-3**, 235
Cinclus cinclus 67, **186-7**
Circus
  C. aeruginosus 185, **198-9**
  C. cyaneus 97, **140-1**, 159, 185
Clangula hyemalis **238-9**
coal tit 87
Coccothraustes coccothraustes **94-5**, 96, 97
collared dove 48
common tern 217
coot 184
corncrake **46-7**
Corvus
  C. corax 67, 146, **156-7**
  C. frugilegus **62-3**
Coturnix coturnix **60-1**
crested tit **86-7**, 147
Crex crex **46-7**
crossbill **88-9**, 96
cuckoo **48-9**, 145
Cuculus canorus **48-9**, 145
curlew **50-1**, 66, 146, 185
Cyanistes caeruleus **12-13**
Cygnus
  C. columbianus **176-7**
  C. olor 177, **200-1**

D

Dartford warbler 96, **130-1**
Delichon urbicum **20-1**, 22
Dendrocopos minor 31, 96, 97, **102-3**
dipper 67, **186-7**
dotterel **132-3**, 146
dunlin 66, 185
dunnock 11, 48

E

eider **224-5**, 230
Emberiza citrinella **74-5**
Erithacus rubecula **26-7**

F

Falco
  F. columbarius 66, 143, **148-9**
  F. peregrinus 66, 143, 146, **152-3**, 185, 227
  F. subbuteo 31, 96, 97, **142-3**, 207
  F. tinnunculus 31, **54-5**, 143
fens 184-5
fieldfare 31
firecrest 96
Fratercula arctica 230, 234, 235, **242-3**
Fringilla montifringilla **80-1**
fulmar **226-7**, 235
Fulmarus glacialis **226-7**, 235

G

gadwall 31, 184
Gallinago gallinago **166-7**
gannet **228-9**, 235
garganey 184
Garulus glandarius 37, 96, **100-1**
Gavia arctica **182-3**
goldcrest 13, **90-1**, 96, 103
golden eagle **134-5**, 146, 147
golden plover 56, 66, **136-7**, 185
goldfinch **14-15**
goosander 31
goshawk **92-3**, 96
great black-backed gull **230-1**
great crested grebe **188-9**
great grey shrike 31, 97
great spotted woodpecker 31, 103
green woodpecker **16-17**, 30-1
greenshank **138-9**
grey heron 185, **190-1**
grey partridge **52-3**
grey wagtail 67, **192-3**
guillemot 235

H

Haliaeetus albicilla **252-3**
hawfinch **94-5**, 96, 97
hen harrier 97, **140-1**, 159, 185
Hirundo rustica 31, **70-1**
hobby 31, 96, 97, **142-3**, 207
honey buzzard 96, **98-9**
hoopoe **18-19**
house martin **20-1**, 22
house sparrow **22-3**
Hydrobates pelagicus 235, **248-9**

J&K

jay 37, 96, **100-1**
kestrel 31, **54-5**, 143
kingfisher **194-5**
kittiwake **232-3**, 235
knot 185, **236-7**

L

Lagopus
  L. lagopus **158-9**
  L. mutus 146, **154-5**
landrail *see* corncrake
lapwing **56-7**, 66, 136, 146, 185
Larus marinus **230-1**
lesser spotted woodpecker 31, 96, 97, **102-3**
Limosa limosa **180-1**, 185
linnet **144-5**
little grebe 184
little owl 31
long-eared owl **104-5**
long-tailed duck **238-9**
long-tailed tit **106-7**
Lophophanes cristatus **86-7**, 147
Loxia
  L. curvirostra **88-9**, 96
  L. leucoptera 88
  L. scotica 88, 147
Lullula arborea 96, **172-3**
Luscinia megarhynchos **110-11**

M

mallard 31
mandarin duck 31, **196-7**
Manx shearwater 230, 235, **240-1**
marsh harrier 185, **198-9**
marsh tit 96
meadow pipit 31, 48, 66
Mergus serrator **244-5**
merlin 66, 143, **148-9**
Milvus milvus 66, **160-1**
mistle thrush **108-9**
moorhen 184
Morus bassanus **228-9**, 235
Motacilla cinerea 67, **192-3**
mute swan 177, **200-1**

N

New Forest 96-7
nightingale **110-11**
nightjar 96-7, **150-1**
Numenius arquata **50-1**, 66, 146, 185
nuthatch 13, 25, 31, 96, 103, **112-13**

O

Oenanthe oenanthe 96, **170–1**
ortolan bunting 31
osprey 147, **202–3**
oystercatcher 146, 185

P&Q

Pandion haliaetus 147, **202–3**
parrot crossbill 88
Passer domesticus **22–3**
Pembrokeshire 234–5
Perdix perdix **52–3**
peregrine 66, 143, 146,
    152–3, 185, 227
Pernis apivorus 96, **98–9**
Phasianus colchicus **58–9**
pheasant **58–9**
Philomachus pugnax **204–5**
Phoenicurus phoenicurus 96,
    114–15
Phylloscopus sibilatrix 96,
    124–5
Picus viridis **16–17**, 30–1
Plectrophenax nivalis 146,
    168–9
Pluvialis apricarius 56, 66,
    136–7, 185
pochard 31
Podiceps cristatus **188–9**
Psittacula krameri **24–5**, 30
ptarmigan 146, **154–5**
puffin 230, 234, 235,
    242–3
Puffinus puffinus 230, 235,
    240–1
purple heron 191
Pyrrhocorax pyrrhocorax
    222–3, 235
Pyrrhula pyrrhula **82–3**
quail **60–1**

R

Rallus aquaticus 184, 185,
    210–11
raven 67, 146, **156–7**
razorbill 235
Recurvirostra avosetta
    218–19
red-breasted merganser
    244–5
red grouse **158–9**
red kite 66, **160–1**
redpoll 31, 96
redshank 66, 185
redstart 96, **114–15**
redwing 31
reed warbler 31, 48
Regulus regulus 13, **90–1**,
    96, 103
Richmond Park 30–1
ring-necked parakeet
    24–5, 30
ring ouzel **162–3**
Riparia riparia 31, **206–7**
Rissa tridactyla **232–3**, 235
robin **26–7**
rook **62–3**
rose-ringed parakeet see
    ring-necked parakeet
ruff **204–5**

S

sanderling **246–7**
sand martin 31, **206–7**
Scolopax rusticola **122–3**
Scottish crossbill 88, 147
sedge warbler 31
short-eared owl 97,
    164–5, 185, 235
shoveler 184, **208–9**
siskin 31, 96, **116–17**

Sitta europaea 13, 25, 31,
    96, 103, **112–13**
skylark 31, **64–5**, 66
snipe 66, **166–7**, 185
snow bunting 146, **168–9**
snowy owl 146
Somateria mollissima
    224–5, 230
song thrush **28–9**
sparrowhawk 96,
    118–19, 207
spotted flycatcher 96
starling **32–3**, 199
Stercorarius parasiticus
    214–15
Sterna
    S. hirundo 217
    S. paradisaea **216–17**
stonechat 31, 96
stone-curlew **68–9**
storm petrel 235, **248–9**
Streptopelia turtur **72–3**
Strix aluco 31, **36–7**,
    104–5
Sturnus vulgaris **32–3**, 199
swallow 31, **70–1**
swan-upping 201
swift 31, **34–5**, 71
Sylvia
    S. atricapilla **78–9**
    S. undata 96, **130–1**

T

taiga bean goose 185
tawny owl 31, **36–7**,
    104–5
Tetrao
    T. tetrix **128–9**, 146
    T. urogallus **84–5**, 146
treecreeper 13, 31, 96,
    120–1

tree pipit 96
Tringa nebularia **138–9**
Troglodytes troglodytes
    11, **40–1**
tufted duck 31
Turdus
    T. merula **10–11**, 31,
        37, 162
    T. philomelos **28–9**
    T. torquatus **162–3**
    T. viscivorus **108–9**
turnstone **250–1**
turtle dove **72–3**
Tyto alba **44–5**, 66, 67

U&V

Upupa epops **18–19**
Vanellus vanellus **56–7**, 66,
    136, 146, 185

W&Y

water rail 184, 185,
    210–11
waxwing **38–9**
wheatear 96, **170–1**
whinchat 96
white-tailed eagle **252–3**
whooper swan 176–7
wigeon 31
willow tit 87
willow warbler 124
woodcock **122–3**
woodlark 96, **172–3**
wood warbler 96, **124–5**
wren 11, **40–1**
yellowhammer **74–5**
yellow wagtail 66
Yorkshire Dales 66–7

Acknowledgments

Front Cover: rspb-images.com/Mark Hamblin (golden eagle); **Back Cover**: Getty Images/Robert Orchard (starlings); **1** David Tipling Photography (avocet); **2-3** Peter Cairns/www.northshots.com (capercaillie); **4-5** David Tipling Photography (wren); **6-7** naturepl.com/Geoff Simpson (grouse); **8-9** naturepl.com/Gary K. Smith; **10** rspb-images.com/Roger Wilmshurst; **12-13** naturepl.com/Colin Varndell; **15** Frank Lane Picture Agency/Gianpiero Ferrari; **16** naturepl.com/Roger Powell; **18-19** Thierry Vezon; **20-21** naturepl.com/Markus Varesvuo; **23** rspb-images.com/David Tipling; **24** David Tipling Photography/Terry Whittaker; **26-27** iStockphoto/Andrew Howe; **28** naturepl.com/William Osborn; **30-31** rspb-images.com/David Kjaer; **33** rspb-images.com/Jeroen Stel; **34-35** rspb-images.com/Tony Hamblin; **36** David Tipling Photography; **39** rspb-images.com/Andrew Parkinson; **40-41** Photoshot/David Chapman/ Woodfall Wild Images; **42-43** Frank Lane Picture Agency/Wayne Hutchinson; **45** David Tipling Photography; **46** Frank Lane Picture Agency/Michael Callan; **48-49** Peter Cairns/www.northshots.com; **50** Frank Lane Picture Agency/Derek Middleton; **53** David Tipling Photography; **54-55** naturepl.com/John Waters; **57** naturepl.com/Adrian Davies; **58** Frank Lane Picture Agency/Malcolm Schuyl; **60-61** Frank Lane Picture Agency/Dietmar Nill/Minden Pictures; **62** Photoshot/Laurie Campbell; **65** David Tipling Photography; **67** Getty Images/David Tipling; **68** naturepl.com/Paul Hobson; **70-71** rspb-images.com/Mark Hamblin; **72** Rudi Debruyne; **75** naturepl.com/Roger Powell; **76-77** Photoshot/Stephen Dalton/ NHPA; **78** David Tipling Photography; **80-81** naturepl.com/David Kjaer; **82** Peter Cairns/www.northshots.com; **85** David Tipling Photography; **86** rspb-images.com/Mark Hamblin; **88-91** David Tipling Photography; **92-93** Peter Cairns/www.northshots.com; **94** Photoshot/David Slater/ NHPA; **97** naturepl.com/David Kjaer; **98-99** naturepl.com/Markus Varesvuo; **101** Frank Lane Picture Agency/John Hawkins; **102** Steven Round Bird Photography; **105-105** Peter Cairns/www.northshots.com; **106-107** Frank Lane Picture Agency/John Watkins; **108** Frank Lane Picture Agency/John Hawkins; **111** Frank Lane Picture Agency/FotoNatura/FN/Minden; **112** naturepl.com/David Kjaer; **114-115** naturepl.com/Paul Hobson; **116-117** David Tipling Photography; **119** Photolibrary.com/Gerhard Schultz; **120-121** David Tipling Photography; **122** rspb-images.com/Chris Knights; **125** rspb-images.com/Steve Round; **126-127** Frank Lane Picture Agency/Michael Callan; **128-129** Peter Cairns/www.northshots.com; **131-132** David Tipling Photography; **134-135** Peter Cairns/www.northshots.com; **137-138** David Tipling Photography; **140-141** Peter Cairns/www.northshots.com; **142-143** Photolibrary.com/Manfred Delpho/Picture Press; **144** rspb-images.com/Steve Knell; **147** naturepl.com/Peter Cairns; **149** naturepl.com/Paul Hobson; **150-151** rspb-images.com/David Tipling; **153-160** David Tipling Photography; **162-163** ardea.com/Dennis Avon; **165** naturepl.com/David Kjaer; **166-167** David Tipling Photography; **168-169** naturepl.com/Andy Sands; **170-171** rspb-images.com/David Kjaer; **173** David Tipling Photography**174-175** Frank Lane Picture Agency/Erica Olsen ; **176-177** David Tipling Photography; **179** Steven Round Bird Photography; **180** ardea.com/Chris Knights; **182-185** naturepl.com/David Kjaer; **187** naturepl.com/Michael Hutchson; **188-189** rspb-images.com/Andrew Parkinson; **190** rspb-images.com/Malcolm Hunt; **192-193** Frank Lane Picture Agency/Simon Litten; **195-196** Steven Round Bird Photography; **198-201** David Tipling Photography; **202-203** Peter Cairns/www.northshots.com; **205** David Tipling Photography; **206-209** Steven Round Bird Photography; **210** Frank Lane Picture Agency/Adri Hoogendijk; **212-215** David Tipling Photography; **216** Steven Round Bird Photography; **218-219** David Tipling Photography; **220-221** naturepl.com/Colin Varndell; **223** rspb-images.com/David Tipling; **224-225** Peter Cairns/www.northshots.com; **226** David Tipling Photography; **228-229** rspb-images.com/Niall Benvie; **231-232** David Tipling Photography; **234-235** Alamy Images/Philip Mugridge; **236-243** David Tipling Photography; **244-245** rspb-images.com/David Kjaer; **246-247** David Tipling Photography; **248** Frank Lane Picture Agency/Roger Tidman; **250-253** David Tipling Photography

Contributors

Project Editor Marion Paull
Project Manager Caroline McDonald
Art Editor Conorde Clarke
Design Shark Attack
Consultant Jonathan Elphick
Feature Writer John Woodward
Picture Editor Christine Hinze
Proofreader Ron Pankhurst
Indexer Marie Lorimer

READER'S DIGEST GENERAL BOOKS
Editorial Director Julian Browne
Art Director Anne-Marie Bulat
Managing Editor Nina Hathway
Head of Book Development Sarah Bloxham
Picture Resource Manager Sarah Stewart-
   Richardson
Pre-press Account Manager Dean Russell
Product Production Manager
   Claudette Bramble
Production Controller Katherine Tibbals

Colour origination by FMG
Printed in China

The Most Amazing Birds to See in Britain is published by The Reader's Digest Association Limited, 11 Westferry Circus, Canary Wharf, London E14 4HE

Copyright © 2010 The Reader's Digest Association Limited
Copyright © 2010 Reader's Digest Association Far East Limited
Philippines Copyright © 2010 Reader's Digest Association Far East Limited
Copyright © 2010 Reader's Digest (Australia) Pty Limited
Copyright © 2010 Reader's Digest India Pvt Limited
Copyright © 2010 Reader's Digest Asia Pvt Limited

The Most Amazing Birds to See in Britain is based on material taken from **Book of British Birds** and **Wild Britain: Birds**, both published by The Reader's Digest Association Limited, London

We are committed both to the quality of our products and the service we provide to our customers. We value your comments, so please do contact us on **08705 113366** or via our website at **www.readersdigest.co.uk**

If you have any comments or suggestions about the content of our books, email us at gbeditiorial@readersdigest.co.uk

ISBN 978 0 276 44587 3
Book Code 400-473 UP0000-1
Oracle Code 250014440S.00.24